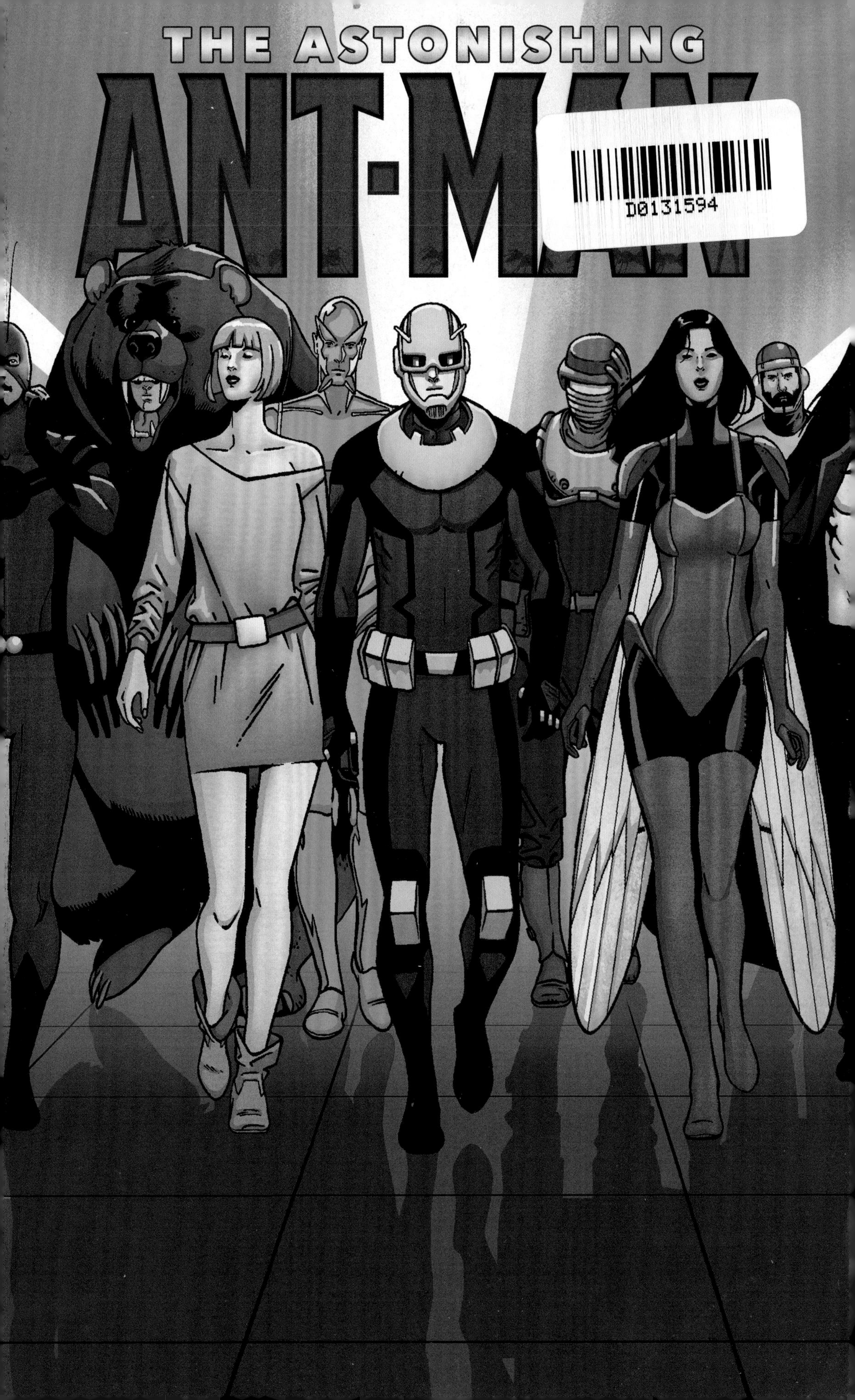
THE ASTONISHING
ANT-MAN

THE ASTONISHING ANT-MAN

SMALL-TIME CRIMINAL

WITHDRAWN

WRITER: NICK SPENCER

ARTISTS: RAMON ROSANAS (#5, #7 & #9),
ANNAPAOLA MARTELLO (#6)
& BRENT SCHOONOVER (#8)

COLOR ARTISTS: JORDAN BOYD WITH WIL QUINTANA (#5 & #7)

LETTERER: VC'S TRAVIS LANHAM

COVER ART: MARK BROOKS (#5-7) & JULIAN TOTINO TEDESCO (#8-9)

ASSISTANT EDITORS: CHRIS ROBINSON & CHARLES BEACHAM

EDITOR: WIL MOSS

PREVIOUSLY

Scott Lang is Ant-Man, a trusted super hero with the ability to shrink and talk to ants. But he wasn't always! Scott had a great teacher in Dr. Hank Pym (former Ant-Man, former Giant-Man, formerly living), who shared his years of Avengers experience and training.

Recently, after a chance encounter, Scott entrusted the Giant-Man suit and powers to computer technician Raz Malhotra. Meanwhile, San Francisco is abuzz with new apps Hench and its copycat competitor Lackey, making hiring super villains both available and affordable to the average consumer (but mostly causing trouble for Scott).

Eventually this'll all somehow land Scott back in prison, but we're not quite there yet...

ANT-MAN CREATED BY **STAN LEE**, **LARRY LIEBER** & **JACK KIRBY**

COLLECTION EDITOR
JENNIFER GRÜNWALD

ASSOCIATE EDITOR
SARAH BRUNSTAD

EDITOR, SPECIAL PROJECTS
MARK D. BEAZLEY

VP, PRODUCTION & SPECIAL PROJECTS
JEFF YOUNGQUIST

SVP PRINT, SALES & MARKETING
DAVID GABRIEL

EDITOR IN CHIEF
AXEL ALONSO

CHIEF CREATIVE OFFICE:
JOE QUESADA

PUBLISHER
DAN BUCKLEY

EXECUTIVE PRODUCER
ALAN FINE

THE ASTONISHING ANT-MAN VOL. 2: SMALL-TIME CRIMINAL. Contains material originally published in magazine form as THE ASTONISHING ANT-MAN #5-9. First printing 2016. ISBN# 978-0-7851-9949-6. Published by MARVEL WORLDWIDE, INC., a subsidiary of MARVEL ENTERTAINMENT, LLC. OFFICE OF PUBLICATION: 135 West 50th Street, New York, NY 10020. Copyright © 2016 MARVEL No similarity between any of the names, characters, persons, and/or institutions in this magazine with those of any living or dead person or institution is intended, and any such similarity which may exist is purely coincidental. **Printed in Canada.** ALAN FINE, President, Marvel Entertainment; DAN BUCKLEY, President, TV, Publishing & Brand Management; JOE QUESADA, Chief Creative Officer; TOM BREVOORT, SVP of Publishing; DAVID BOGART, SVP of Business Affairs & Operations, Publishing & Partnership; C.B. CEBULSKI, VP of Brand Management & Development, Asia; DAVID GABRIEL, SVP of Sales & Marketing, Publishing; JEFF YOUNGQUIST, VP of Production & Special Projects; DAN CARR, Executive Director of Publishing Technology; ALEX MORALES, Director of Publishing Operations; SUSAN CRESPI, Production Manager; STAN LEE, Chairman Emeritus. For information regarding advertising in Marvel Comics or on Marvel.com, please contact Vit DeBellis, Integrated Sales Manager, at vdebellis@marvel.com. For Marvel subscription inquiries, please call 888-511-5480. **Manufactured between 7/29/2016 and 9/5/2016 by SOLISCO PRINTERS, SCOTT, QC, CANADA.**

10 9 8 7 6 5 4 3 2 1

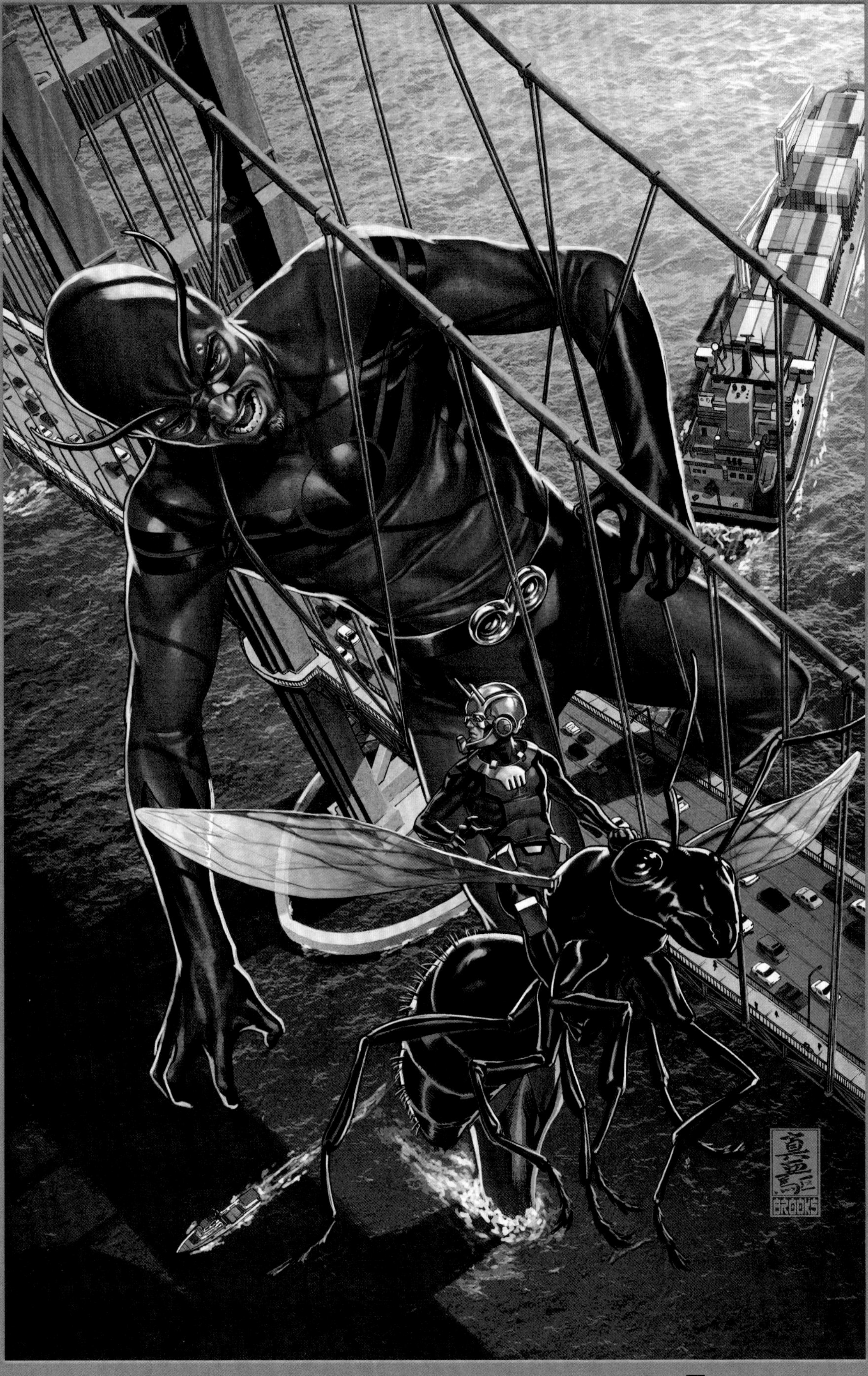
BROOKS

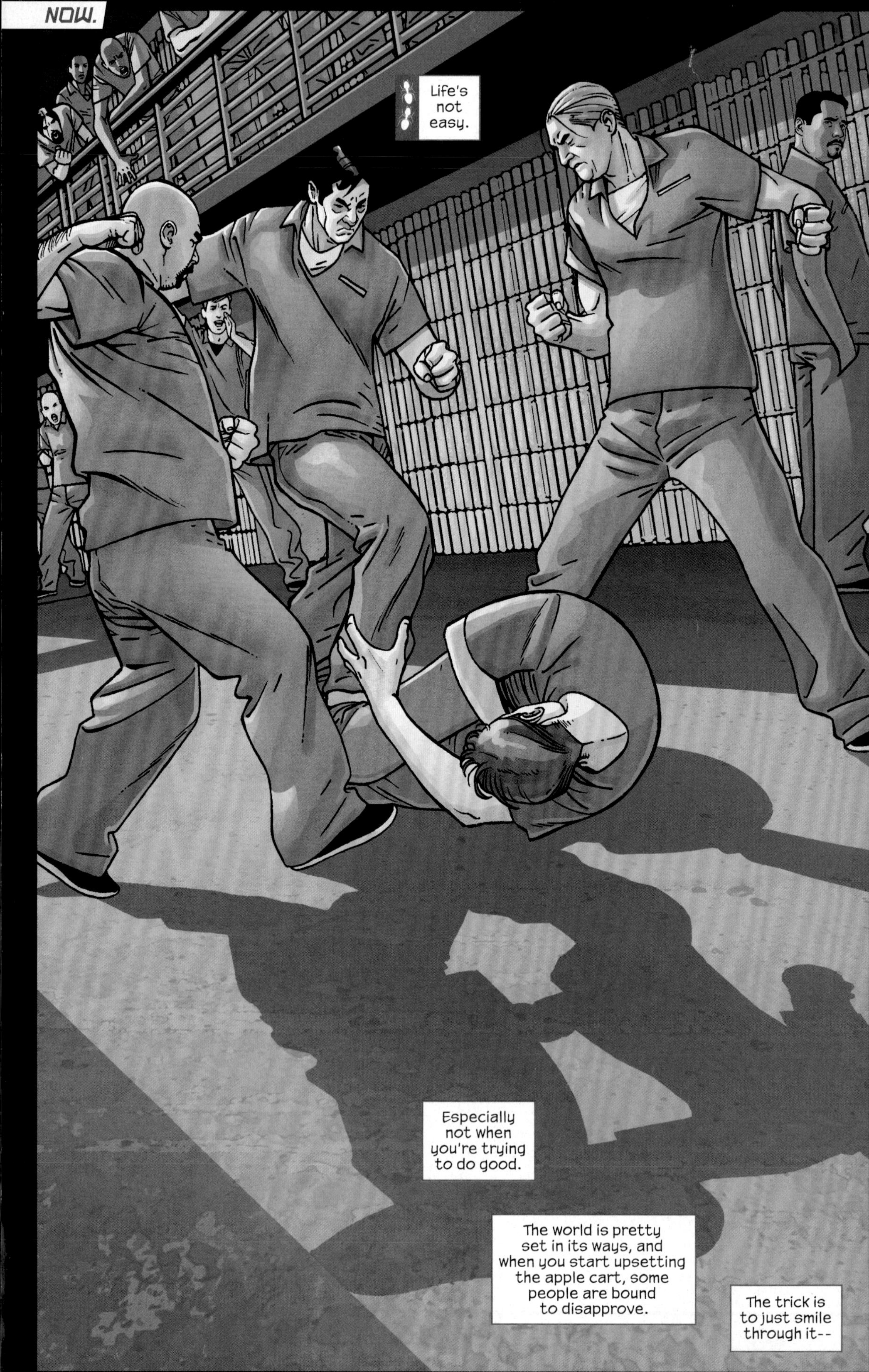
NOW.
Life's not easy.
Especially not when you're trying to do good.
The world is pretty set in its ways, and when you start upsetting the apple cart, some people are bound to disapprove.
The trick is to just smile through it--

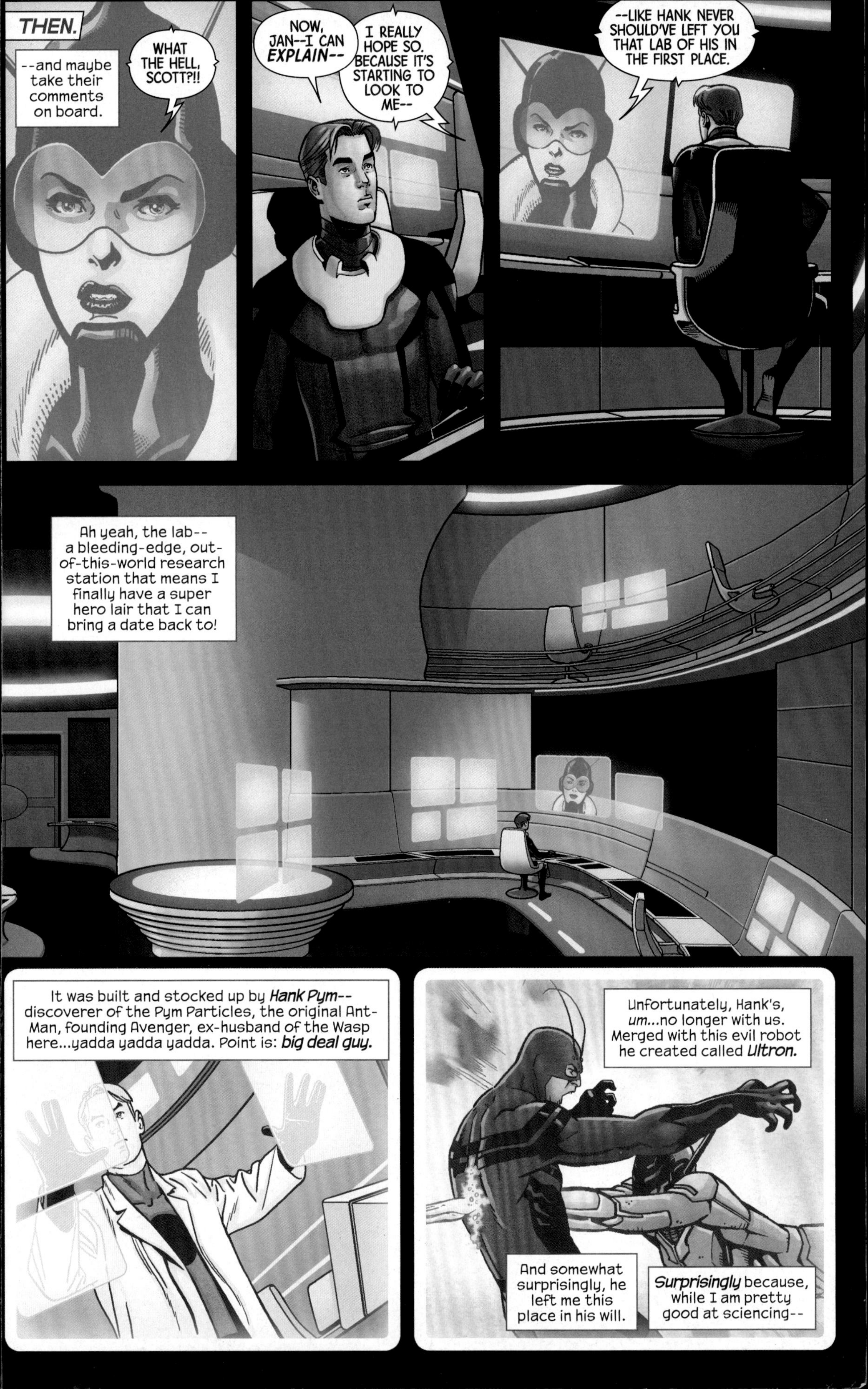
THEN.
--and maybe take their comments on board.
WHAT THE HELL, SCOTT?!!
NOW, JAN--I CAN EXPLAIN--
I REALLY HOPE SO. BECAUSE IT'S STARTING TO LOOK TO ME--
--LIKE HANK NEVER SHOULD'VE LEFT YOU THAT LAB OF HIS IN THE FIRST PLACE.
Ah yeah, the lab--a bleeding-edge, out-of-this-world research station that means I finally have a super hero lair that I can bring a date back to!
It was built and stocked up by Hank Pym--discoverer of the Pym Particles, the original Ant-Man, founding Avenger, ex-husband of the Wasp here...yadda yadda yadda. Point is: big deal guy.
Unfortunately, Hank's, um...no longer with us. Merged with this evil robot he created called Ultron.
And somewhat surprisingly, he left me this place in his will.
Surprisingly because, while I am pretty good at sciencing--

--most of this stuff definitely falls above my paygrade.

INITIATING SINGULARITY/ APOCALYPTIC PROTOCOLS... SIXTY SECONDS TO EXTINCTION-LEVEL EVENT--

OKAY-- TROUBLESHOOTING, PAGE FORTY-FOUR... NO, NOT IN *FRENCH*... NO, NOT *GERMAN*...

But there was one thing in the lab--one thing I knew *exactly* what to do with.

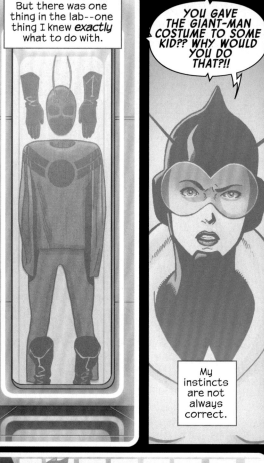

YOU GAVE THE GIANT-MAN COSTUME TO SOME KID?? WHY WOULD YOU DO THAT?!!

My instincts are not always correct.

My last adventure with Hank, we met this guy-- *Raz Malhotra.* Worked for this Techbusters outfit fixing computers and whatnot.

See, this bad guy called *Egghead* had brainwashed him and used him to revive these evil robot versions of the Avengers that Hank had once built--

And no, I have no idea *why* the guy built so many evil robots, okay? Point is--

After Hank died, I gave the *Giant-Man* suit to Raz. Mostly because--

To Raz, from Scott
You can't do worse than I did !

...HE SEEMED COOL?

"COOL"?!!

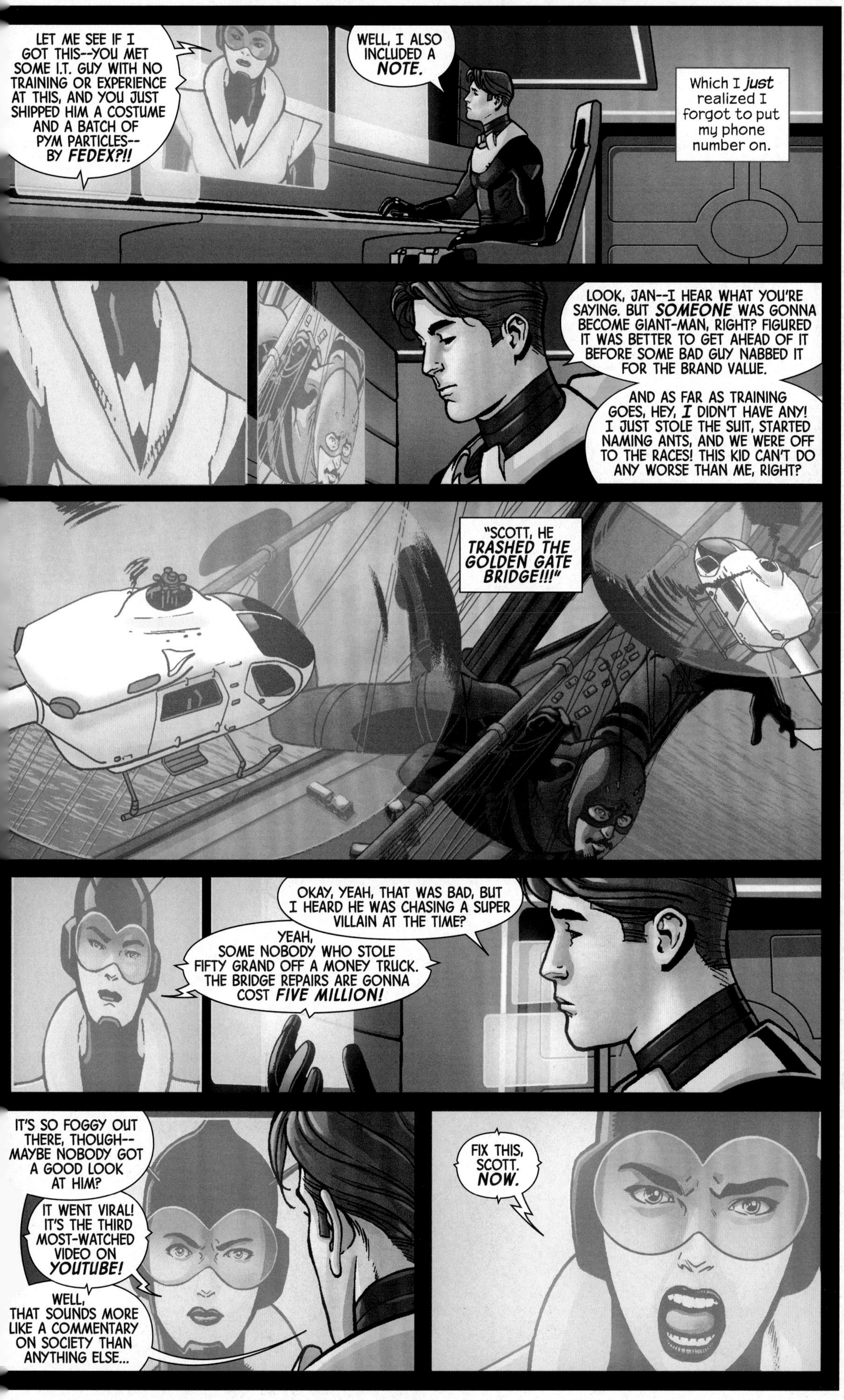
LET ME SEE IF I GOT THIS--YOU MET SOME I.T. GUY WITH NO TRAINING OR EXPERIENCE AT THIS, AND YOU JUST SHIPPED HIM A COSTUME AND A BATCH OF PYM PARTICLES-- BY *FEDEX?!!*
WELL, I ALSO INCLUDED A *NOTE.*
Which I *just* realized I forgot to put my phone number on.
LOOK, JAN--I HEAR WHAT YOU'RE SAYING. BUT *SOMEONE* WAS GONNA BECOME GIANT-MAN, RIGHT? FIGURED IT WAS BETTER TO GET AHEAD OF IT BEFORE SOME BAD GUY NABBED IT FOR THE BRAND VALUE.
AND AS FAR AS TRAINING GOES, HEY, *I* DIDN'T HAVE ANY! I JUST STOLE THE SUIT, STARTED NAMING ANTS, AND WE WERE OFF TO THE RACES! THIS KID CAN'T DO ANY WORSE THAN ME, RIGHT?
"SCOTT, HE *TRASHED THE GOLDEN GATE BRIDGE!!!"*
OKAY, YEAH, THAT WAS BAD, BUT I HEARD HE WAS CHASING A SUPER VILLAIN AT THE TIME?
YEAH, SOME NOBODY WHO STOLE FIFTY GRAND OFF A MONEY TRUCK. THE BRIDGE REPAIRS ARE GONNA COST *FIVE MILLION!*
IT'S SO FOGGY OUT THERE, THOUGH-- MAYBE NOBODY GOT A GOOD LOOK AT HIM?
IT WENT VIRAL! IT'S THE THIRD MOST-WATCHED VIDEO ON *YOUTUBE!*
WELL, THAT SOUNDS MORE LIKE A COMMENTARY ON SOCIETY THAN ANYTHING ELSE...
FIX THIS, SCOTT. *NOW.*

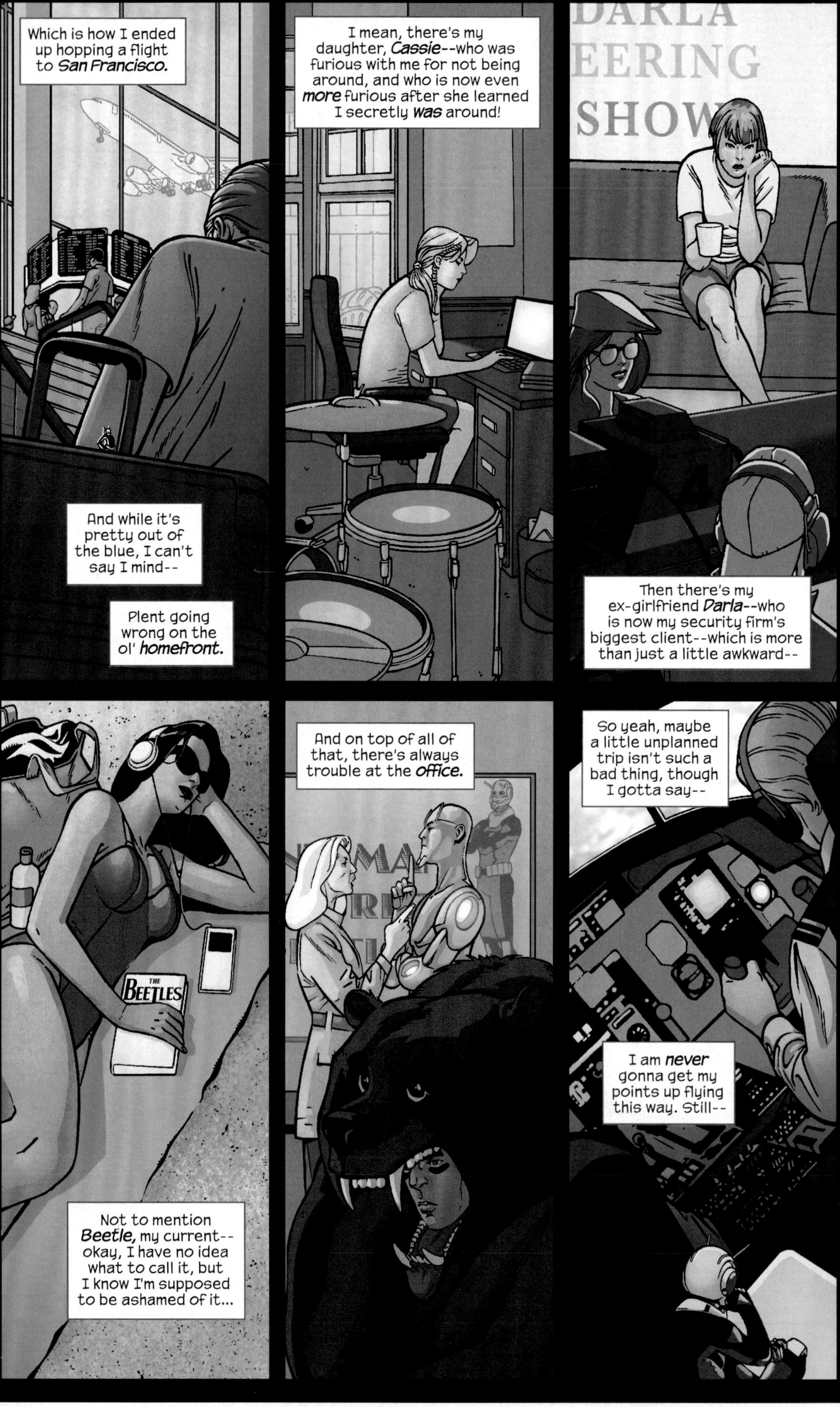

Which is how I ended up hopping a flight to *San Francisco.*
And while it's pretty out of the blue, I can't say I mind--
Plent going wrong on the ol' *homefront.*
I mean, there's my daughter, *Cassie*--who was furious with me for not being around, and who is now even *more* furious after she learned I secretly *was* around!
DARLA
Then there's my ex-girlfriend *Darla*--who is now my security firm's biggest client--which is more than just a little awkward--
THE BEETLES
Not to mention *Beetle,* my current-- okay, I have no idea what to call it, but I know I'm supposed to be ashamed of it...
And on top of all of that, there's always trouble at the *office.*
So yeah, maybe a little unplanned trip isn't such a bad thing, though I gotta say--
I am *never* gonna get my points up flying this way. Still--

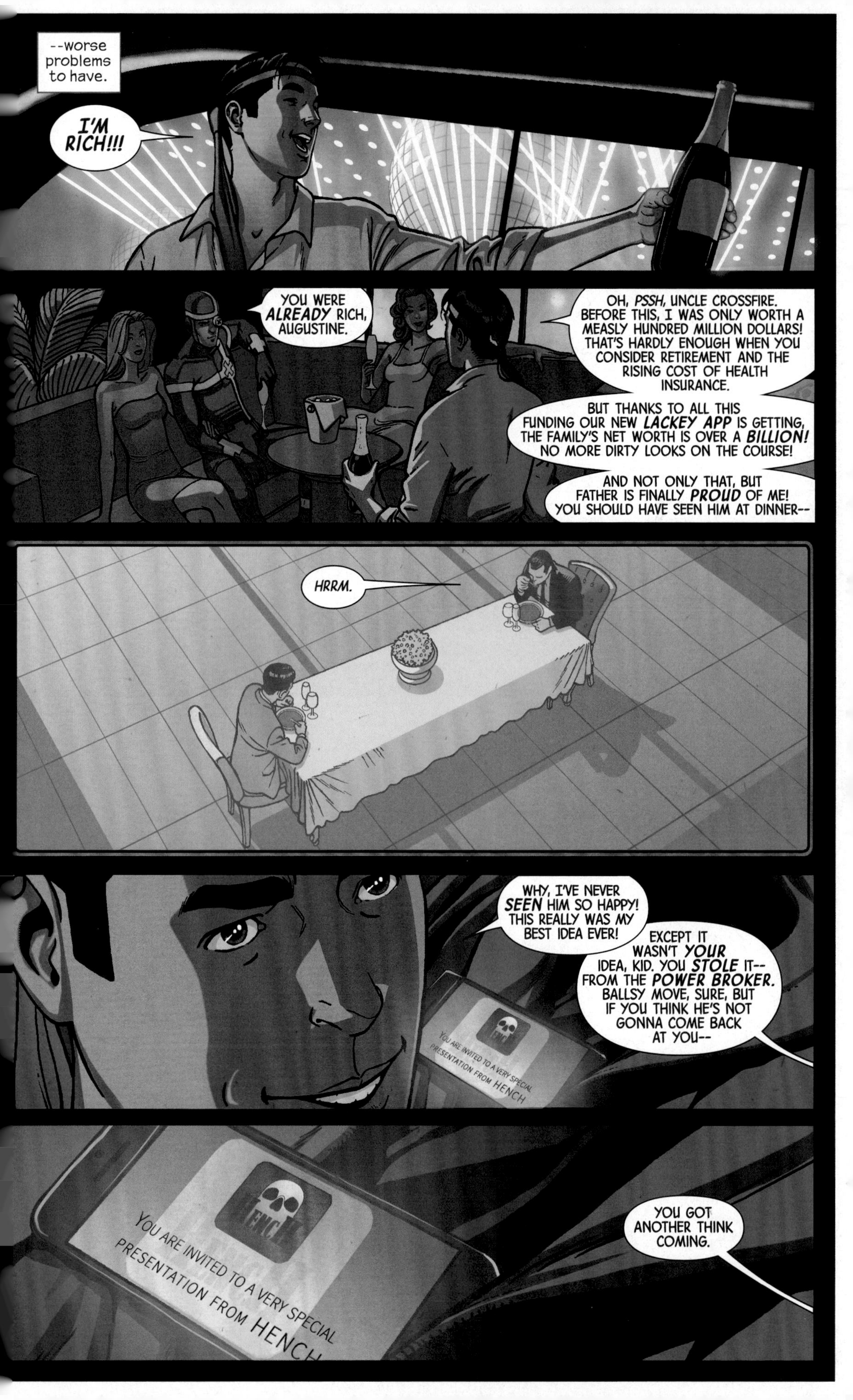
--worse problems to have.
I'M RICH!!!
YOU WERE ALREADY RICH, AUGUSTINE.
OH, PSSH, UNCLE CROSSFIRE. BEFORE THIS, I WAS ONLY WORTH A MEASLY HUNDRED MILLION DOLLARS! THAT'S HARDLY ENOUGH WHEN YOU CONSIDER RETIREMENT AND THE RISING COST OF HEALTH INSURANCE.
BUT THANKS TO ALL THIS FUNDING OUR NEW LACKEY APP IS GETTING, THE FAMILY'S NET WORTH IS OVER A BILLION! NO MORE DIRTY LOOKS ON THE COURSE!
AND NOT ONLY THAT, BUT FATHER IS FINALLY PROUD OF ME! YOU SHOULD HAVE SEEN HIM AT DINNER--
HRRM.
WHY, I'VE NEVER SEEN HIM SO HAPPY! THIS REALLY WAS MY BEST IDEA EVER!
EXCEPT IT WASN'T YOUR IDEA, KID. YOU STOLE IT--FROM THE POWER BROKER. BALLSY MOVE, SURE, BUT IF YOU THINK HE'S NOT GONNA COME BACK AT YOU--
YOU ARE INVITED TO A VERY SPECIAL PRESENTATION FROM HENCH
HENCH
YOU ARE INVITED TO A VERY SPECIAL PRESENTATION FROM HENCH
YOU GOT ANOTHER THINK COMING.

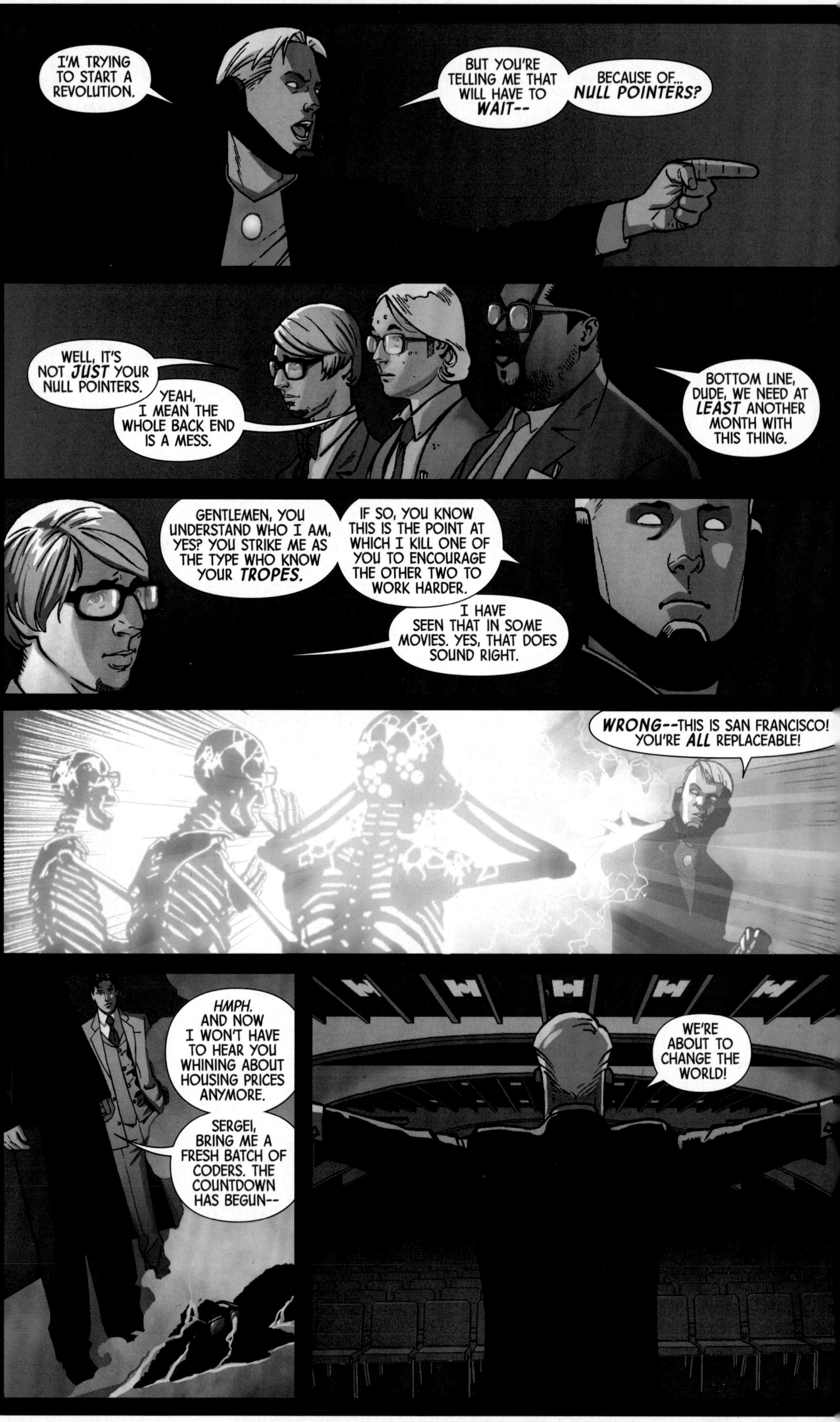

I'M TRYING TO START A REVOLUTION.
BUT YOU'RE TELLING ME THAT WILL HAVE TO WAIT--
BECAUSE OF... NULL POINTERS?
WELL, IT'S NOT JUST YOUR NULL POINTERS.
YEAH, I MEAN THE WHOLE BACK END IS A MESS.
BOTTOM LINE, DUDE, WE NEED AT LEAST ANOTHER MONTH WITH THIS THING.
GENTLEMEN, YOU UNDERSTAND WHO I AM, YES? YOU STRIKE ME AS THE TYPE WHO KNOW YOUR TROPES.
IF SO, YOU KNOW THIS IS THE POINT AT WHICH I KILL ONE OF YOU TO ENCOURAGE THE OTHER TWO TO WORK HARDER.
I HAVE SEEN THAT IN SOME MOVIES. YES, THAT DOES SOUND RIGHT.
WRONG--THIS IS SAN FRANCISCO! YOU'RE ALL REPLACEABLE!
HMPH. AND NOW I WON'T HAVE TO HEAR YOU WHINING ABOUT HOUSING PRICES ANYMORE.
SERGEI, BRING ME A FRESH BATCH OF CODERS. THE COUNTDOWN HAS BEGUN--
WE'RE ABOUT TO CHANGE THE WORLD!

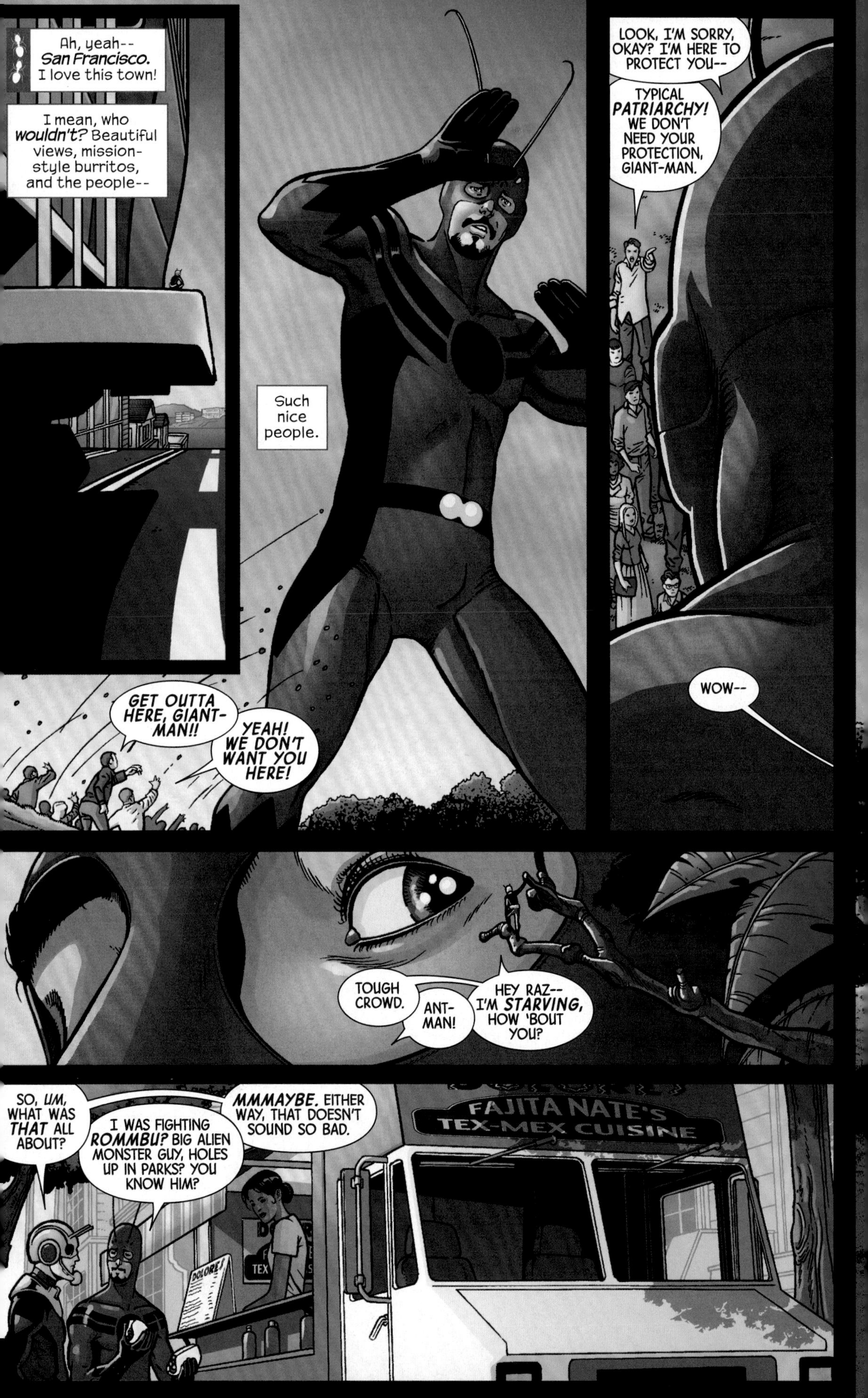
Ah, yeah--
San Francisco.
I love this town!
I mean, who wouldn't? Beautiful views, mission-style burritos, and the people--
Such nice people.
GET OUTTA HERE, GIANT-MAN!!
YEAH! WE DON'T WANT YOU HERE!
LOOK, I'M SORRY, OKAY? I'M HERE TO PROTECT YOU--
TYPICAL PATRIARCHY! WE DON'T NEED YOUR PROTECTION, GIANT-MAN.
WOW--
TOUGH CROWD.
ANT-MAN!
HEY RAZ-- I'M STARVING, HOW 'BOUT YOU?
SO, UM, WHAT WAS THAT ALL ABOUT?
I WAS FIGHTING ROMMBU? BIG ALIEN MONSTER GUY, HOLES UP IN PARKS? YOU KNOW HIM?
MMMAYBE. EITHER WAY, THAT DOESN'T SOUND SO BAD.
FAJITA NATE'S
TEX-MEX CUISINE

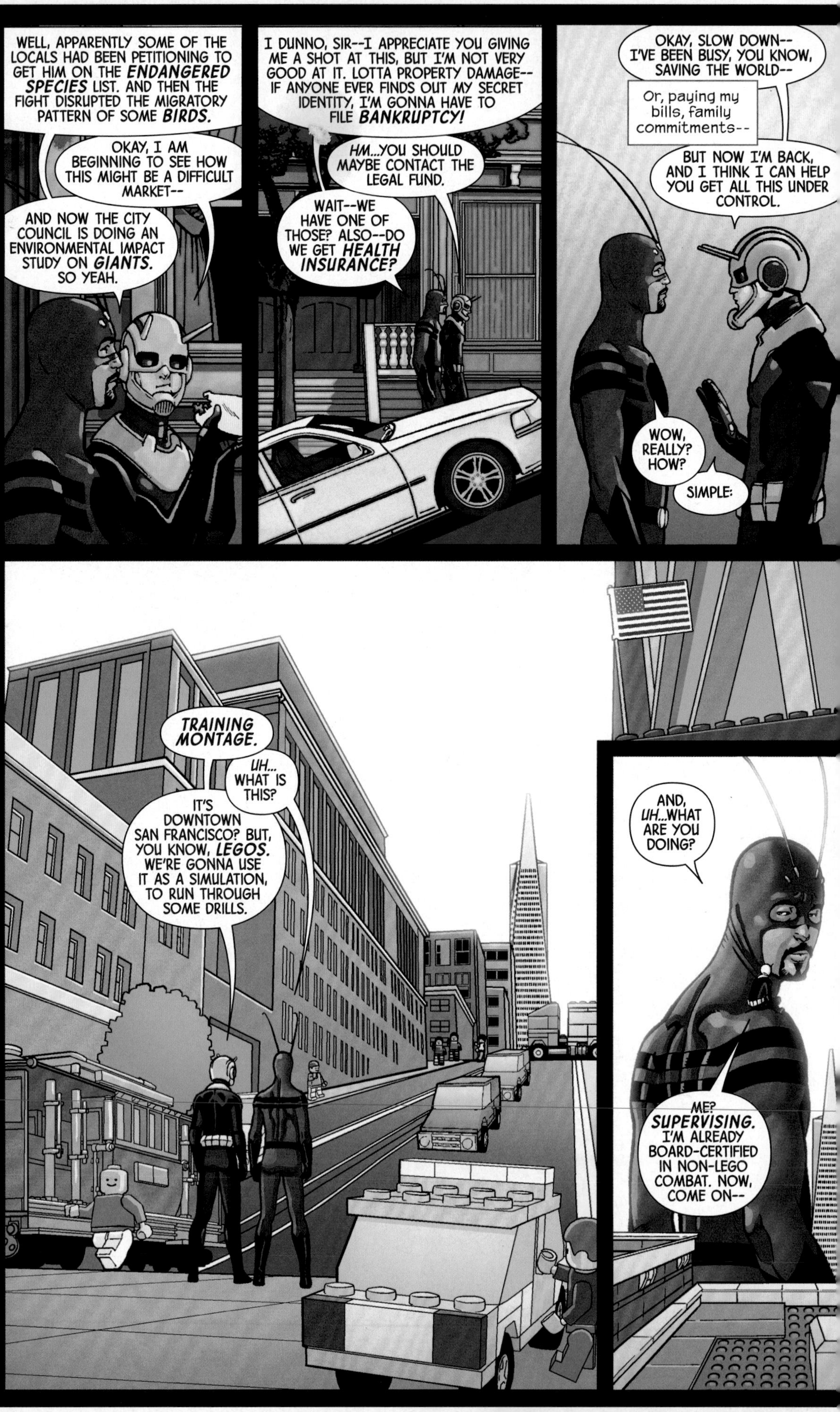
WELL, APPARENTLY SOME OF THE LOCALS HAD BEEN PETITIONING TO GET HIM ON THE ENDANGERED SPECIES LIST. AND THEN THE FIGHT DISRUPTED THE MIGRATORY PATTERN OF SOME BIRDS.
OKAY, I AM BEGINNING TO SEE HOW THIS MIGHT BE A DIFFICULT MARKET--
AND NOW THE CITY COUNCIL IS DOING AN ENVIRONMENTAL IMPACT STUDY ON GIANTS. SO YEAH.
I DUNNO, SIR--I APPRECIATE YOU GIVING ME A SHOT AT THIS, BUT I'M NOT VERY GOOD AT IT. LOTTA PROPERTY DAMAGE--IF ANYONE EVER FINDS OUT MY SECRET IDENTITY, I'M GONNA HAVE TO FILE BANKRUPTCY!
HM...YOU SHOULD MAYBE CONTACT THE LEGAL FUND.
WAIT--WE HAVE ONE OF THOSE? ALSO--DO WE GET HEALTH INSURANCE?
OKAY, SLOW DOWN--I'VE BEEN BUSY, YOU KNOW, SAVING THE WORLD--
Or, paying my bills, family commitments--
BUT NOW I'M BACK, AND I THINK I CAN HELP YOU GET ALL THIS UNDER CONTROL.
WOW, REALLY? HOW?
SIMPLE:
TRAINING MONTAGE.
UH... WHAT IS THIS?
IT'S DOWNTOWN SAN FRANCISCO? BUT, YOU KNOW, LEGOS. WE'RE GONNA USE IT AS A SIMULATION, TO RUN THROUGH SOME DRILLS.
AND, UH...WHAT ARE YOU DOING?
ME? SUPERVISING. I'M ALREADY BOARD-CERTIFIED IN NON-LEGO COMBAT. NOW, COME ON--

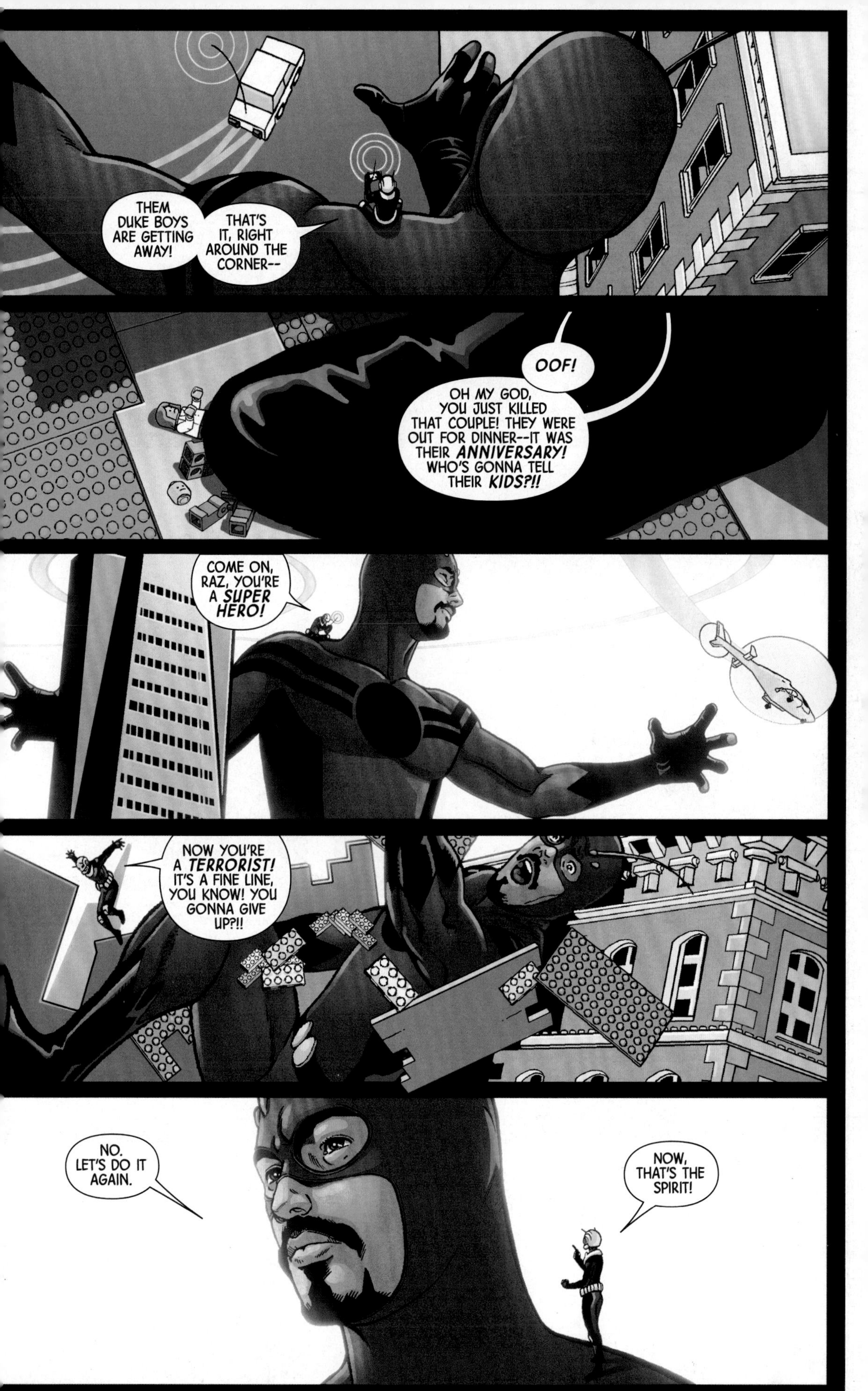
THEM DUKE BOYS ARE GETTING AWAY!
THAT'S IT, RIGHT AROUND THE CORNER--
OOF!
OH MY GOD, YOU JUST KILLED THAT COUPLE! THEY WERE OUT FOR DINNER--IT WAS THEIR *ANNIVERSARY!* WHO'S GONNA TELL THEIR *KIDS?!!*
COME ON, RAZ, YOU'RE A *SUPER HERO!*
NOW YOU'RE A *TERRORIST!* IT'S A FINE LINE, YOU KNOW! YOU GONNA GIVE UP?!!
NO. LET'S DO IT AGAIN.
NOW, THAT'S THE SPIRIT!

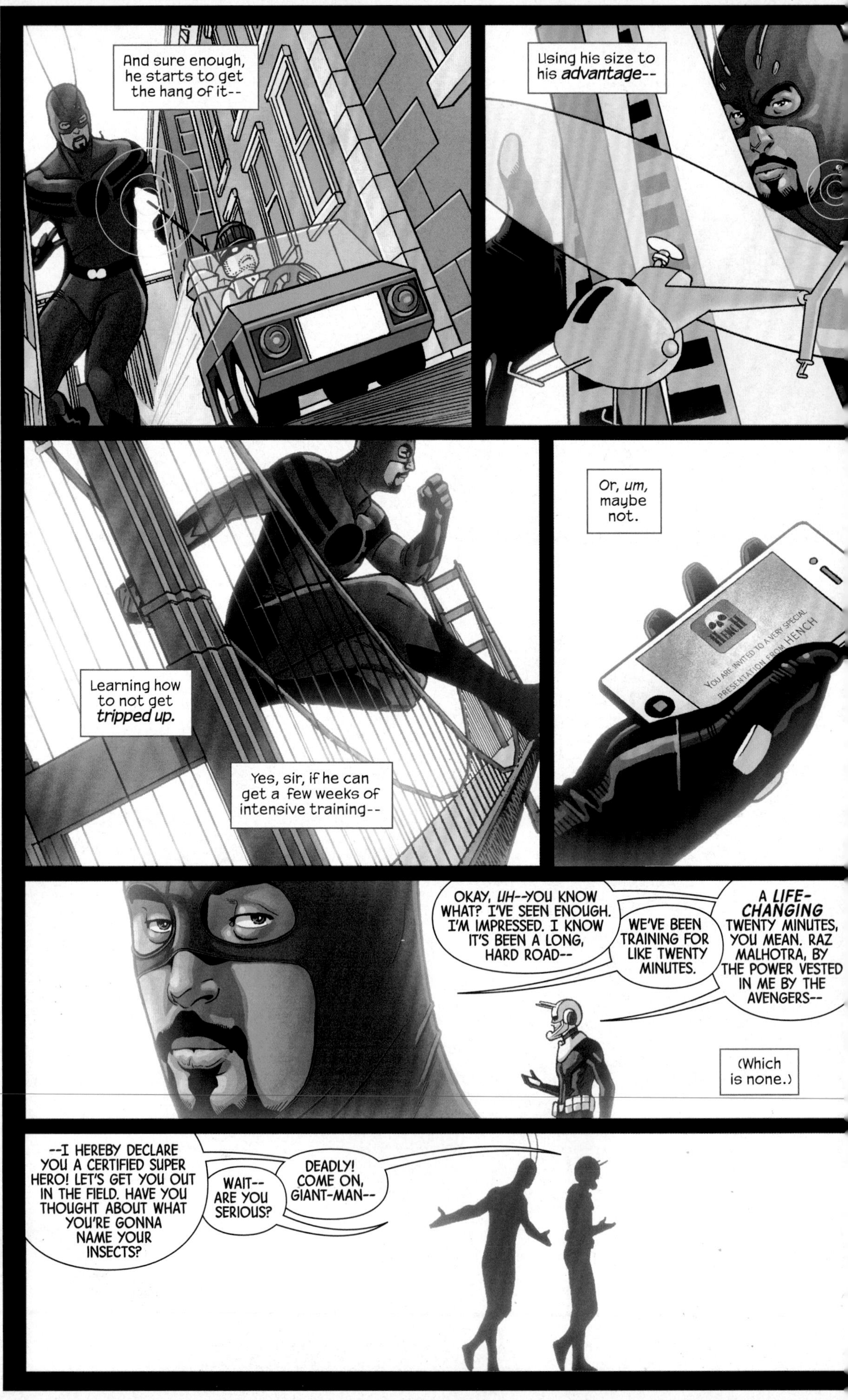
And sure enough, he starts to get the hang of it--
Using his size to his *advantage*--
Learning how to not get *tripped up.*
Yes, sir, if he can get a few weeks of intensive training--
Or, um, maybe not.
HENCH
YOU ARE INVITED TO A VERY SPECIAL PRESENTATION FROM HENCH
OKAY, *UH*--YOU KNOW WHAT? I'VE SEEN ENOUGH. I'M IMPRESSED. I KNOW IT'S BEEN A LONG, HARD ROAD--
WE'VE BEEN TRAINING FOR LIKE TWENTY MINUTES.
A *LIFE-CHANGING* TWENTY MINUTES, YOU MEAN. RAZ MALHOTRA, BY THE POWER VESTED IN ME BY THE AVENGERS--
(Which is none.)
--I HEREBY DECLARE YOU A CERTIFIED SUPER HERO! LET'S GET YOU OUT IN THE FIELD. HAVE YOU THOUGHT ABOUT WHAT YOU'RE GONNA NAME YOUR INSECTS?
WAIT-- ARE YOU SERIOUS?
DEADLY! COME ON, GIANT-MAN--

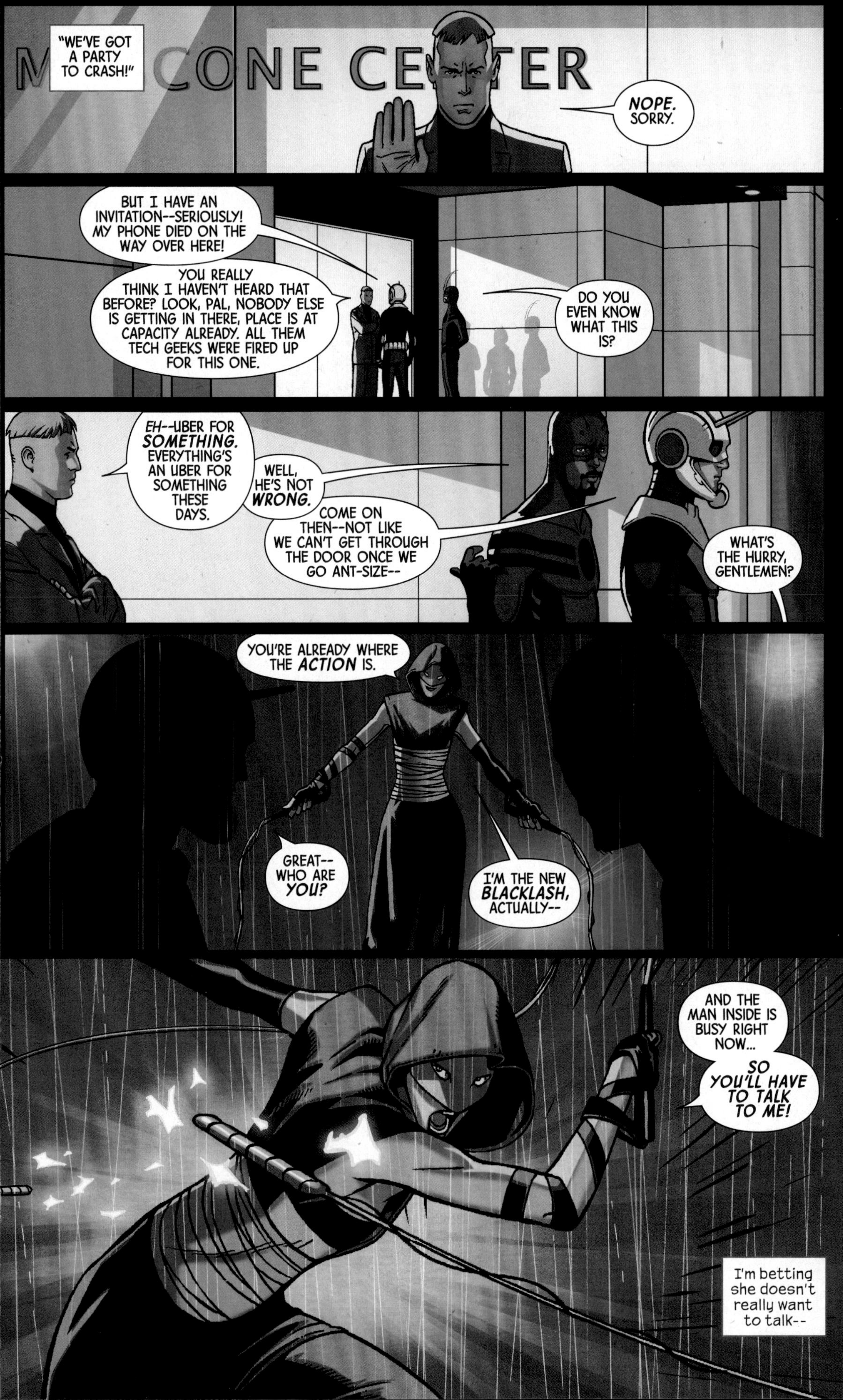
"WE'VE GOT A PARTY TO CRASH!"
CONE CENTER
NOPE. SORRY.
BUT I HAVE AN INVITATION--SERIOUSLY! MY PHONE DIED ON THE WAY OVER HERE!
YOU REALLY THINK I HAVEN'T HEARD THAT BEFORE? LOOK, PAL, NOBODY ELSE IS GETTING IN THERE, PLACE IS AT CAPACITY ALREADY. ALL THEM TECH GEEKS WERE FIRED UP FOR THIS ONE.
DO YOU EVEN KNOW WHAT THIS IS?
EH--UBER FOR SOMETHING. EVERYTHING'S AN UBER FOR SOMETHING THESE DAYS.
WELL, HE'S NOT WRONG.
COME ON THEN--NOT LIKE WE CAN'T GET THROUGH THE DOOR ONCE WE GO ANT-SIZE--
WHAT'S THE HURRY, GENTLEMEN?
YOU'RE ALREADY WHERE THE ACTION IS.
GREAT--WHO ARE YOU?
I'M THE NEW BLACKLASH, ACTUALLY--
AND THE MAN INSIDE IS BUSY RIGHT NOW...
SO YOU'LL HAVE TO TALK TO ME!
I'm betting she doesn't really want to talk--

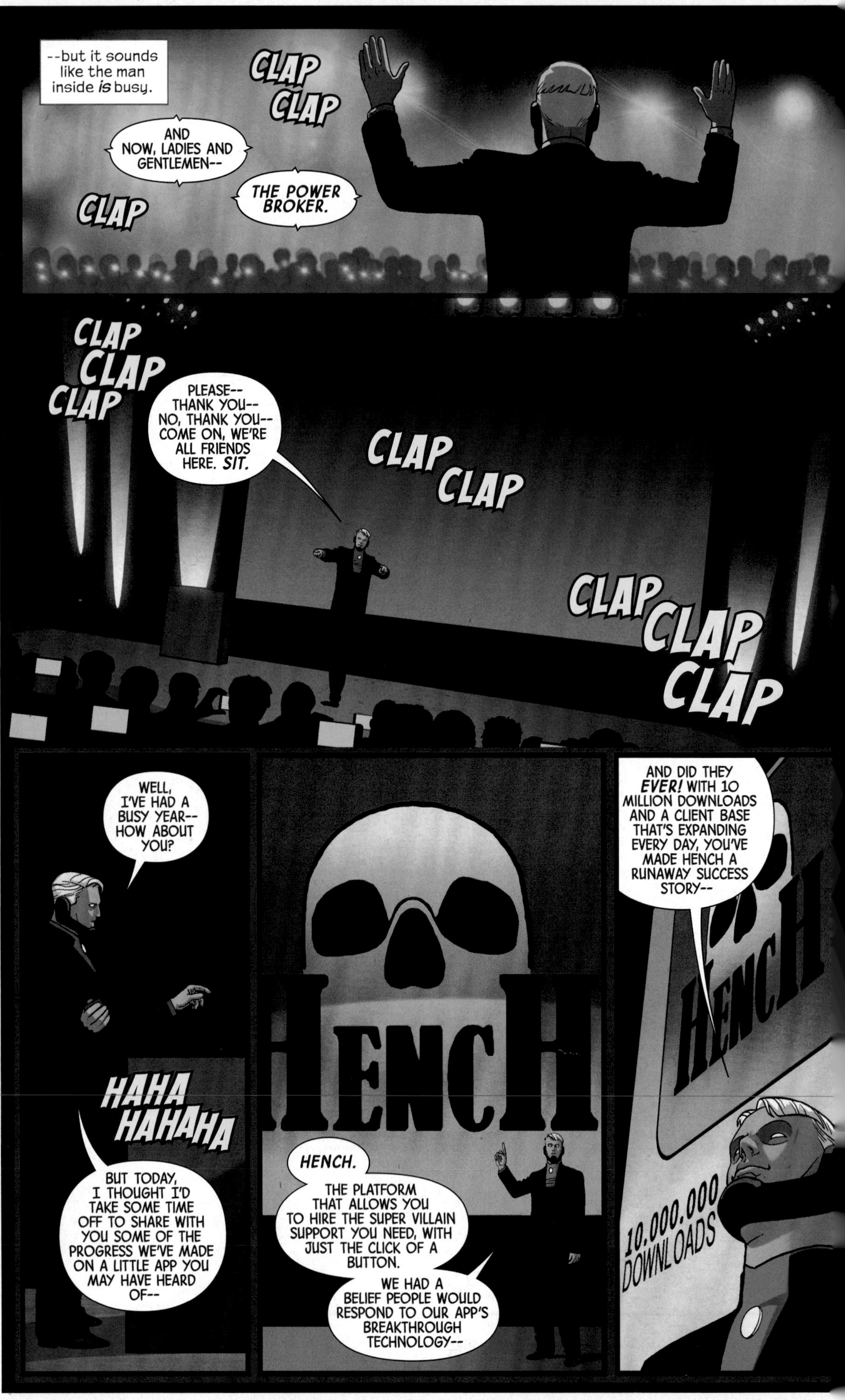
--but it sounds like the man inside *is* busy.
CLAP CLAP
AND NOW, LADIES AND GENTLEMEN--
CLAP
THE POWER BROKER.
CLAP CLAP CLAP
PLEASE-- THANK YOU-- NO, THANK YOU-- COME ON, WE'RE ALL FRIENDS HERE. *SIT.*
CLAP CLAP
CLAP CLAP CLAP
WELL, I'VE HAD A BUSY YEAR-- HOW ABOUT YOU?
HAHA HAHAHA
BUT TODAY, I THOUGHT I'D TAKE SOME TIME OFF TO SHARE WITH YOU SOME OF THE PROGRESS WE'VE MADE ON A LITTLE APP YOU MAY HAVE HEARD OF--
HENCH
HENCH.
THE PLATFORM THAT ALLOWS YOU TO HIRE THE SUPER VILLAIN SUPPORT YOU NEED, WITH JUST THE CLICK OF A BUTTON.
WE HAD A BELIEF PEOPLE WOULD RESPOND TO OUR APP'S BREAKTHROUGH TECHNOLOGY--
AND DID THEY *EVER!* WITH 10 MILLION DOWNLOADS AND A CLIENT BASE THAT'S EXPANDING EVERY DAY, YOU'VE MADE HENCH A RUNAWAY SUCCESS STORY--
HENCH
10.000.000 DOWNLOADS

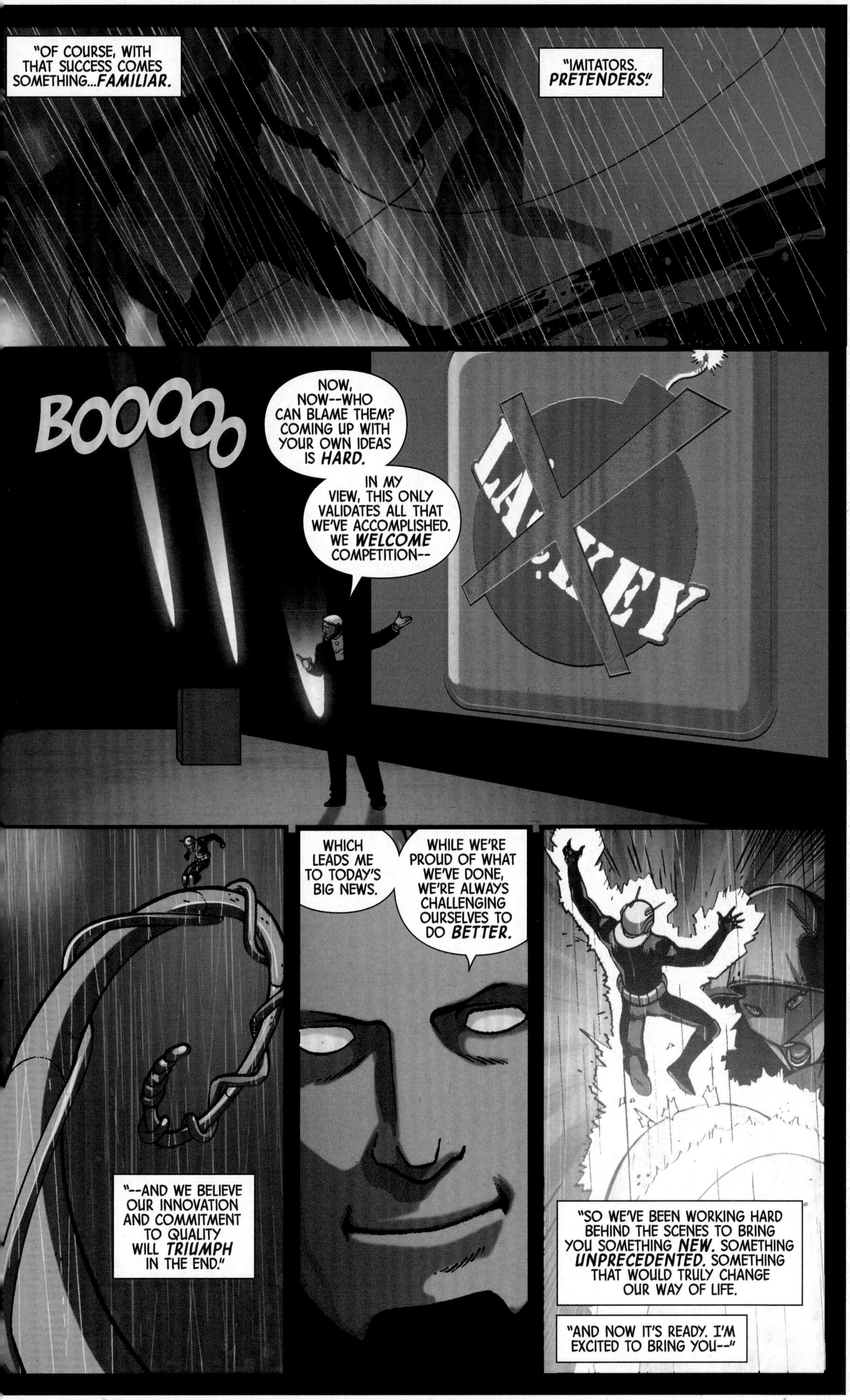
"OF COURSE, WITH THAT SUCCESS COMES SOMETHING...FAMILIAR.
"IMITATORS. PRETENDERS!"
BOOOOO
NOW, NOW--WHO CAN BLAME THEM? COMING UP WITH YOUR OWN IDEAS IS HARD.
IN MY VIEW, THIS ONLY VALIDATES ALL THAT WE'VE ACCOMPLISHED. WE WELCOME COMPETITION--
"--AND WE BELIEVE OUR INNOVATION AND COMMITMENT TO QUALITY WILL TRIUMPH IN THE END."
WHICH LEADS ME TO TODAY'S BIG NEWS.
WHILE WE'RE PROUD OF WHAT WE'VE DONE, WE'RE ALWAYS CHALLENGING OURSELVES TO DO BETTER.
"SO WE'VE BEEN WORKING HARD BEHIND THE SCENES TO BRING YOU SOMETHING NEW. SOMETHING UNPRECEDENTED. SOMETHING THAT WOULD TRULY CHANGE OUR WAY OF LIFE.
"AND NOW IT'S READY. I'M EXCITED TO BRING YOU--"

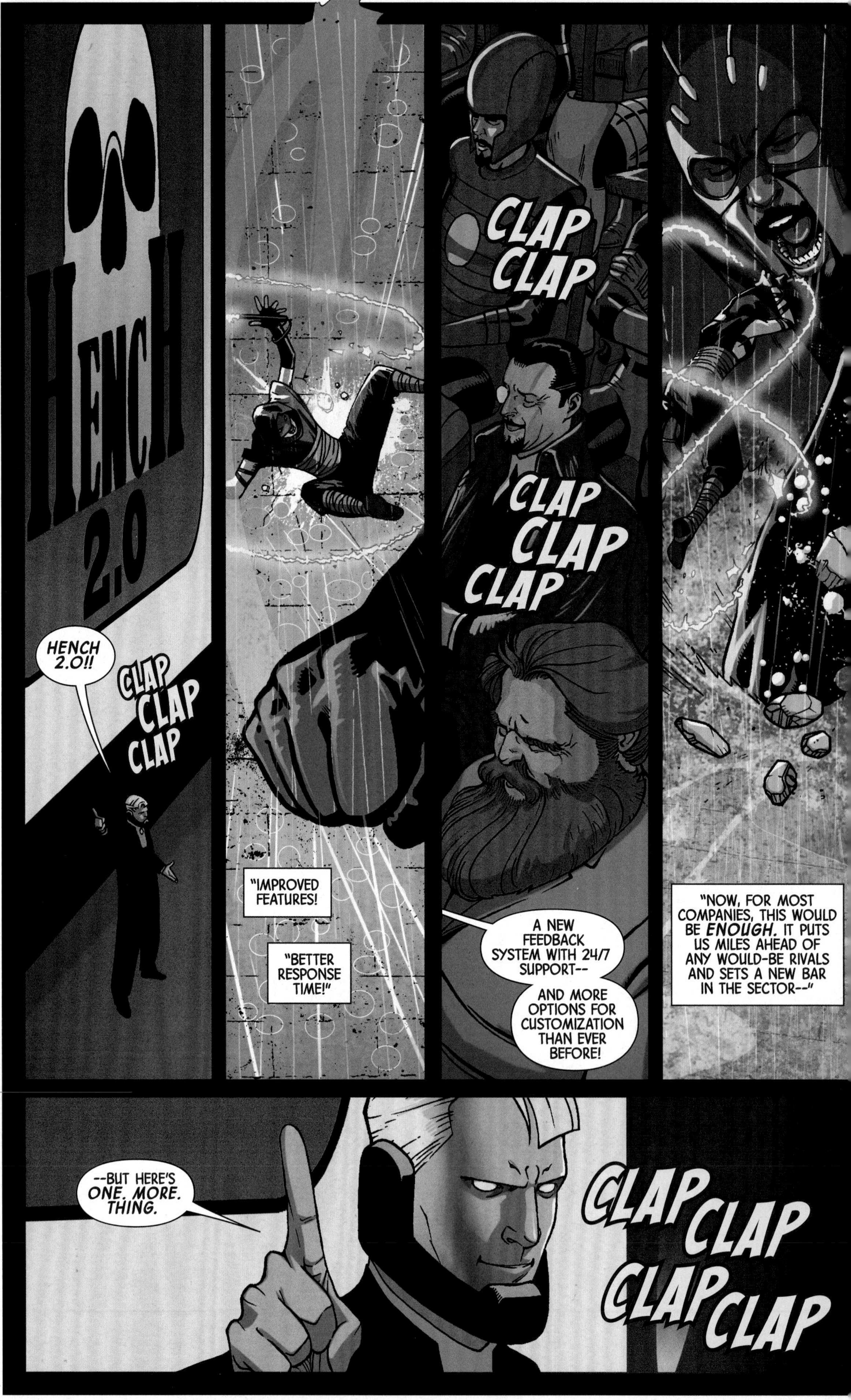
HENCH 2.0
HENCH 2.0!!
CLAP CLAP CLAP
"IMPROVED FEATURES!
"BETTER RESPONSE TIME!"
CLAP CLAP
CLAP CLAP CLAP
A NEW FEEDBACK SYSTEM WITH 24/7 SUPPORT--
AND MORE OPTIONS FOR CUSTOMIZATION THAN EVER BEFORE!
"NOW, FOR MOST COMPANIES, THIS WOULD BE ENOUGH. IT PUTS US MILES AHEAD OF ANY WOULD-BE RIVALS AND SETS A NEW BAR IN THE SECTOR--"
--BUT HERE'S ONE. MORE. THING.
CLAP CLAP CLAP CLAP

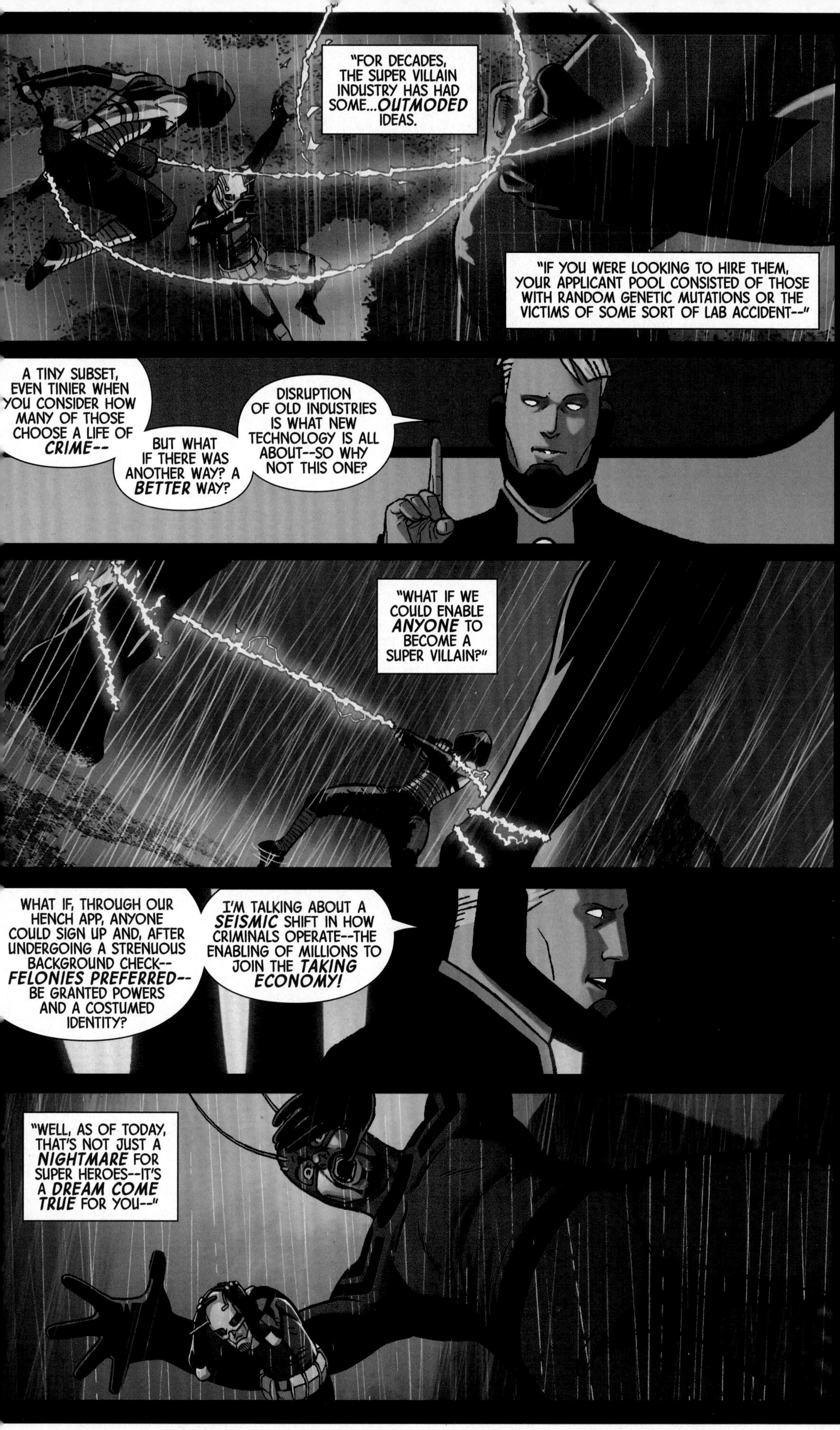
"FOR DECADES, THE SUPER VILLAIN INDUSTRY HAS HAD SOME...OUTMODED IDEAS.
"IF YOU WERE LOOKING TO HIRE THEM, YOUR APPLICANT POOL CONSISTED OF THOSE WITH RANDOM GENETIC MUTATIONS OR THE VICTIMS OF SOME SORT OF LAB ACCIDENT--"
A TINY SUBSET, EVEN TINIER WHEN YOU CONSIDER HOW MANY OF THOSE CHOOSE A LIFE OF CRIME--
BUT WHAT IF THERE WAS ANOTHER WAY? A BETTER WAY?
DISRUPTION OF OLD INDUSTRIES IS WHAT NEW TECHNOLOGY IS ALL ABOUT--SO WHY NOT THIS ONE?
"WHAT IF WE COULD ENABLE ANYONE TO BECOME A SUPER VILLAIN?"
WHAT IF, THROUGH OUR HENCH APP, ANYONE COULD SIGN UP AND, AFTER UNDERGOING A STRENUOUS BACKGROUND CHECK--FELONIES PREFERRED--BE GRANTED POWERS AND A COSTUMED IDENTITY?
I'M TALKING ABOUT A SEISMIC SHIFT IN HOW CRIMINALS OPERATE--THE ENABLING OF MILLIONS TO JOIN THE TAKING ECONOMY!
"WELL, AS OF TODAY, THAT'S NOT JUST A NIGHTMARE FOR SUPER HEROES--IT'S A DREAM COME TRUE FOR YOU--"

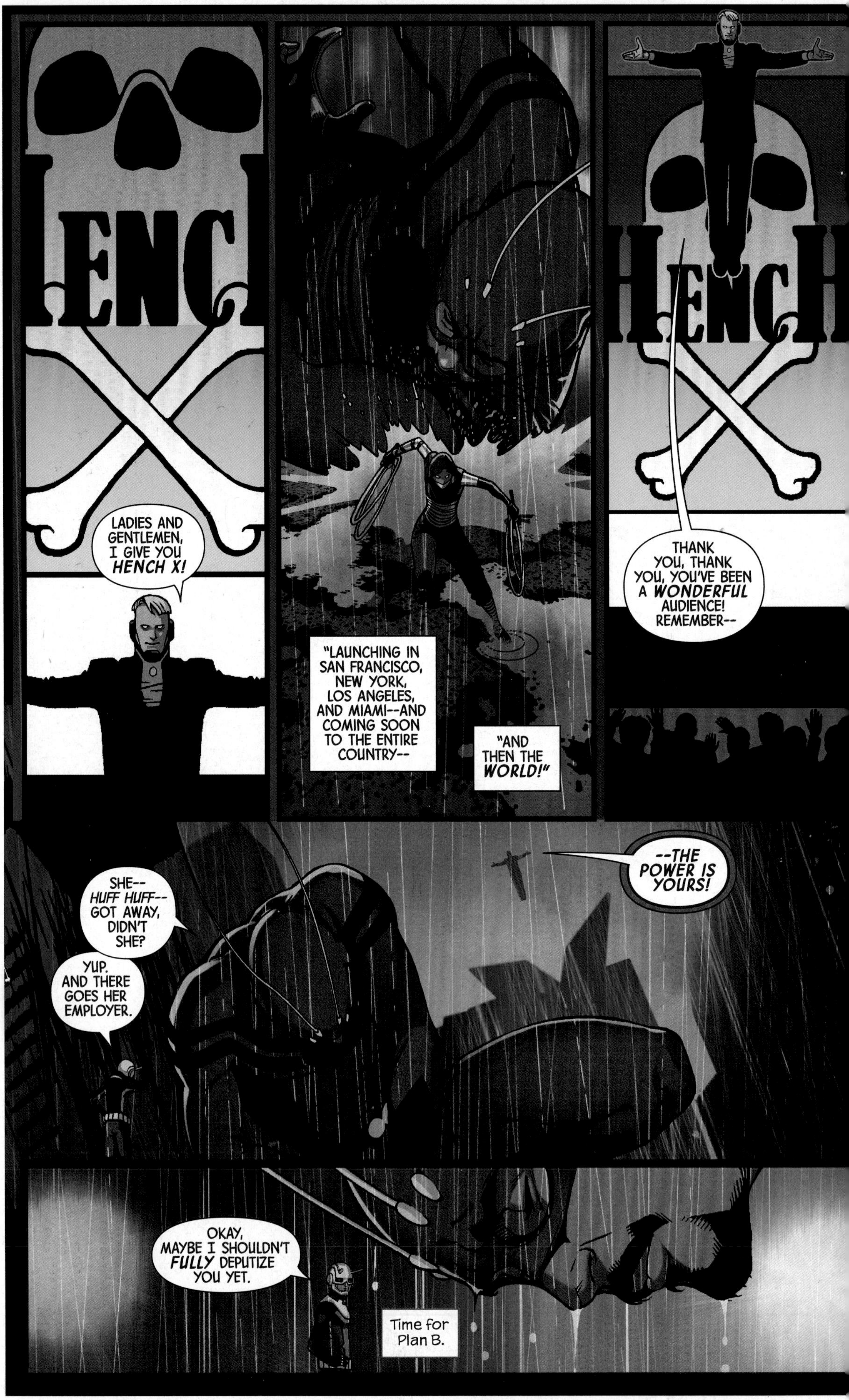

LADIES AND GENTLEMEN, I GIVE YOU HENCH X!
"LAUNCHING IN SAN FRANCISCO, NEW YORK, LOS ANGELES, AND MIAMI--AND COMING SOON TO THE ENTIRE COUNTRY--
"AND THEN THE WORLD!"
THANK YOU, THANK YOU, YOU'VE BEEN A WONDERFUL AUDIENCE! REMEMBER--
--THE POWER IS YOURS!
SHE-- HUFF HUFF-- GOT AWAY, DIDN'T SHE?
YUP. AND THERE GOES HER EMPLOYER.
OKAY, MAYBE I SHOULDN'T FULLY DEPUTIZE YOU YET.
Time for Plan B.

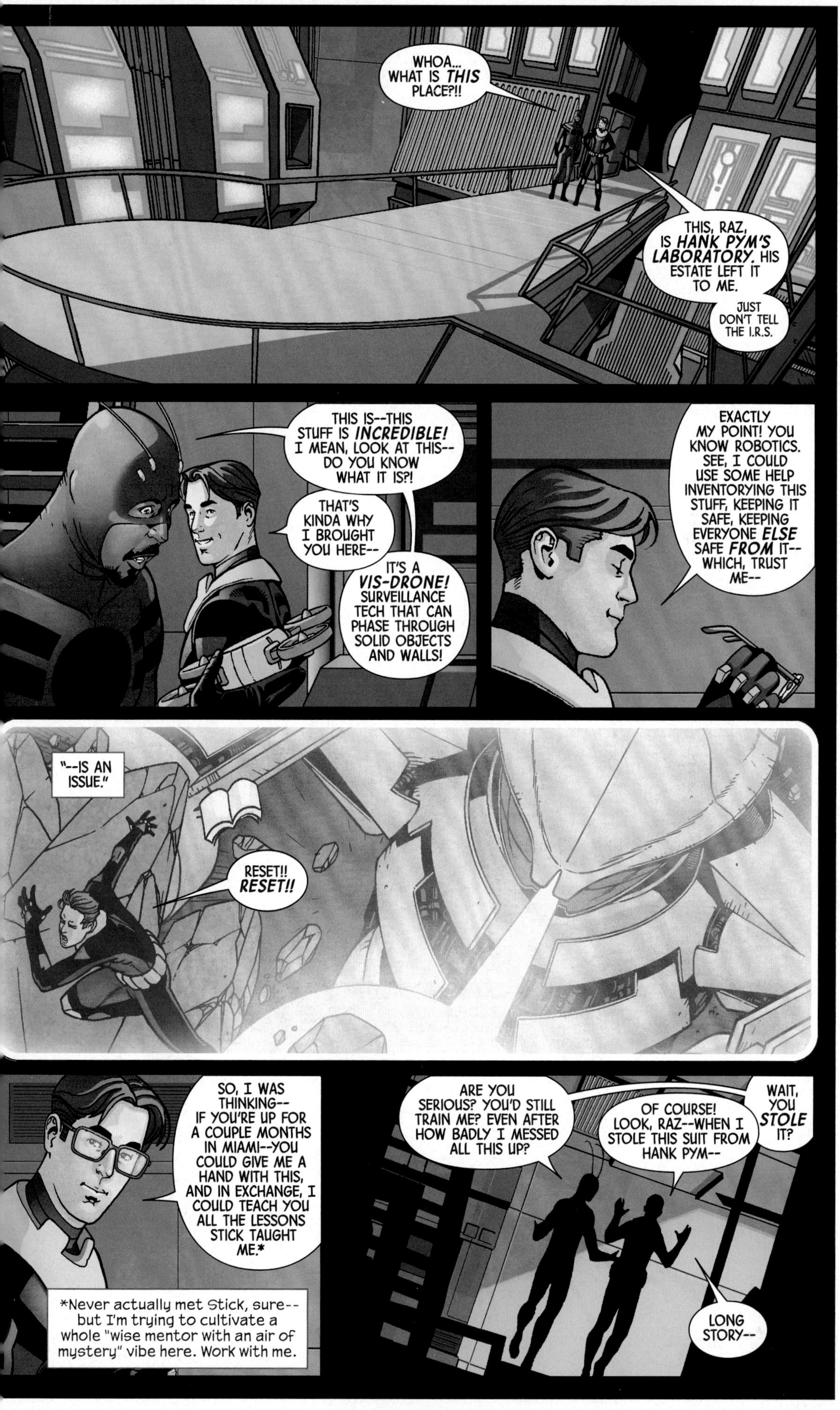
WHOA... WHAT IS THIS PLACE?!!
THIS, RAZ, IS HANK PYM'S LABORATORY. HIS ESTATE LEFT IT TO ME.
JUST DON'T TELL THE I.R.S.
THIS IS--THIS STUFF IS INCREDIBLE! I MEAN, LOOK AT THIS-- DO YOU KNOW WHAT IT IS?!
THAT'S KINDA WHY I BROUGHT YOU HERE--
IT'S A VIS-DRONE! SURVEILLANCE TECH THAT CAN PHASE THROUGH SOLID OBJECTS AND WALLS!
EXACTLY MY POINT! YOU KNOW ROBOTICS. SEE, I COULD USE SOME HELP INVENTORYING THIS STUFF, KEEPING IT SAFE, KEEPING EVERYONE ELSE SAFE FROM IT-- WHICH, TRUST ME--
"--IS AN ISSUE."
RESET!! RESET!!
SO, I WAS THINKING-- IF YOU'RE UP FOR A COUPLE MONTHS IN MIAMI--YOU COULD GIVE ME A HAND WITH THIS, AND IN EXCHANGE, I COULD TEACH YOU ALL THE LESSONS STICK TAUGHT ME.*
*Never actually met Stick, sure-- but I'm trying to cultivate a whole "wise mentor with an air of mystery" vibe here. Work with me.
ARE YOU SERIOUS? YOU'D STILL TRAIN ME? EVEN AFTER HOW BADLY I MESSED ALL THIS UP?
OF COURSE! LOOK, RAZ--WHEN I STOLE THIS SUIT FROM HANK PYM--
WAIT, YOU STOLE IT?
LONG STORY--

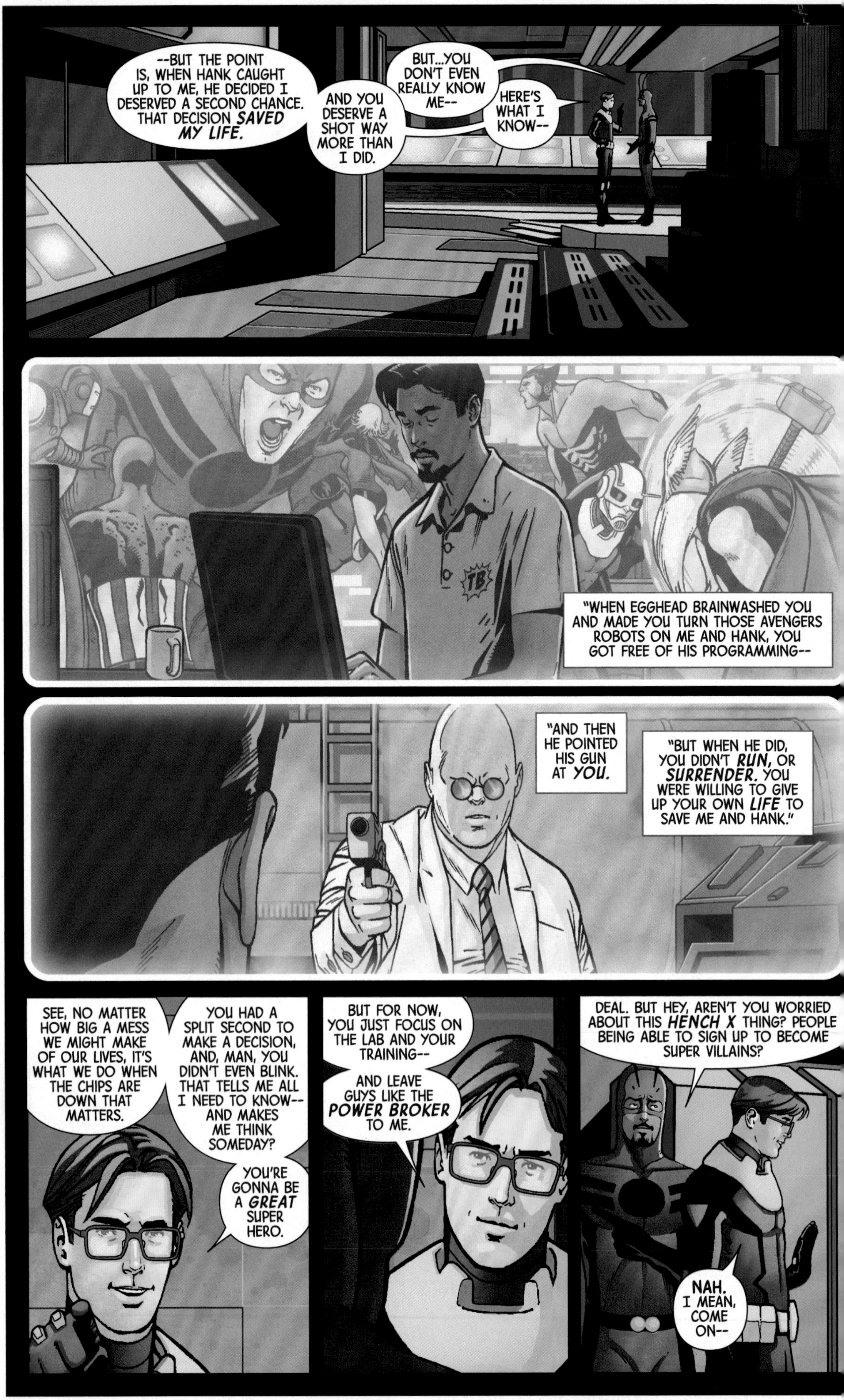
--BUT THE POINT IS, WHEN HANK CAUGHT UP TO ME, HE DECIDED I DESERVED A SECOND CHANCE. THAT DECISION SAVED MY LIFE.
AND YOU DESERVE A SHOT WAY MORE THAN I DID.
BUT...YOU DON'T EVEN REALLY KNOW ME--
HERE'S WHAT I KNOW--
"WHEN EGGHEAD BRAINWASHED YOU AND MADE YOU TURN THOSE AVENGERS ROBOTS ON ME AND HANK, YOU GOT FREE OF HIS PROGRAMMING--
TB
"AND THEN HE POINTED HIS GUN AT YOU.
"BUT WHEN HE DID, YOU DIDN'T RUN, OR SURRENDER. YOU WERE WILLING TO GIVE UP YOUR OWN LIFE TO SAVE ME AND HANK."
SEE, NO MATTER HOW BIG A MESS WE MIGHT MAKE OF OUR LIVES, IT'S WHAT WE DO WHEN THE CHIPS ARE DOWN THAT MATTERS.
YOU HAD A SPLIT SECOND TO MAKE A DECISION, AND, MAN, YOU DIDN'T EVEN BLINK. THAT TELLS ME ALL I NEED TO KNOW-- AND MAKES ME THINK SOMEDAY?
YOU'RE GONNA BE A GREAT SUPER HERO.
BUT FOR NOW, YOU JUST FOCUS ON THE LAB AND YOUR TRAINING--
AND LEAVE GUYS LIKE THE POWER BROKER TO ME.
DEAL. BUT HEY, AREN'T YOU WORRIED ABOUT THIS HENCH X THING? PEOPLE BEING ABLE TO SIGN UP TO BECOME SUPER VILLAINS?
NAH. I MEAN, COME ON--

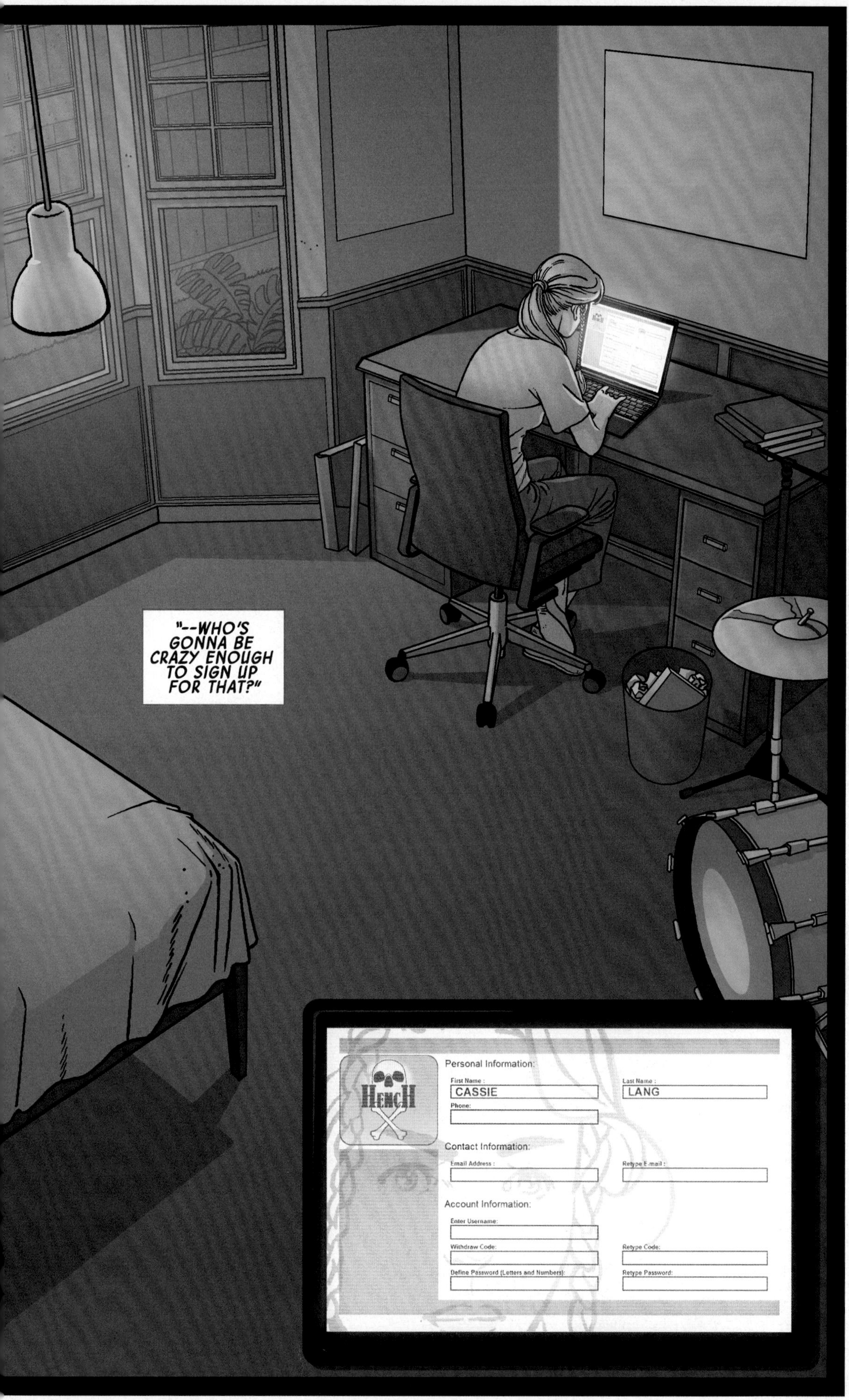
"--WHO'S GONNA BE CRAZY ENOUGH TO SIGN UP FOR THAT?"
HENCH
Personal Information:
First Name :
CASSIE
Last Name :
LANG
Phone:
Contact Information:
Email Address :
Retype E-mail :
Account Information:
Enter Username:
Withdraw Code:
Retype Code:
Define Password (Letters and Numbers):
Retype Password:

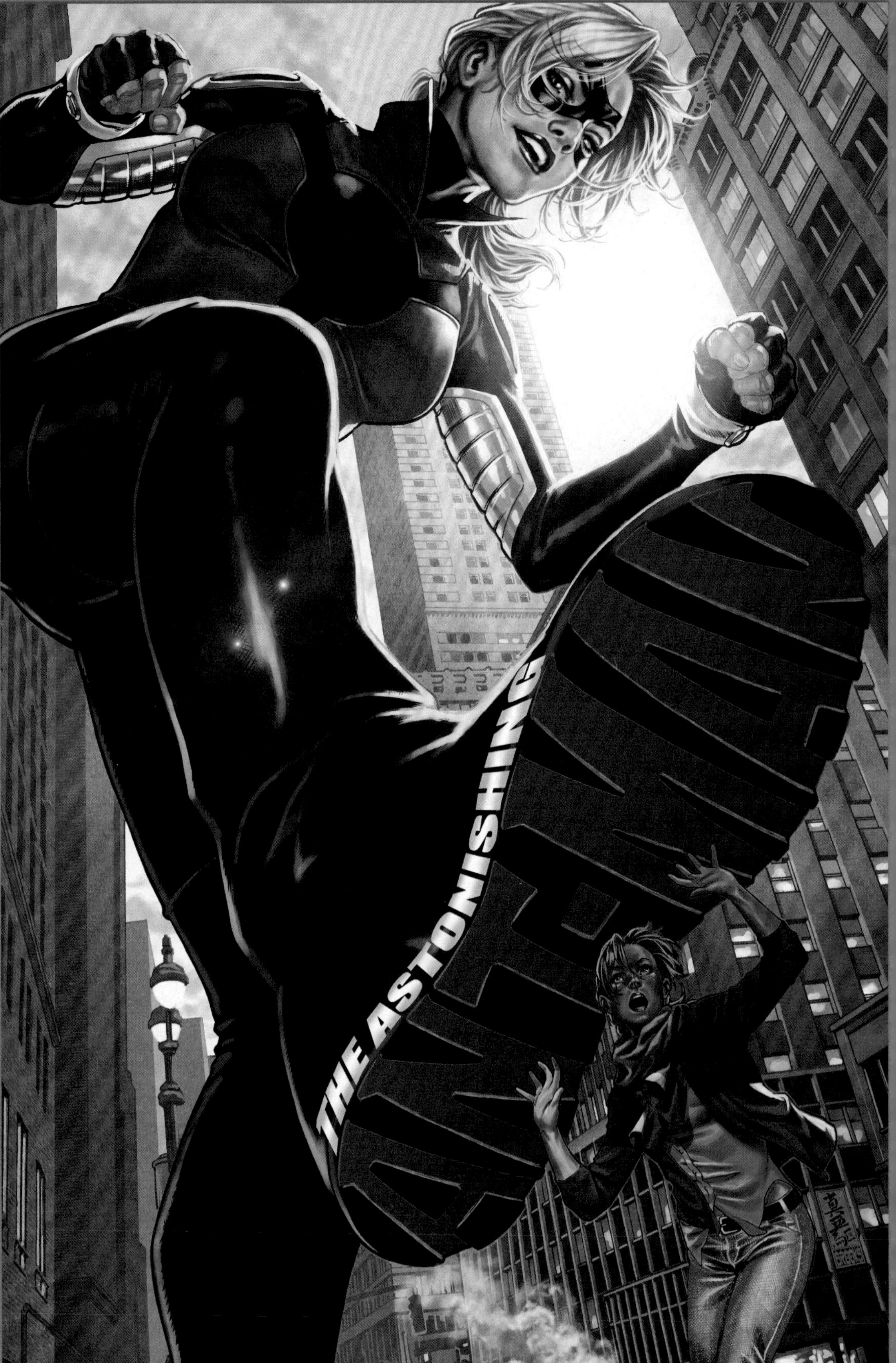
THE ASTONISHING

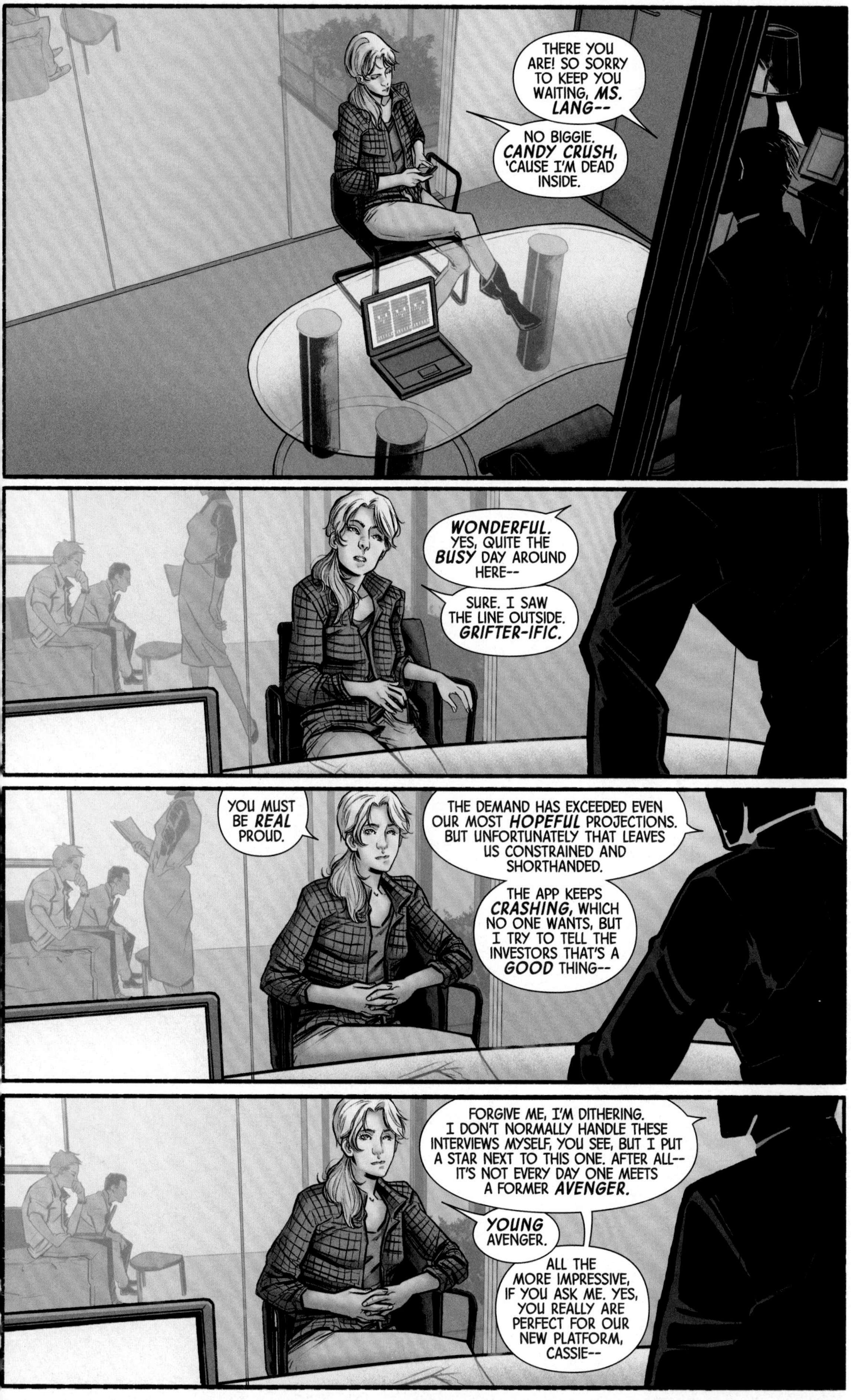
THERE YOU ARE! SO SORRY TO KEEP YOU WAITING, MS. LANG--
NO BIGGIE. CANDY CRUSH, 'CAUSE I'M DEAD INSIDE.
WONDERFUL. YES, QUITE THE BUSY DAY AROUND HERE--
SURE. I SAW THE LINE OUTSIDE. GRIFTER-IFIC.
YOU MUST BE REAL PROUD.
THE DEMAND HAS EXCEEDED EVEN OUR MOST HOPEFUL PROJECTIONS. BUT UNFORTUNATELY THAT LEAVES US CONSTRAINED AND SHORTHANDED.
THE APP KEEPS CRASHING, WHICH NO ONE WANTS, BUT I TRY TO TELL THE INVESTORS THAT'S A GOOD THING--
FORGIVE ME, I'M DITHERING. I DON'T NORMALLY HANDLE THESE INTERVIEWS MYSELF, YOU SEE, BUT I PUT A STAR NEXT TO THIS ONE. AFTER ALL-- IT'S NOT EVERY DAY ONE MEETS A FORMER AVENGER.
YOUNG AVENGER.
ALL THE MORE IMPRESSIVE, IF YOU ASK ME. YES, YOU REALLY ARE PERFECT FOR OUR NEW PLATFORM, CASSIE--

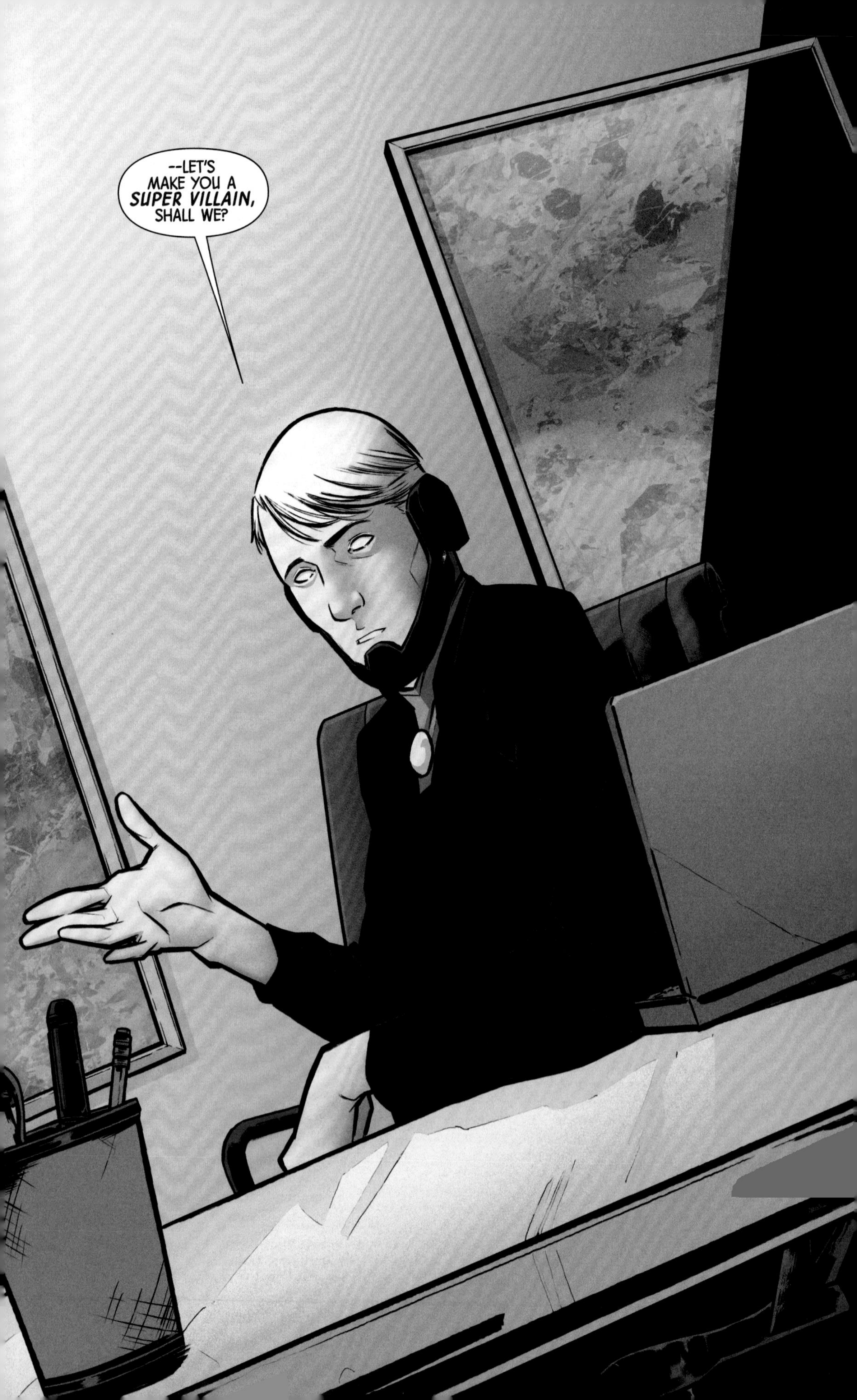
--LET'S MAKE YOU A *SUPER VILLAIN,* SHALL WE?

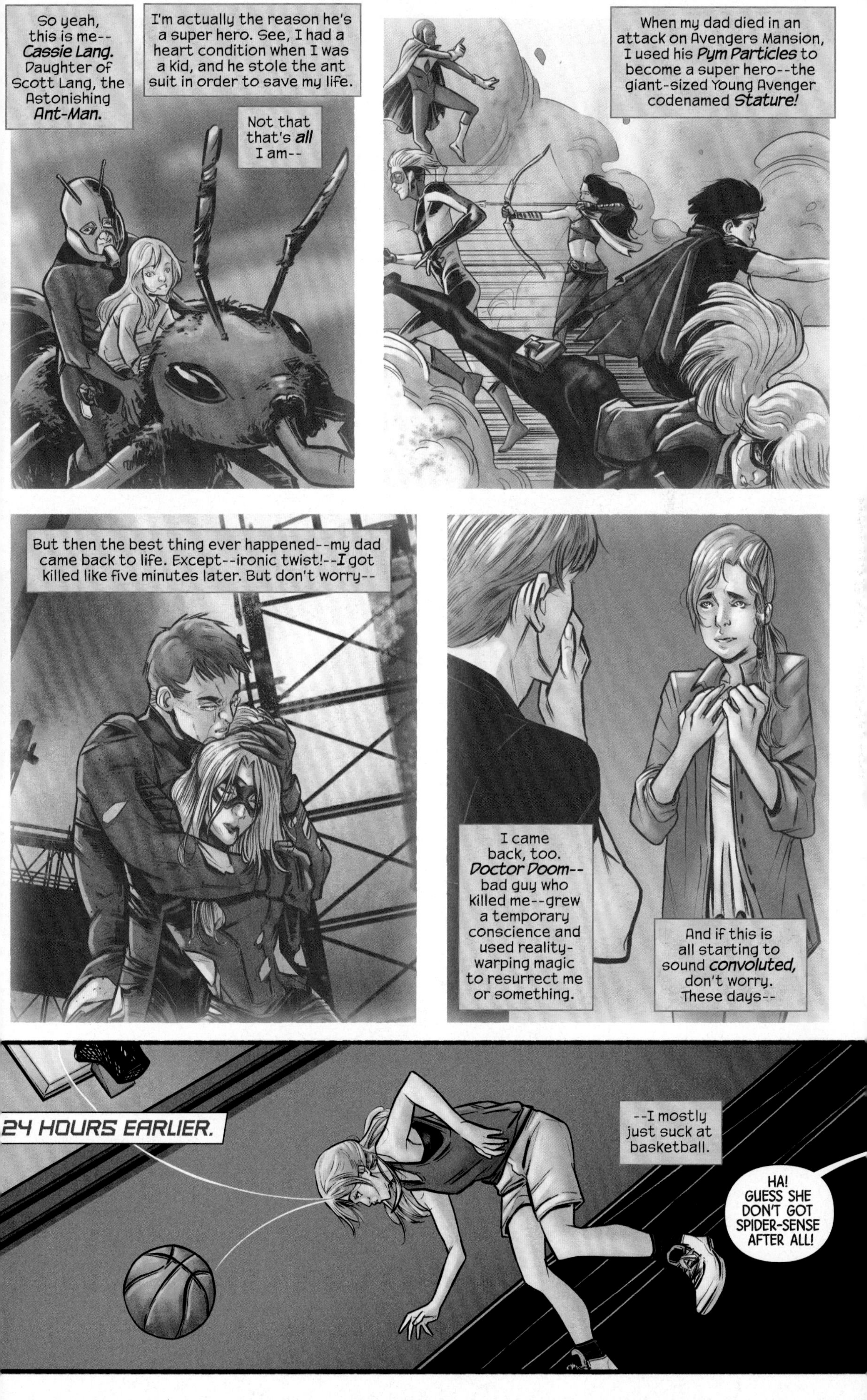

So yeah, this is me-- Cassie Lang. Daughter of Scott Lang, the Astonishing Ant-Man.
I'm actually the reason he's a super hero. See, I had a heart condition when I was a kid, and he stole the ant suit in order to save my life.
Not that that's all I am--
When my dad died in an attack on Avengers Mansion, I used his Pym Particles to become a super hero--the giant-sized Young Avenger codenamed Stature!
But then the best thing ever happened--my dad came back to life. Except--ironic twist!--I got killed like five minutes later. But don't worry--
I came back, too. Doctor Doom-- bad guy who killed me--grew a temporary conscience and used reality-warping magic to resurrect me or something.
And if this is all starting to sound convoluted, don't worry. These days--
24 HOURS EARLIER.
--I mostly just suck at basketball.
HA! GUESS SHE DON'T GOT SPIDER-SENSE AFTER ALL!

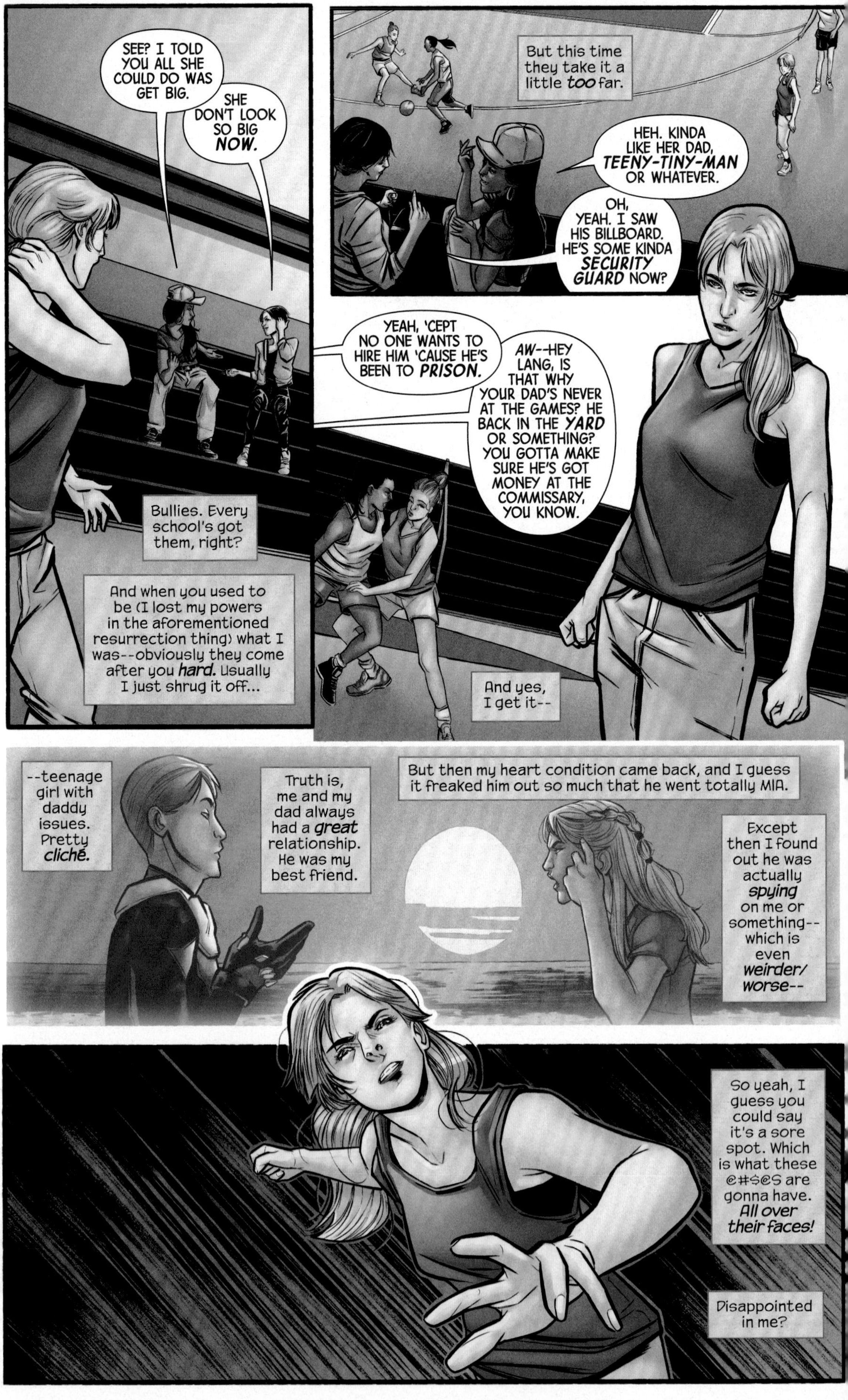
SEE? I TOLD YOU ALL SHE COULD DO WAS GET BIG.
SHE DON'T LOOK SO BIG NOW.
Bullies. Every school's got them, right?
And when you used to be (I lost my powers in the aforementioned resurrection thing) what I was--obviously they come after you hard. Usually I just shrug it off...
But this time they take it a little too far.
HEH. KINDA LIKE HER DAD, TEENY-TINY-MAN OR WHATEVER.
OH, YEAH. I SAW HIS BILLBOARD. HE'S SOME KINDA SECURITY GUARD NOW?
YEAH, 'CEPT NO ONE WANTS TO HIRE HIM 'CAUSE HE'S BEEN TO PRISON.
AW--HEY LANG, IS THAT WHY YOUR DAD'S NEVER AT THE GAMES? HE BACK IN THE YARD OR SOMETHING? YOU GOTTA MAKE SURE HE'S GOT MONEY AT THE COMMISSARY, YOU KNOW.
And yes, I get it--
--teenage girl with daddy issues. Pretty cliché.
Truth is, me and my dad always had a great relationship. He was my best friend.
But then my heart condition came back, and I guess it freaked him out so much that he went totally MIA.
Except then I found out he was actually spying on me or something--which is even weirder/worse--
So yeah, I guess you could say it's a sore spot. Which is what these @#$@S are gonna have. All over their faces!
Disappointed in me?

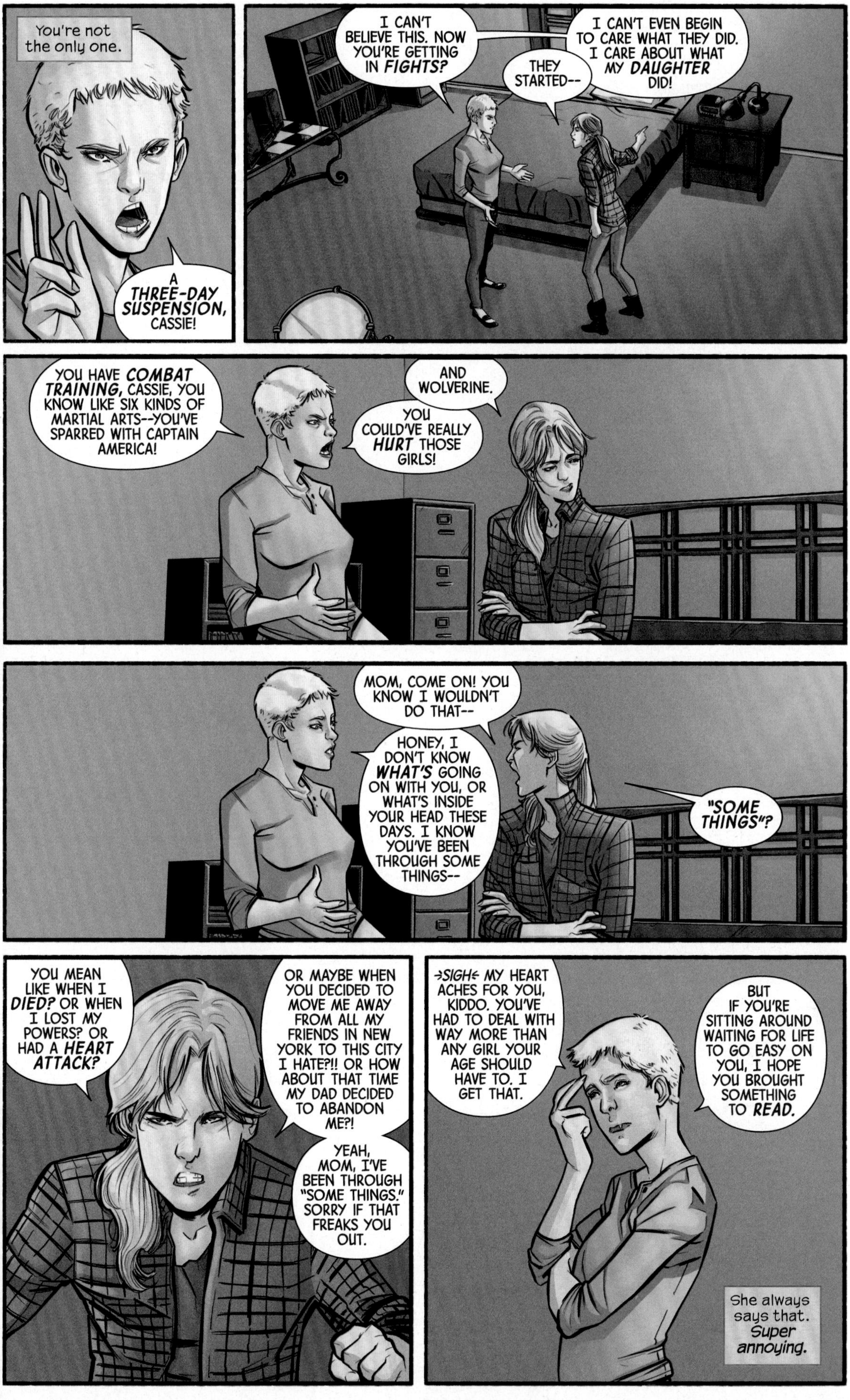
You're not the only one.
A THREE-DAY SUSPENSION, CASSIE!
I CAN'T BELIEVE THIS. NOW YOU'RE GETTING IN FIGHTS?
THEY STARTED--
I CAN'T EVEN BEGIN TO CARE WHAT THEY DID. I CARE ABOUT WHAT MY DAUGHTER DID!
YOU HAVE COMBAT TRAINING, CASSIE, YOU KNOW LIKE SIX KINDS OF MARTIAL ARTS--YOU'VE SPARRED WITH CAPTAIN AMERICA!
AND WOLVERINE.
YOU COULD'VE REALLY HURT THOSE GIRLS!
MOM, COME ON! YOU KNOW I WOULDN'T DO THAT--
HONEY, I DON'T KNOW WHAT'S GOING ON WITH YOU, OR WHAT'S INSIDE YOUR HEAD THESE DAYS. I KNOW YOU'VE BEEN THROUGH SOME THINGS--
"SOME THINGS"?
YOU MEAN LIKE WHEN I DIED? OR WHEN I LOST MY POWERS? OR HAD A HEART ATTACK?
OR MAYBE WHEN YOU DECIDED TO MOVE ME AWAY FROM ALL MY FRIENDS IN NEW YORK TO THIS CITY I HATE?!! OR HOW ABOUT THAT TIME MY DAD DECIDED TO ABANDON ME?!
YEAH, MOM, I'VE BEEN THROUGH "SOME THINGS." SORRY IF THAT FREAKS YOU OUT.
→SIGH← MY HEART ACHES FOR YOU, KIDDO. YOU'VE HAD TO DEAL WITH WAY MORE THAN ANY GIRL YOUR AGE SHOULD HAVE TO. I GET THAT.
BUT IF YOU'RE SITTING AROUND WAITING FOR LIFE TO GO EASY ON YOU, I HOPE YOU BROUGHT SOMETHING TO READ.
She always says that. Super annoying.

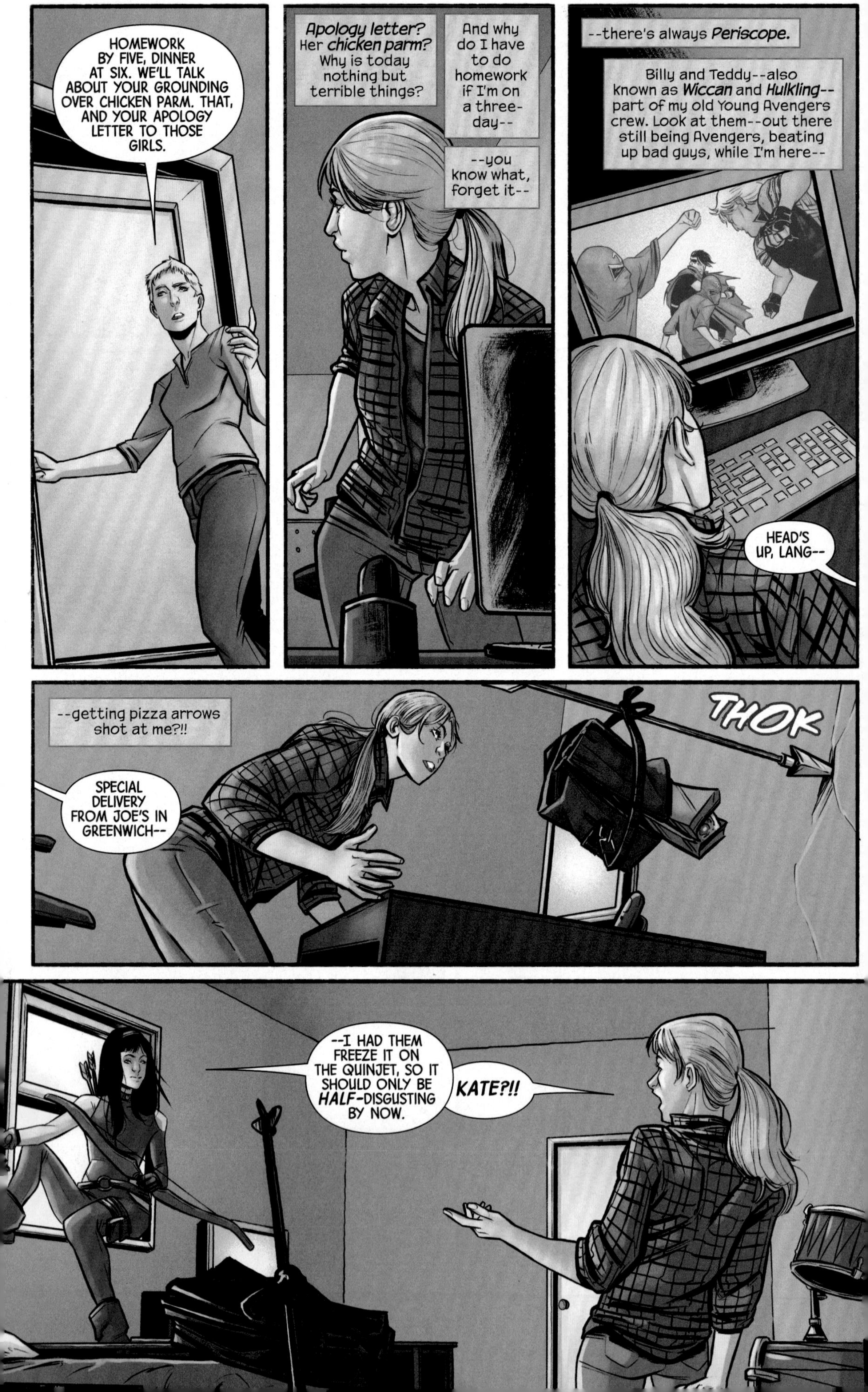
HOMEWORK BY FIVE, DINNER AT SIX. WE'LL TALK ABOUT YOUR GROUNDING OVER CHICKEN PARM. THAT, AND YOUR APOLOGY LETTER TO THOSE GIRLS.
Apology letter? Her chicken parm? Why is today nothing but terrible things?
And why do I have to do homework if I'm on a three-day--
--you know what, forget it--
--there's always Periscope.
Billy and Teddy--also known as Wiccan and Hulkling--part of my old Young Avengers crew. Look at them--out there still being Avengers, beating up bad guys, while I'm here--
HEAD'S UP, LANG--
--getting pizza arrows shot at me?!!
THOK
SPECIAL DELIVERY FROM JOE'S IN GREENWICH--
--I HAD THEM FREEZE IT ON THE QUINJET, SO IT SHOULD ONLY BE HALF-DISGUSTING BY NOW.
KATE?!!

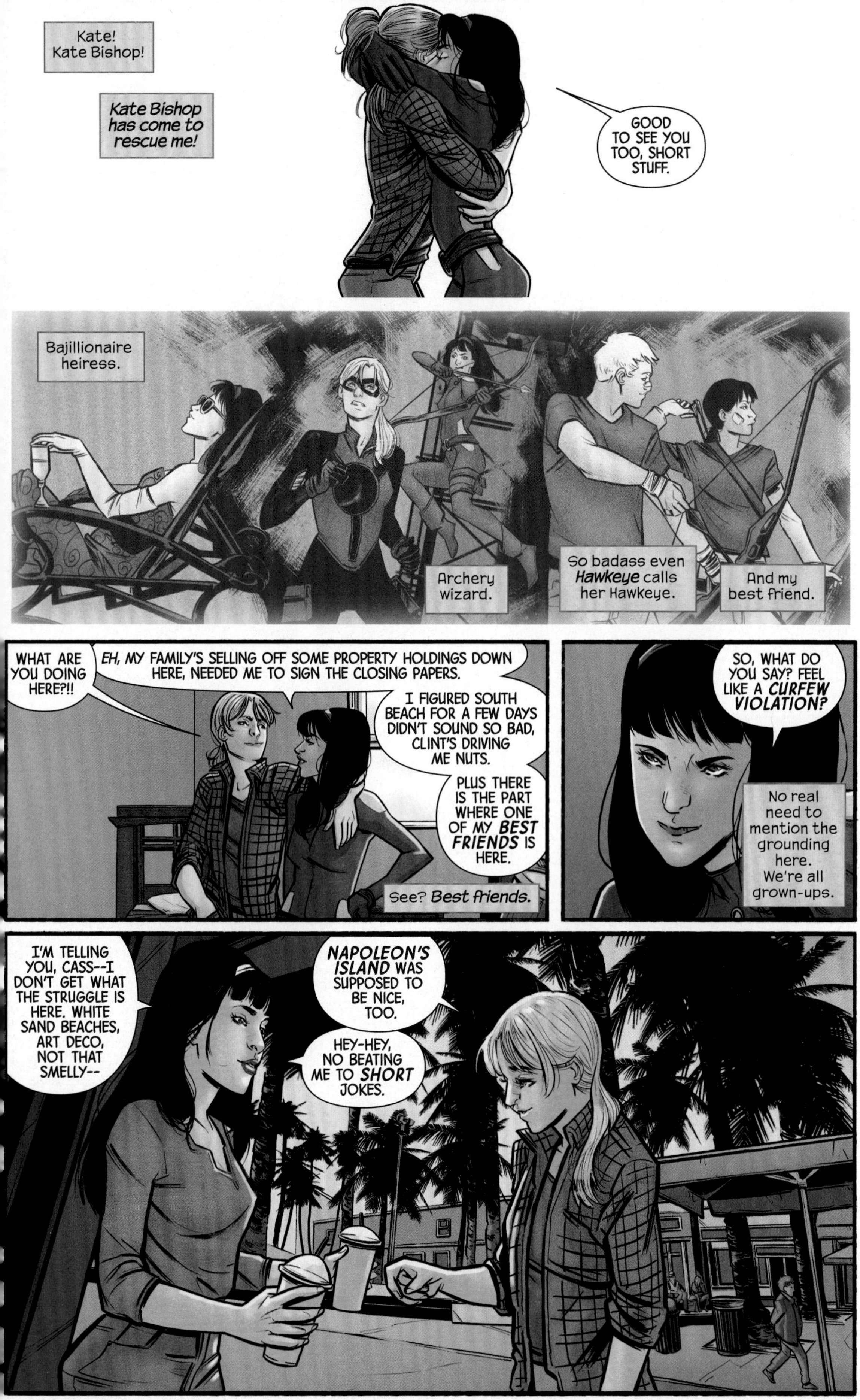

Kate!
Kate Bishop!
Kate Bishop has come to rescue me!
GOOD TO SEE YOU TOO, SHORT STUFF.
Bajillionaire heiress.
Archery wizard.
So badass even Hawkeye calls her Hawkeye.
And my best friend.
WHAT ARE YOU DOING HERE?!!
EH, MY FAMILY'S SELLING OFF SOME PROPERTY HOLDINGS DOWN HERE, NEEDED ME TO SIGN THE CLOSING PAPERS.
I FIGURED SOUTH BEACH FOR A FEW DAYS DIDN'T SOUND SO BAD, CLINT'S DRIVING ME NUTS.
PLUS THERE IS THE PART WHERE ONE OF MY BEST FRIENDS IS HERE.
See? Best friends.
SO, WHAT DO YOU SAY? FEEL LIKE A CURFEW VIOLATION?
No real need to mention the grounding here. We're all grown-ups.
I'M TELLING YOU, CASS--I DON'T GET WHAT THE STRUGGLE IS HERE. WHITE SAND BEACHES, ART DECO, NOT THAT SMELLY--
NAPOLEON'S ISLAND WAS SUPPOSED TO BE NICE, TOO.
HEY-HEY, NO BEATING ME TO SHORT JOKES.

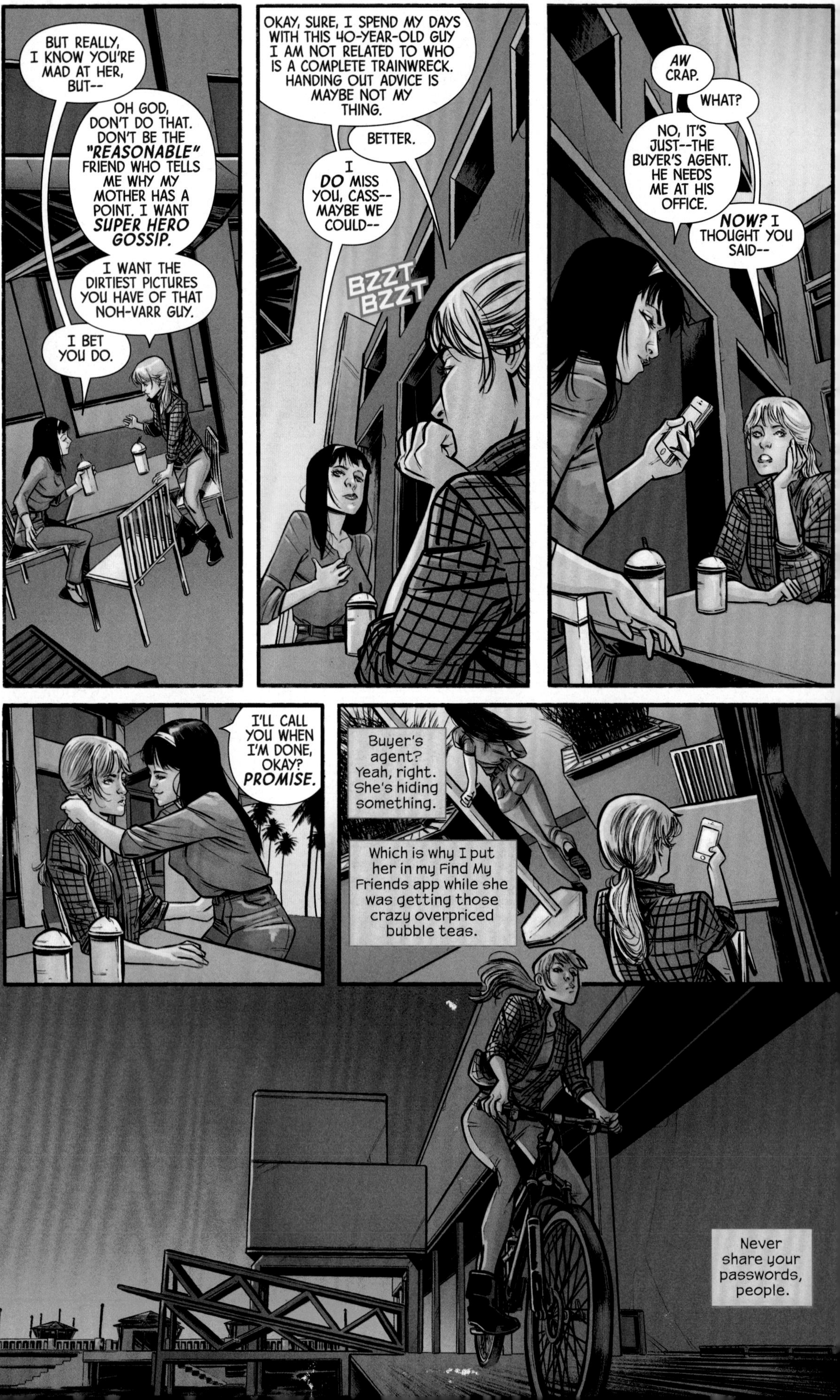

BUT REALLY, I KNOW YOU'RE MAD AT HER, BUT--
OH GOD, DON'T DO THAT. DON'T BE THE "REASONABLE" FRIEND WHO TELLS ME WHY MY MOTHER HAS A POINT. I WANT SUPER HERO GOSSIP.
I WANT THE DIRTIEST PICTURES YOU HAVE OF THAT NOH-VARR GUY.
I BET YOU DO.
OKAY, SURE, I SPEND MY DAYS WITH THIS 40-YEAR-OLD GUY I AM NOT RELATED TO WHO IS A COMPLETE TRAINWRECK. HANDING OUT ADVICE IS MAYBE NOT MY THING.
BETTER.
I DO MISS YOU, CASS-- MAYBE WE COULD--
BZZT BZZT
AW CRAP.
WHAT?
NO, IT'S JUST--THE BUYER'S AGENT. HE NEEDS ME AT HIS OFFICE.
NOW? I THOUGHT YOU SAID--
I'LL CALL YOU WHEN I'M DONE, OKAY? PROMISE.
Buyer's agent? Yeah, right. She's hiding something.
Which is why I put her in my Find My Friends app while she was getting those crazy overpriced bubble teas.
Never share your passwords, people.

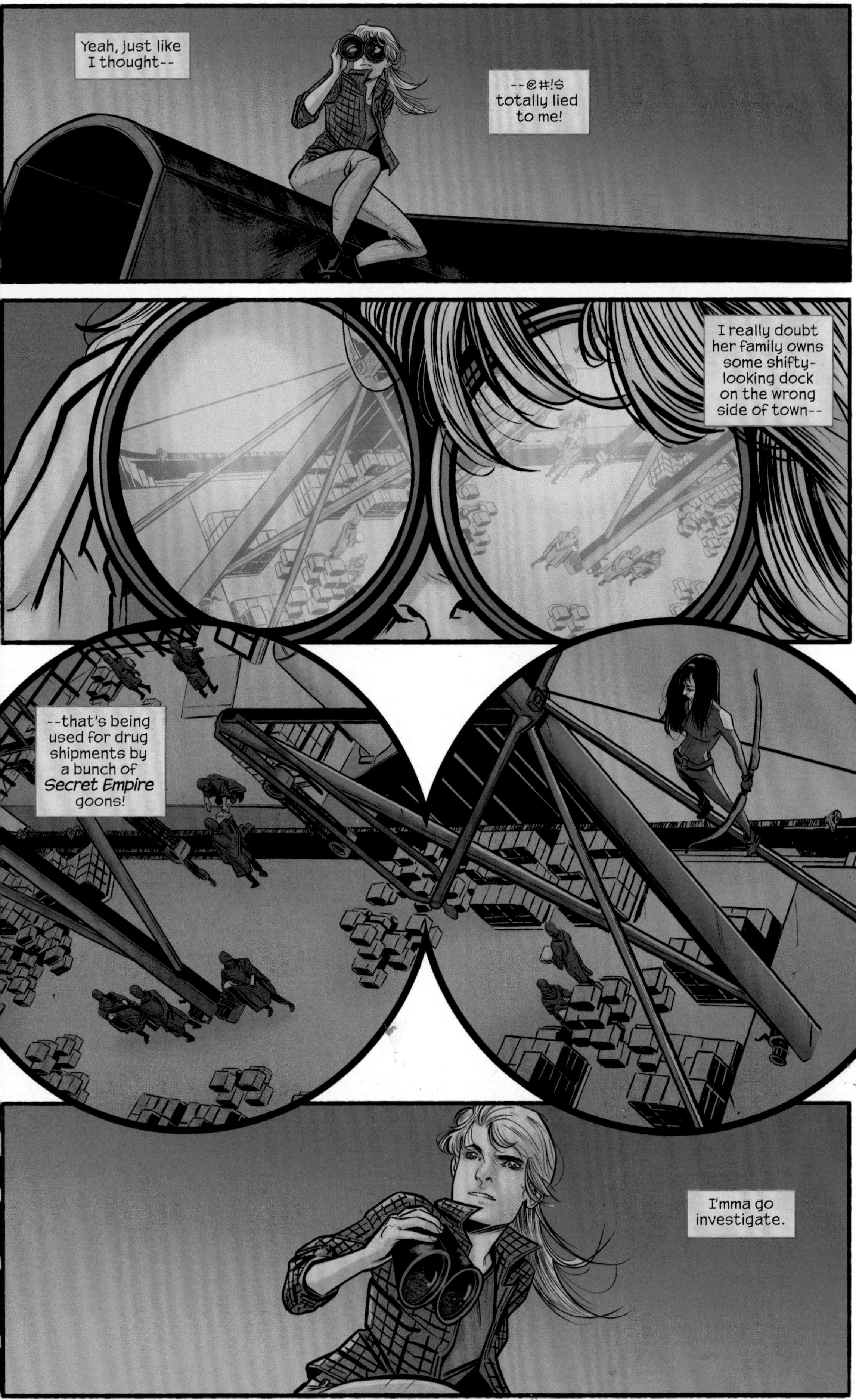
Yeah, just like I thought--
--@#!$ totally lied to me!
I really doubt her family owns some shifty-looking dock on the wrong side of town--
--that's being used for drug shipments by a bunch of *Secret Empire* goons!
I'mma go investigate.

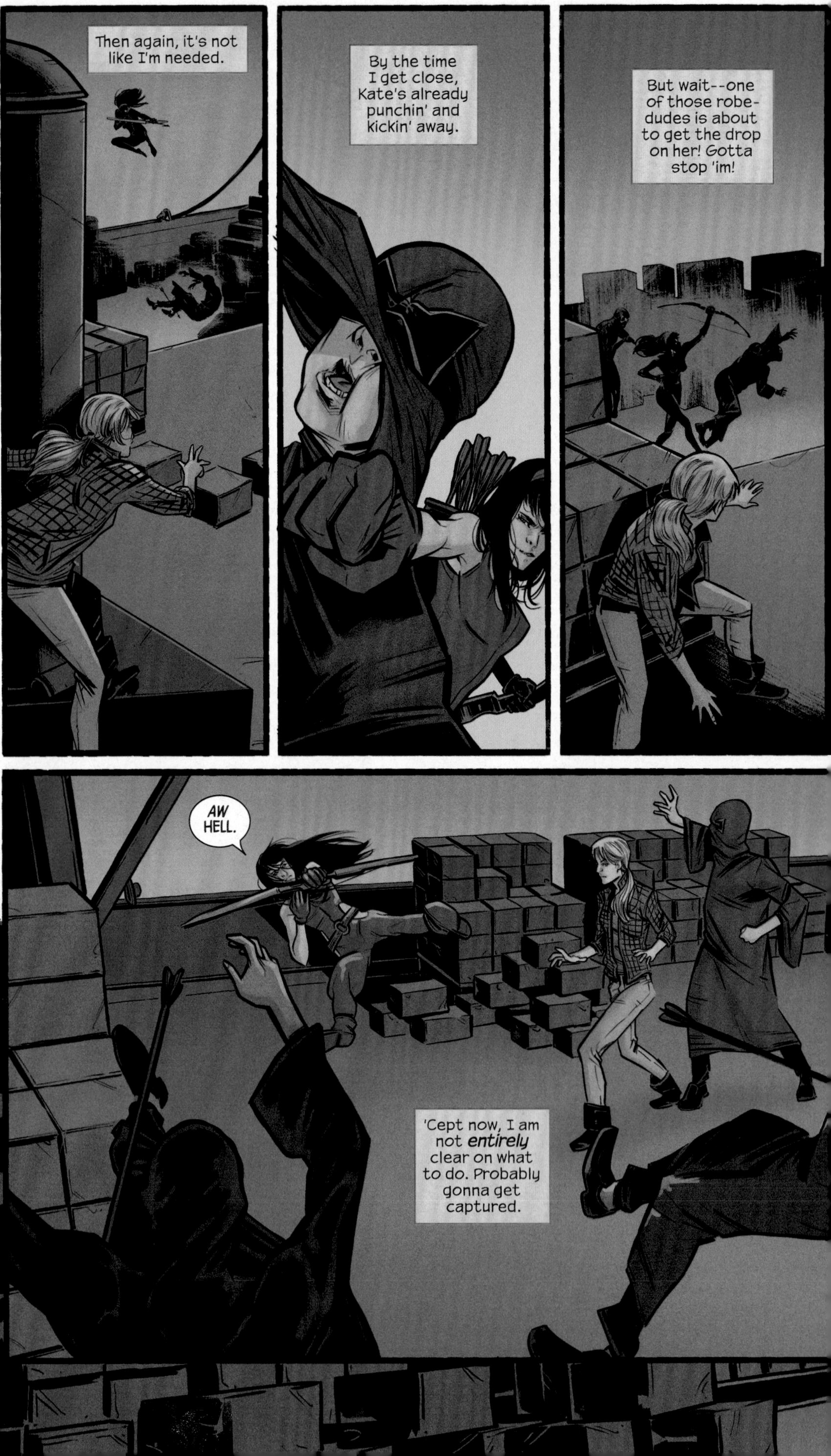

Then again, it's not like I'm needed.
By the time I get close, Kate's already punchin' and kickin' away.
But wait--one of those robe-dudes is about to get the drop on her! Gotta stop 'im!
AW HELL.
'Cept now, I am not *entirely* clear on what to do. Probably gonna get captured.

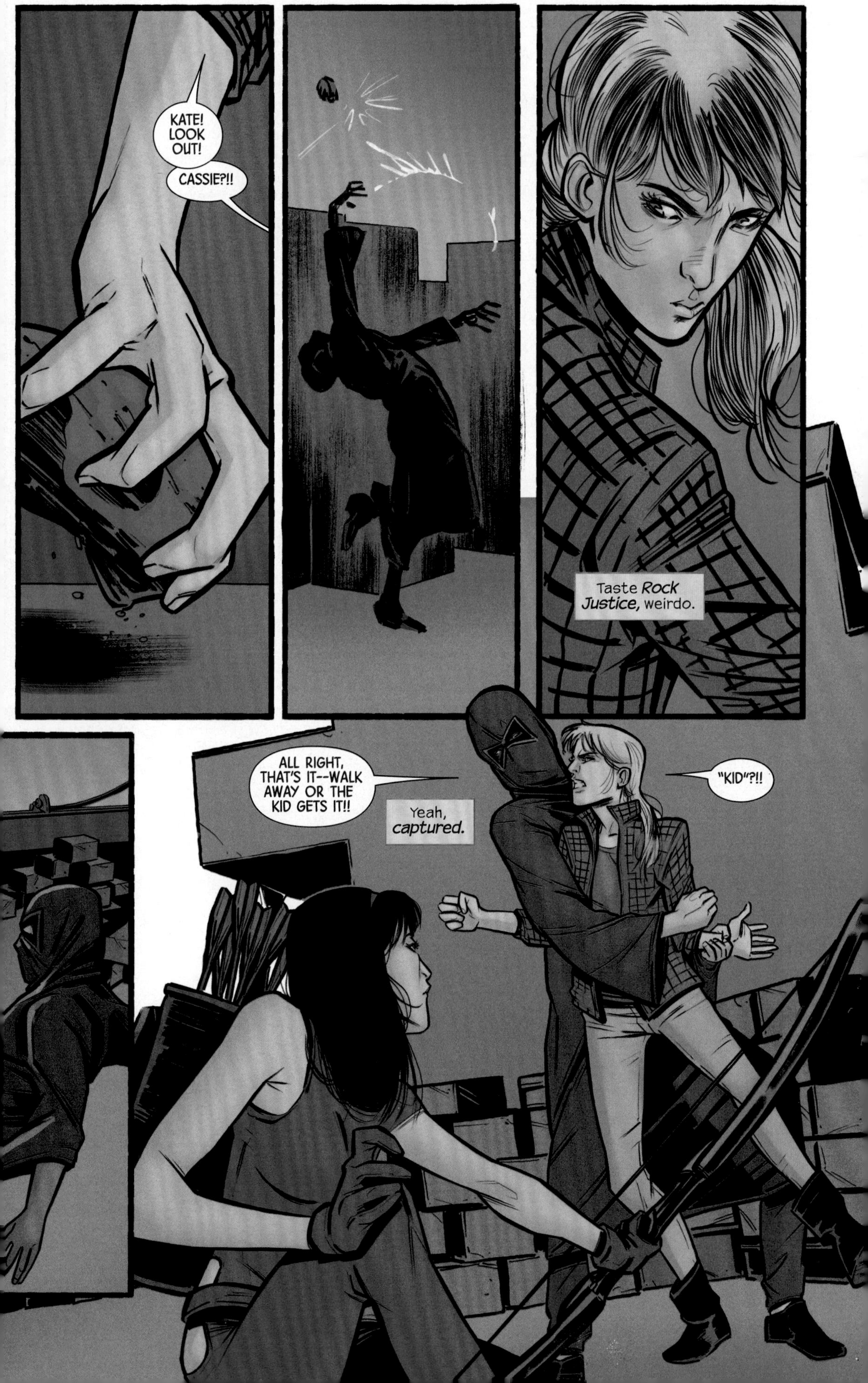
KATE! LOOK OUT!
CASSIE?!!
Taste *Rock Justice,* weirdo.
ALL RIGHT, THAT'S IT--WALK AWAY OR THE KID GETS IT!!
Yeah, *captured.*
"KID"?!!

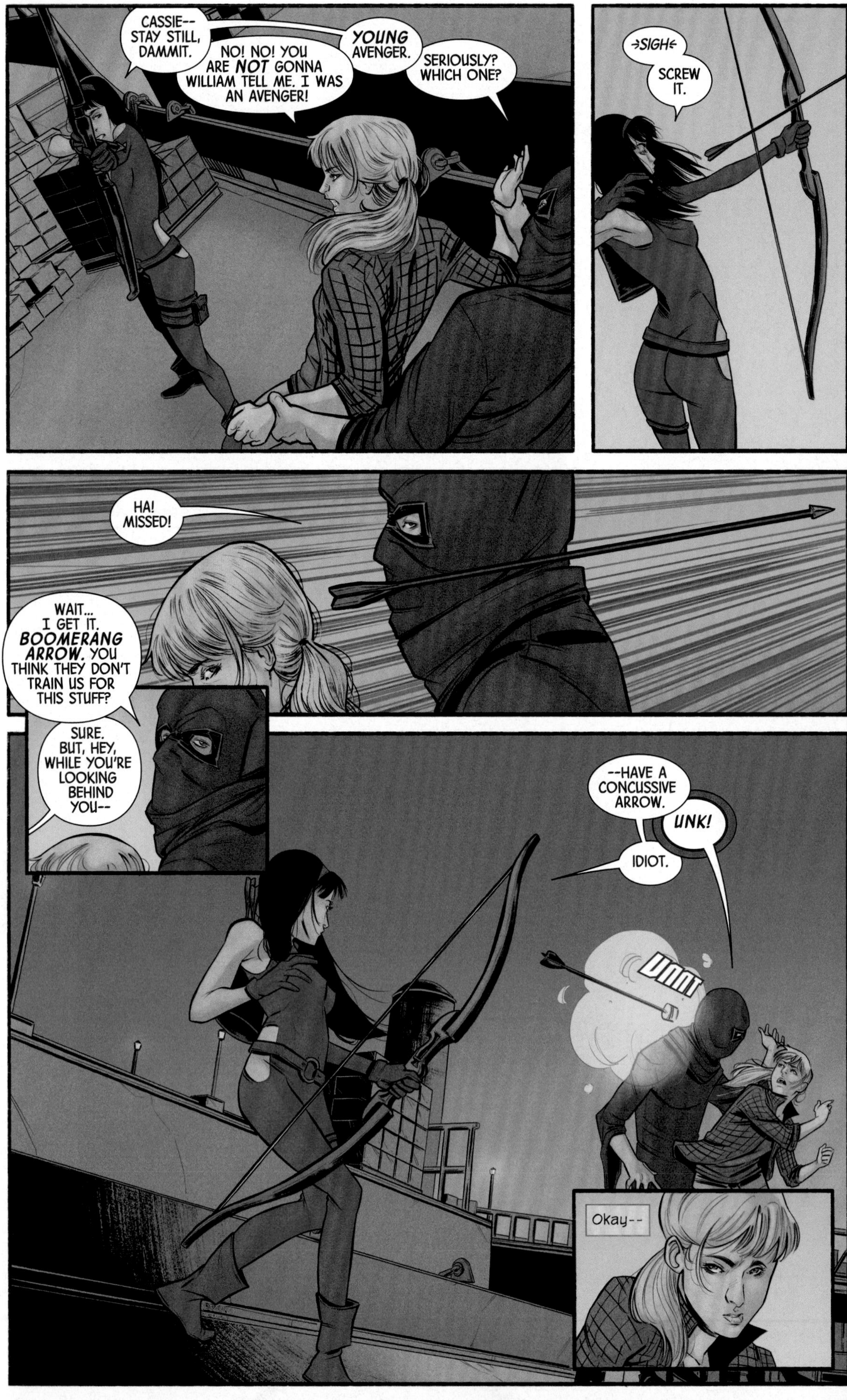
CASSIE-- STAY STILL, DAMMIT.
NO! NO! YOU ARE NOT GONNA WILLIAM TELL ME. I WAS AN AVENGER!
YOUNG AVENGER.
SERIOUSLY? WHICH ONE?
SIGH
SCREW IT.
HA! MISSED!
WAIT... I GET IT. BOOMERANG ARROW. YOU THINK THEY DON'T TRAIN US FOR THIS STUFF?
SURE. BUT, HEY, WHILE YOU'RE LOOKING BEHIND YOU--
--HAVE A CONCUSSIVE ARROW.
UNK!
IDIOT.
UNNT
Okay--

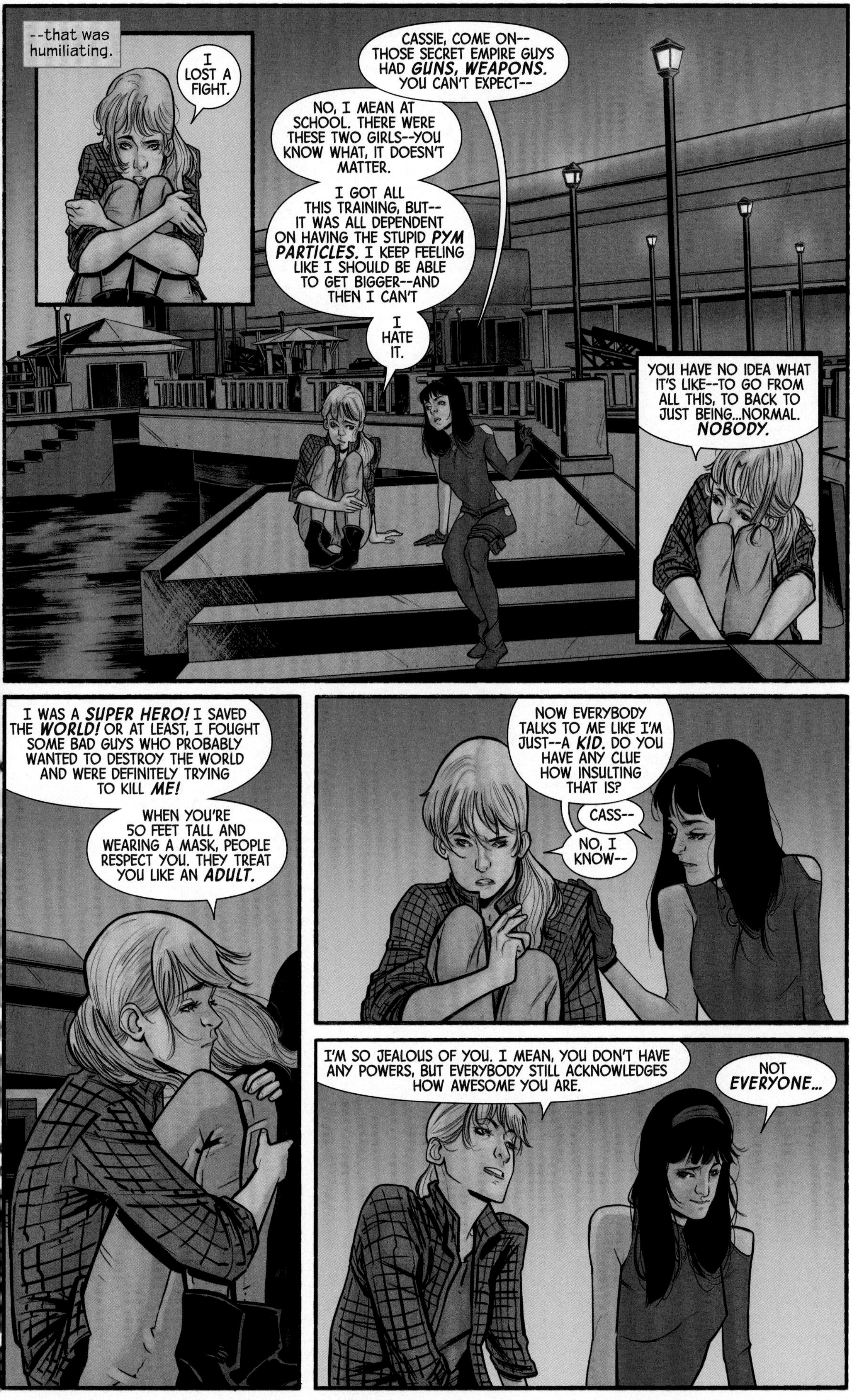
--that was humiliating.
I LOST A FIGHT.
CASSIE, COME ON-- THOSE SECRET EMPIRE GUYS HAD GUNS, WEAPONS. YOU CAN'T EXPECT--
NO, I MEAN AT SCHOOL. THERE WERE THESE TWO GIRLS--YOU KNOW WHAT, IT DOESN'T MATTER.
I GOT ALL THIS TRAINING, BUT-- IT WAS ALL DEPENDENT ON HAVING THE STUPID PYM PARTICLES. I KEEP FEELING LIKE I SHOULD BE ABLE TO GET BIGGER--AND THEN I CAN'T
I HATE IT.
YOU HAVE NO IDEA WHAT IT'S LIKE--TO GO FROM ALL THIS, TO BACK TO JUST BEING...NORMAL. NOBODY.
I WAS A SUPER HERO! I SAVED THE WORLD! OR AT LEAST, I FOUGHT SOME BAD GUYS WHO PROBABLY WANTED TO DESTROY THE WORLD AND WERE DEFINITELY TRYING TO KILL ME!
WHEN YOU'RE 50 FEET TALL AND WEARING A MASK, PEOPLE RESPECT YOU. THEY TREAT YOU LIKE AN ADULT.
NOW EVERYBODY TALKS TO ME LIKE I'M JUST--A KID. DO YOU HAVE ANY CLUE HOW INSULTING THAT IS?
CASS--
NO, I KNOW--
I'M SO JEALOUS OF YOU. I MEAN, YOU DON'T HAVE ANY POWERS, BUT EVERYBODY STILL ACKNOWLEDGES HOW AWESOME YOU ARE.
NOT EVERYONE...

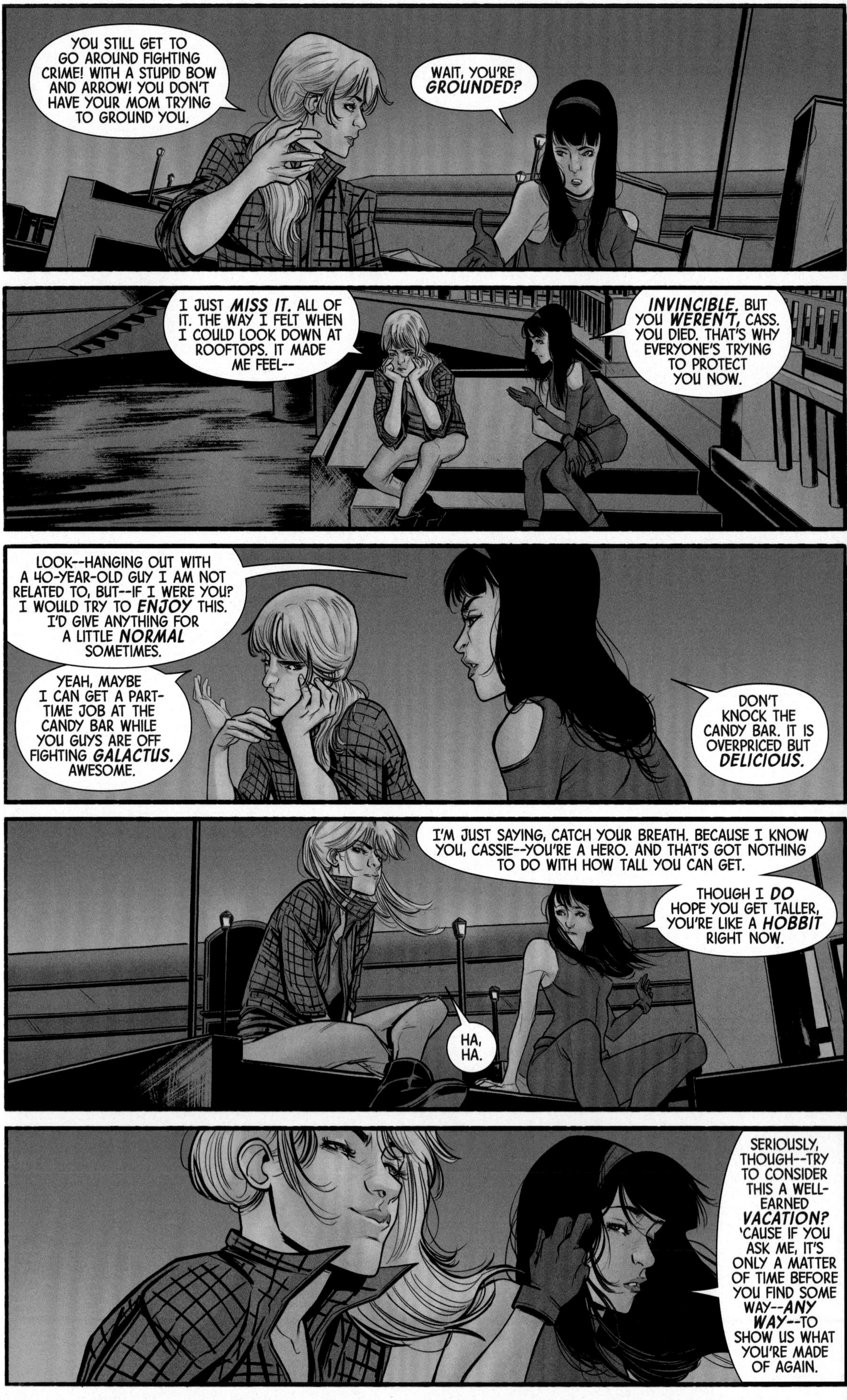
YOU STILL GET TO GO AROUND FIGHTING CRIME! WITH A STUPID BOW AND ARROW! YOU DON'T HAVE YOUR MOM TRYING TO GROUND YOU.
WAIT, YOU'RE GROUNDED?
I JUST MISS IT. ALL OF IT. THE WAY I FELT WHEN I COULD LOOK DOWN AT ROOFTOPS. IT MADE ME FEEL--
INVINCIBLE. BUT YOU WEREN'T, CASS. YOU DIED. THAT'S WHY EVERYONE'S TRYING TO PROTECT YOU NOW.
LOOK--HANGING OUT WITH A 40-YEAR-OLD GUY I AM NOT RELATED TO, BUT--IF I WERE YOU? I WOULD TRY TO ENJOY THIS. I'D GIVE ANYTHING FOR A LITTLE NORMAL SOMETIMES.
YEAH, MAYBE I CAN GET A PART-TIME JOB AT THE CANDY BAR WHILE YOU GUYS ARE OFF FIGHTING GALACTUS. AWESOME.
DON'T KNOCK THE CANDY BAR. IT IS OVERPRICED BUT DELICIOUS.
I'M JUST SAYING, CATCH YOUR BREATH. BECAUSE I KNOW YOU, CASSIE--YOU'RE A HERO. AND THAT'S GOT NOTHING TO DO WITH HOW TALL YOU CAN GET.
THOUGH I DO HOPE YOU GET TALLER, YOU'RE LIKE A HOBBIT RIGHT NOW.
HA, HA.
SERIOUSLY, THOUGH--TRY TO CONSIDER THIS A WELL-EARNED VACATION? 'CAUSE IF YOU ASK ME, IT'S ONLY A MATTER OF TIME BEFORE YOU FIND SOME WAY--ANY WAY--TO SHOW US WHAT YOU'RE MADE OF AGAIN.

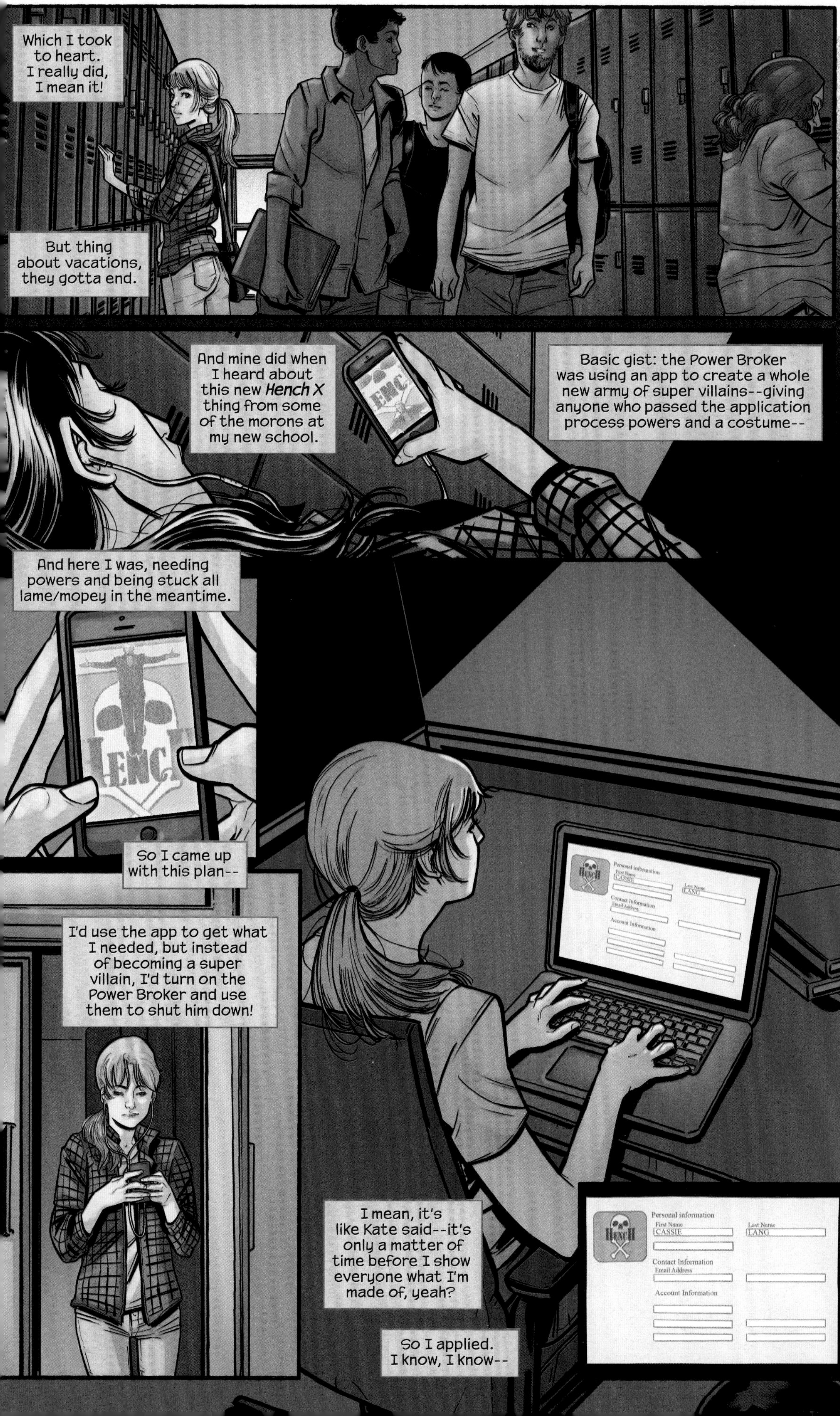

Which I took to heart. I really did, I mean it!
But thing about vacations, they gotta end.
And mine did when I heard about this new *Hench X* thing from some of the morons at my new school.
Basic gist: the Power Broker was using an app to create a whole new army of super villains--giving anyone who passed the application process powers and a costume--
And here I was, needing powers and being stuck all lame/mopey in the meantime.
So I came up with this plan--
I'd use the app to get what I needed, but instead of becoming a super villain, I'd turn on the Power Broker and use them to shut him down!
I mean, it's like Kate said--it's only a matter of time before I show everyone what I'm made of, yeah?
So I applied. I know, I know--
HENCH
Personal information
First Name
CASSIE
Last Name
LANG
Contact Information
Email Address
Account Information

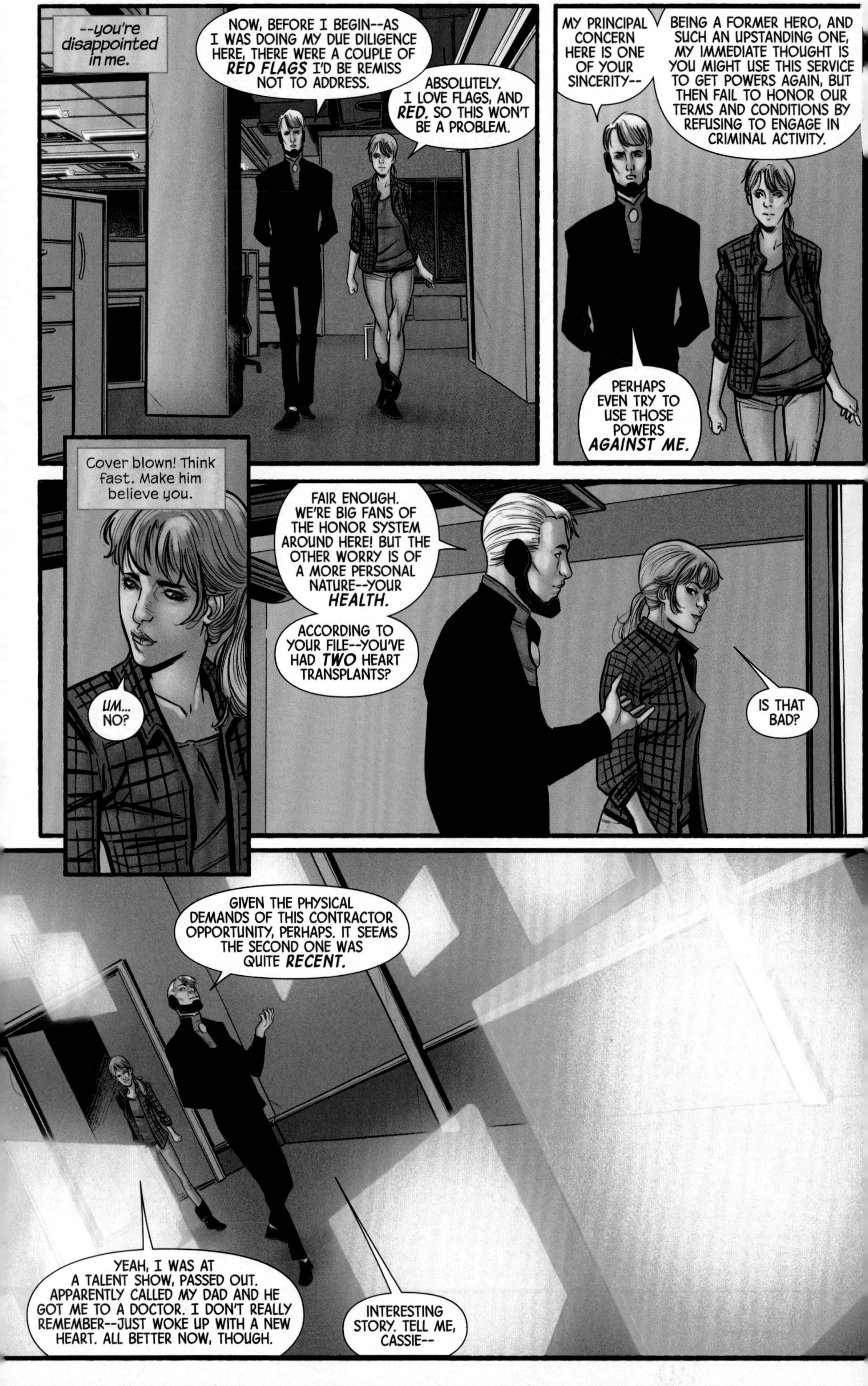
--you're disappointed in me.
NOW, BEFORE I BEGIN--AS I WAS DOING MY DUE DILIGENCE HERE, THERE WERE A COUPLE OF RED FLAGS I'D BE REMISS NOT TO ADDRESS.
ABSOLUTELY. I LOVE FLAGS, AND RED. SO THIS WON'T BE A PROBLEM.
MY PRINCIPAL CONCERN HERE IS ONE OF YOUR SINCERITY--
BEING A FORMER HERO, AND SUCH AN UPSTANDING ONE, MY IMMEDIATE THOUGHT IS YOU MIGHT USE THIS SERVICE TO GET POWERS AGAIN, BUT THEN FAIL TO HONOR OUR TERMS AND CONDITIONS BY REFUSING TO ENGAGE IN CRIMINAL ACTIVITY.
PERHAPS EVEN TRY TO USE THOSE POWERS AGAINST ME.
Cover blown! Think fast. Make him believe you.
UM... NO?
FAIR ENOUGH. WE'RE BIG FANS OF THE HONOR SYSTEM AROUND HERE! BUT THE OTHER WORRY IS OF A MORE PERSONAL NATURE--YOUR HEALTH.
ACCORDING TO YOUR FILE--YOU'VE HAD TWO HEART TRANSPLANTS?
IS THAT BAD?
GIVEN THE PHYSICAL DEMANDS OF THIS CONTRACTOR OPPORTUNITY, PERHAPS. IT SEEMS THE SECOND ONE WAS QUITE RECENT.
YEAH, I WAS AT A TALENT SHOW, PASSED OUT. APPARENTLY CALLED MY DAD AND HE GOT ME TO A DOCTOR. I DON'T REALLY REMEMBER--JUST WOKE UP WITH A NEW HEART. ALL BETTER NOW, THOUGH.
INTERESTING STORY. TELL ME, CASSIE--

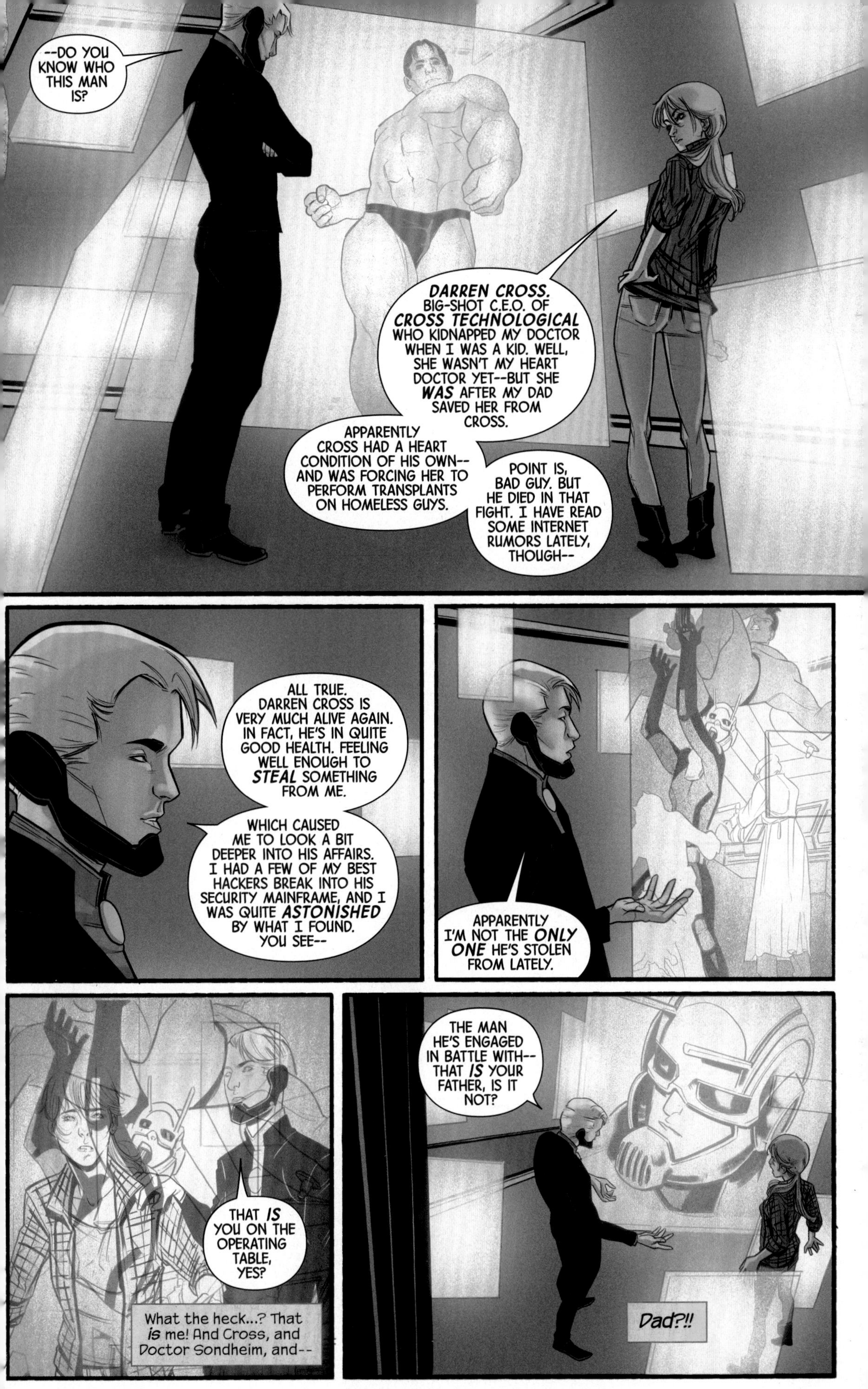
--DO YOU KNOW WHO THIS MAN IS?
DARREN CROSS. BIG-SHOT C.E.O. OF CROSS TECHNOLOGICAL WHO KIDNAPPED MY DOCTOR WHEN I WAS A KID. WELL, SHE WASN'T MY HEART DOCTOR YET--BUT SHE WAS AFTER MY DAD SAVED HER FROM CROSS.
APPARENTLY CROSS HAD A HEART CONDITION OF HIS OWN--AND WAS FORCING HER TO PERFORM TRANSPLANTS ON HOMELESS GUYS.
POINT IS, BAD GUY. BUT HE DIED IN THAT FIGHT. I HAVE READ SOME INTERNET RUMORS LATELY, THOUGH--
ALL TRUE. DARREN CROSS IS VERY MUCH ALIVE AGAIN. IN FACT, HE'S IN QUITE GOOD HEALTH. FEELING WELL ENOUGH TO STEAL SOMETHING FROM ME.
WHICH CAUSED ME TO LOOK A BIT DEEPER INTO HIS AFFAIRS. I HAD A FEW OF MY BEST HACKERS BREAK INTO HIS SECURITY MAINFRAME, AND I WAS QUITE ASTONISHED BY WHAT I FOUND. YOU SEE--
APPARENTLY I'M NOT THE ONLY ONE HE'S STOLEN FROM LATELY.
THAT IS YOU ON THE OPERATING TABLE, YES?
What the heck...? That is me! And Cross, and Doctor Sondheim, and--
THE MAN HE'S ENGAGED IN BATTLE WITH--THAT IS YOUR FATHER, IS IT NOT?
Dad?!!

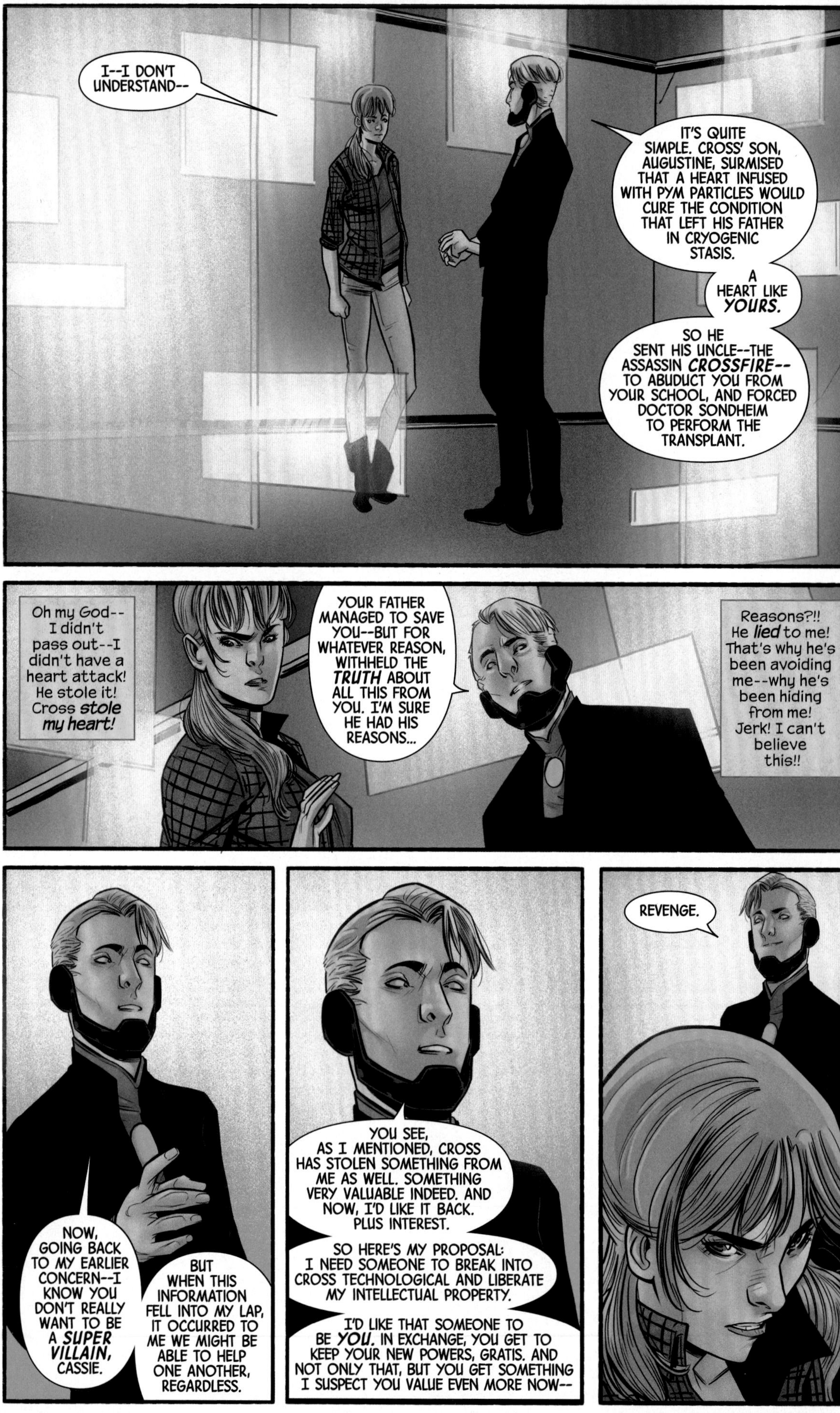

I--I DON'T UNDERSTAND--
IT'S QUITE SIMPLE. CROSS' SON, AUGUSTINE, SURMISED THAT A HEART INFUSED WITH PYM PARTICLES WOULD CURE THE CONDITION THAT LEFT HIS FATHER IN CRYOGENIC STASIS.
A HEART LIKE YOURS.
SO HE SENT HIS UNCLE--THE ASSASSIN CROSSFIRE--TO ABUDUCT YOU FROM YOUR SCHOOL, AND FORCED DOCTOR SONDHEIM TO PERFORM THE TRANSPLANT.
Oh my God--I didn't pass out--I didn't have a heart attack! He stole it! Cross stole my heart!
YOUR FATHER MANAGED TO SAVE YOU--BUT FOR WHATEVER REASON, WITHHELD THE TRUTH ABOUT ALL THIS FROM YOU. I'M SURE HE HAD HIS REASONS...
Reasons?!! He lied to me! That's why he's been avoiding me--why he's been hiding from me! Jerk! I can't believe this!!
NOW, GOING BACK TO MY EARLIER CONCERN--I KNOW YOU DON'T REALLY WANT TO BE A SUPER VILLAIN, CASSIE.
BUT WHEN THIS INFORMATION FELL INTO MY LAP, IT OCCURRED TO ME WE MIGHT BE ABLE TO HELP ONE ANOTHER, REGARDLESS.
YOU SEE, AS I MENTIONED, CROSS HAS STOLEN SOMETHING FROM ME AS WELL. SOMETHING VERY VALUABLE INDEED. AND NOW, I'D LIKE IT BACK. PLUS INTEREST.
SO HERE'S MY PROPOSAL: I NEED SOMEONE TO BREAK INTO CROSS TECHNOLOGICAL AND LIBERATE MY INTELLECTUAL PROPERTY.
I'D LIKE THAT SOMEONE TO BE YOU. IN EXCHANGE, YOU GET TO KEEP YOUR NEW POWERS, GRATIS. AND NOT ONLY THAT, BUT YOU GET SOMETHING I SUSPECT YOU VALUE EVEN MORE NOW--
REVENGE.

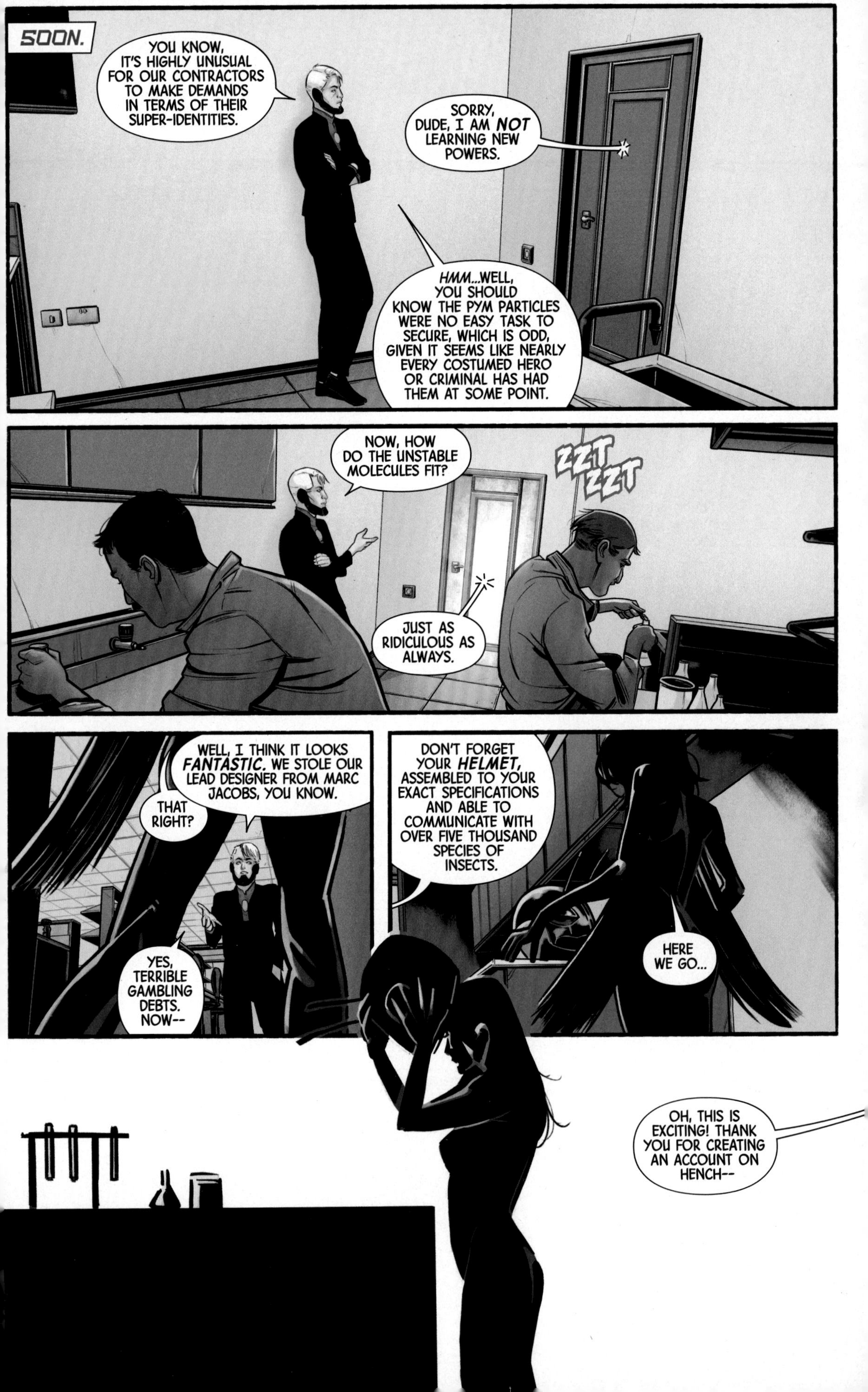
SOON.
YOU KNOW, IT'S HIGHLY UNUSUAL FOR OUR CONTRACTORS TO MAKE DEMANDS IN TERMS OF THEIR SUPER-IDENTITIES.
SORRY, DUDE, I AM NOT LEARNING NEW POWERS.
HMM...WELL, YOU SHOULD KNOW THE PYM PARTICLES WERE NO EASY TASK TO SECURE, WHICH IS ODD, GIVEN IT SEEMS LIKE NEARLY EVERY COSTUMED HERO OR CRIMINAL HAS HAD THEM AT SOME POINT.
NOW, HOW DO THE UNSTABLE MOLECULES FIT?
ZZT ZZT
JUST AS RIDICULOUS AS ALWAYS.
WELL, I THINK IT LOOKS FANTASTIC. WE STOLE OUR LEAD DESIGNER FROM MARC JACOBS, YOU KNOW.
THAT RIGHT?
YES, TERRIBLE GAMBLING DEBTS. NOW--
DON'T FORGET YOUR HELMET, ASSEMBLED TO YOUR EXACT SPECIFICATIONS AND ABLE TO COMMUNICATE WITH OVER FIVE THOUSAND SPECIES OF INSECTS.
HERE WE GO...
OH, THIS IS EXCITING! THANK YOU FOR CREATING AN ACCOUNT ON HENCH--

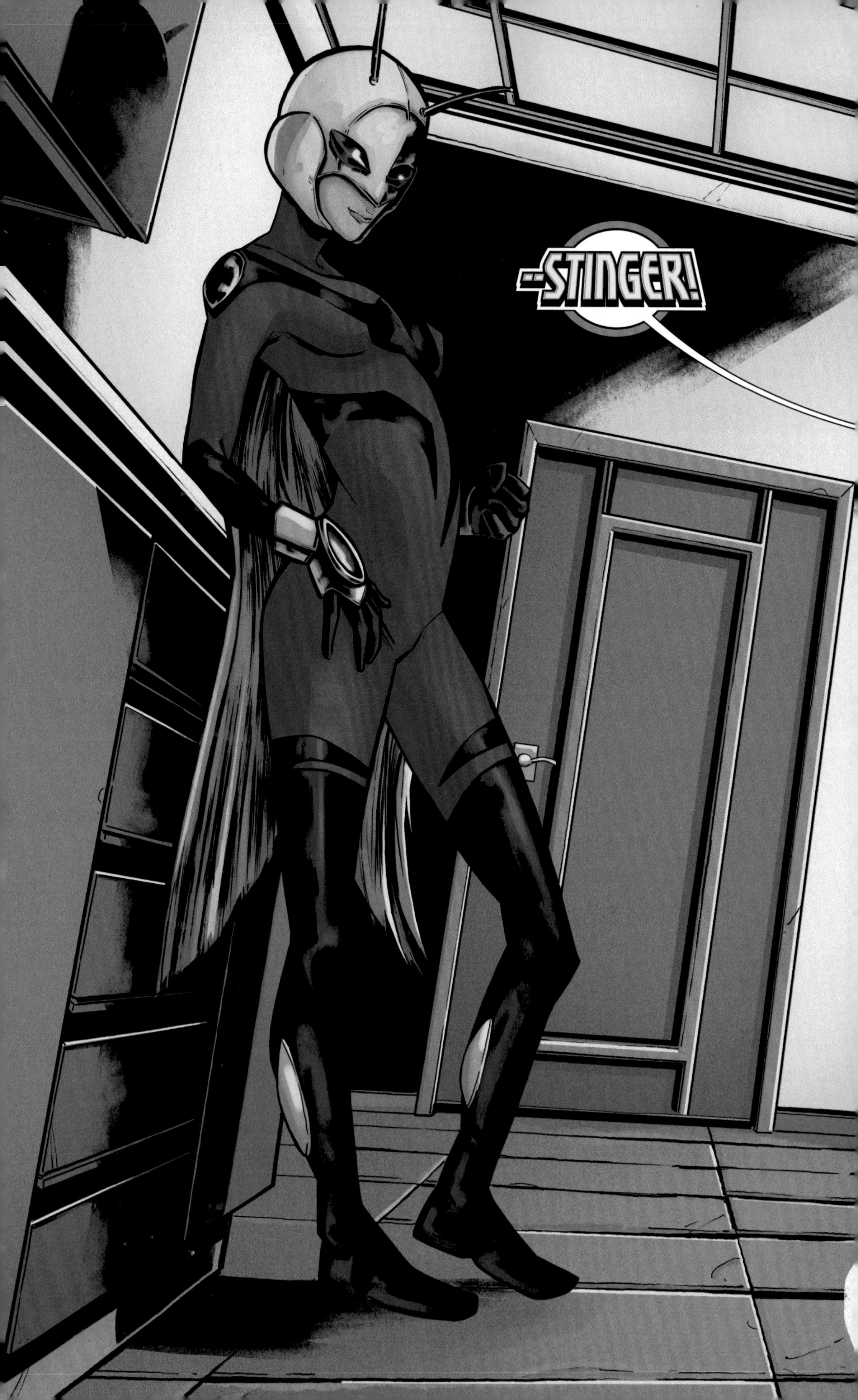
--STINGER!

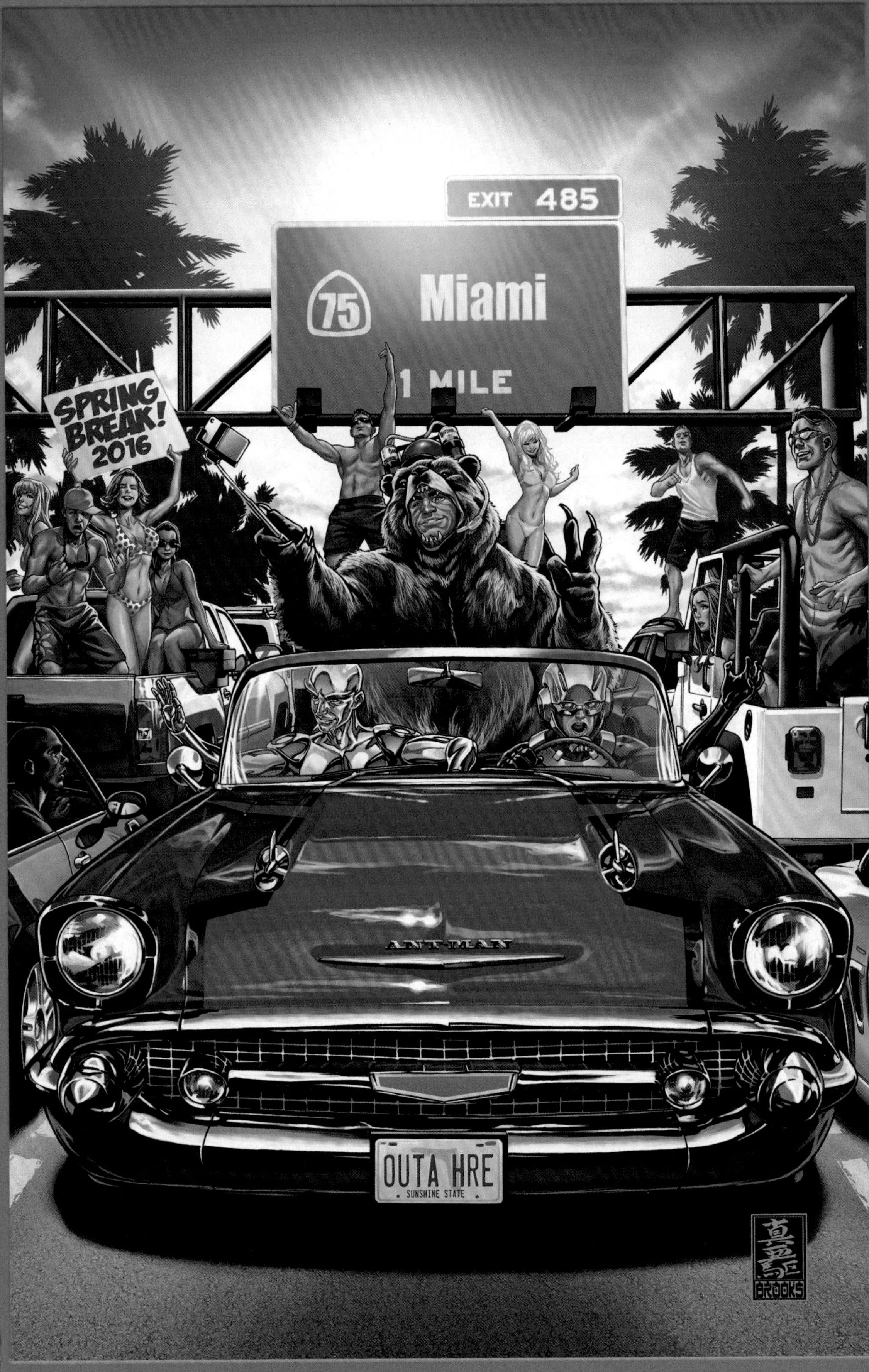

EXIT 485
75
Miami
1 MILE
SPRING BREAK! 2016
ANT-MAN
OUTA T HRE
SUNSHINE STATE
BROOKS

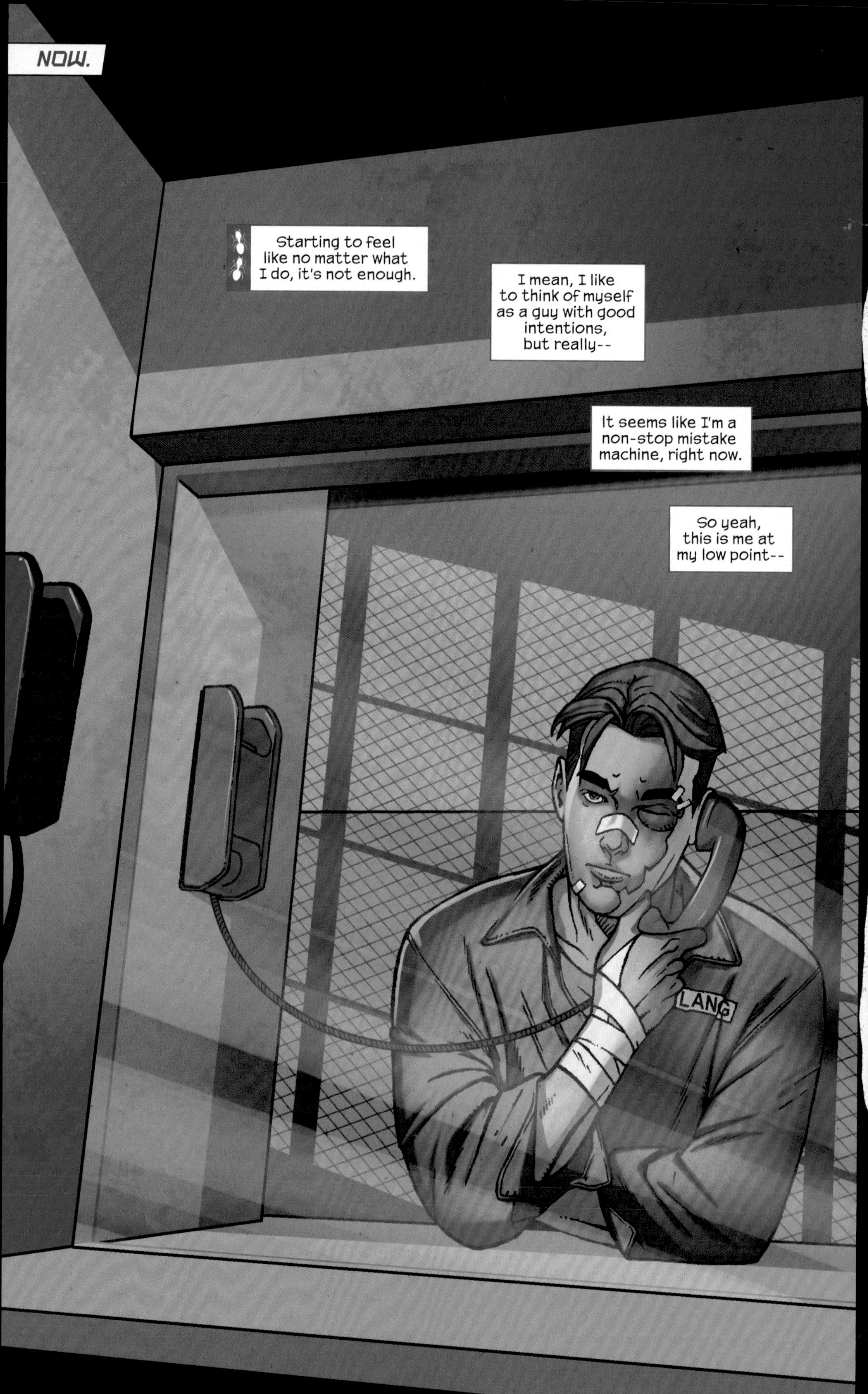
NOW.
Starting to feel like no matter what I do, it's not enough.
I mean, I like to think of myself as a guy with good intentions, but really--
It seems like I'm a non-stop mistake machine, right now.
So yeah, this is me at my low point--
LANG

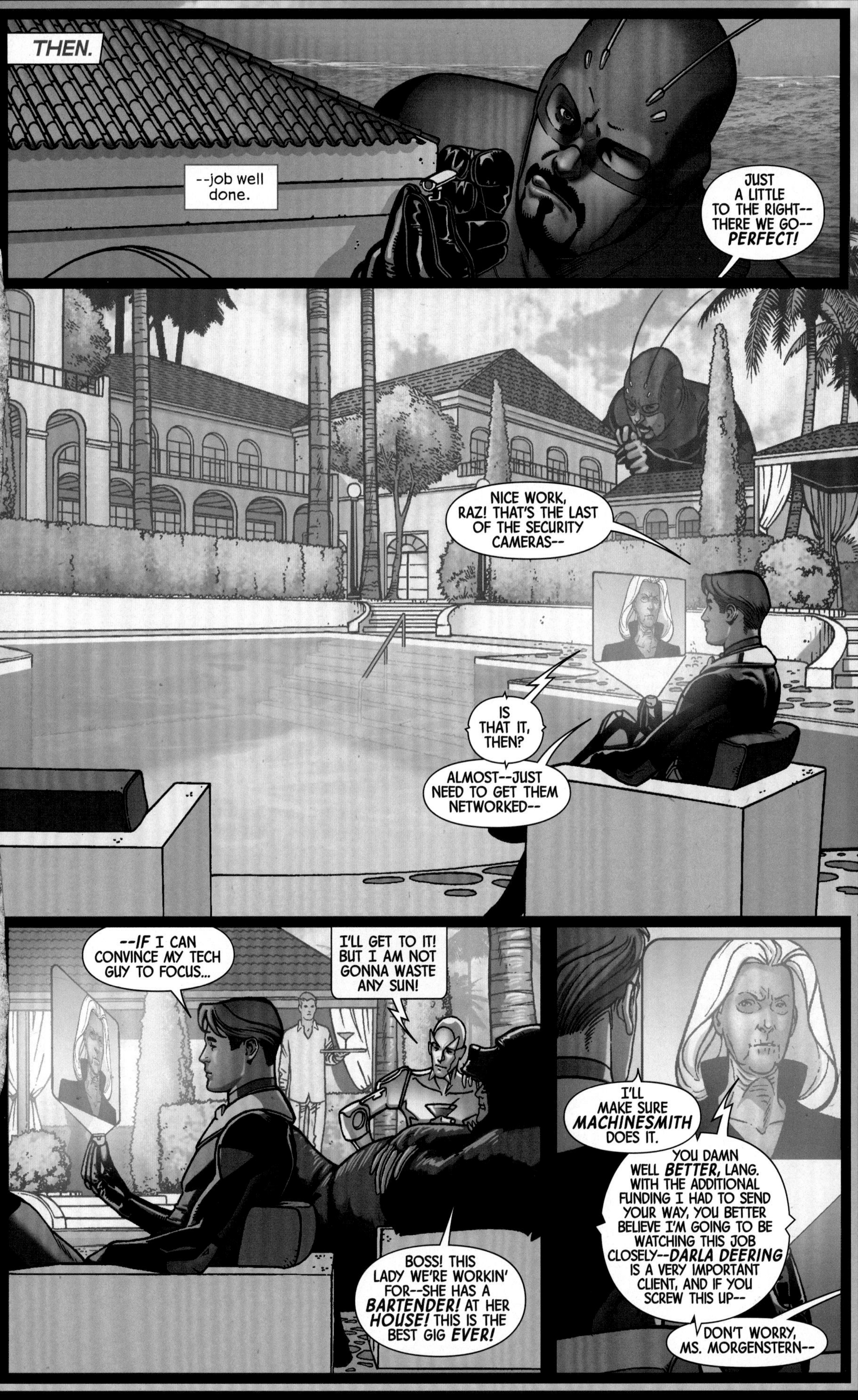
THEN.
--job well done.
JUST A LITTLE TO THE RIGHT-- THERE WE GO-- PERFECT!
NICE WORK, RAZ! THAT'S THE LAST OF THE SECURITY CAMERAS--
IS THAT IT, THEN?
ALMOST--JUST NEED TO GET THEM NETWORKED--
--IF I CAN CONVINCE MY TECH GUY TO FOCUS...
I'LL GET TO IT! BUT I AM NOT GONNA WASTE ANY SUN!
BOSS! THIS LADY WE'RE WORKIN' FOR--SHE HAS A BARTENDER! AT HER HOUSE! THIS IS THE BEST GIG EVER!
I'LL MAKE SURE MACHINESMITH DOES IT.
YOU DAMN WELL BETTER, LANG. WITH THE ADDITIONAL FUNDING I HAD TO SEND YOUR WAY, YOU BETTER BELIEVE I'M GOING TO BE WATCHING THIS JOB CLOSELY--DARLA DEERING IS A VERY IMPORTANT CLIENT, AND IF YOU SCREW THIS UP--
DON'T WORRY, MS. MORGENSTERN--

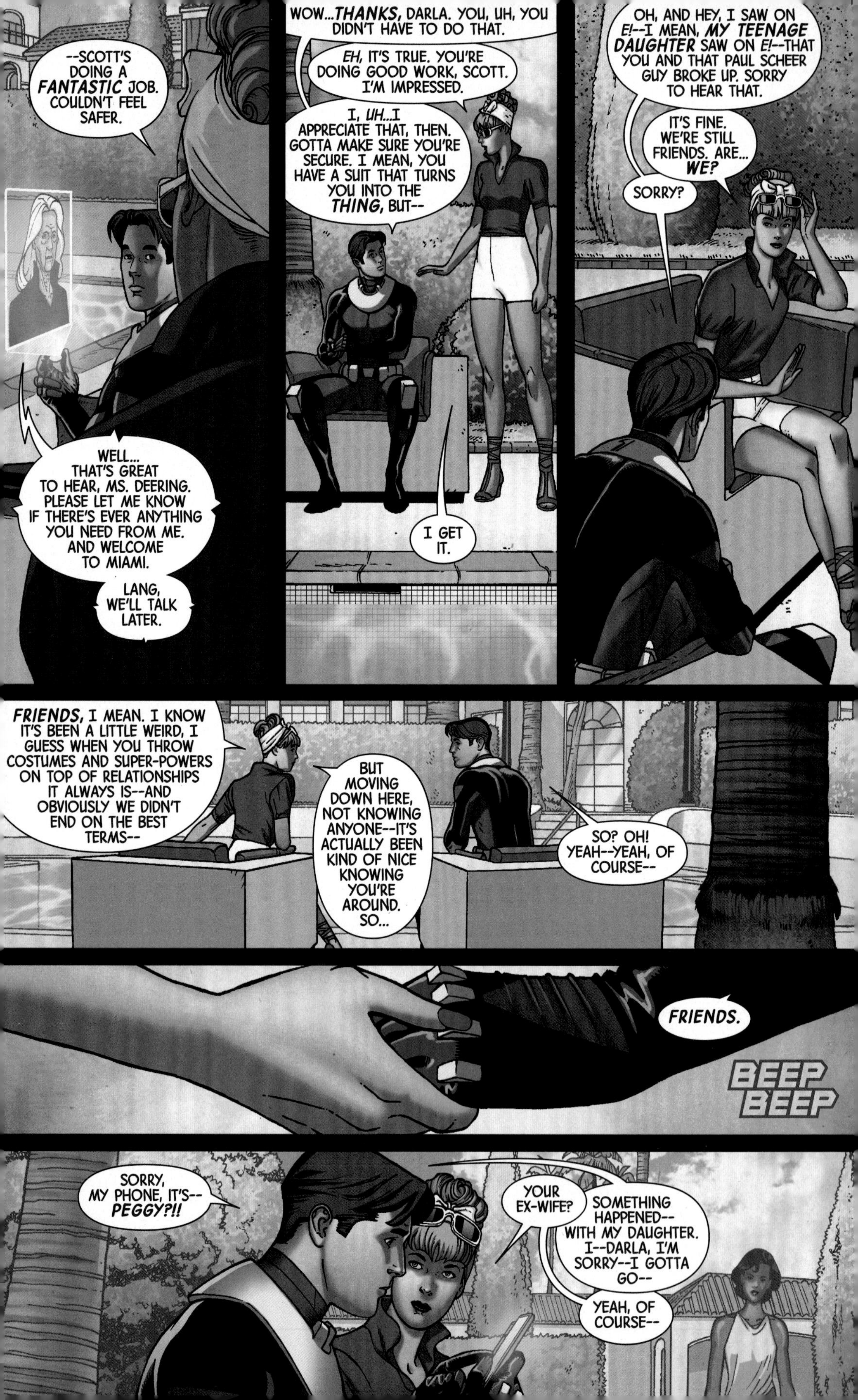
--SCOTT'S DOING A FANTASTIC JOB. COULDN'T FEEL SAFER.
WELL... THAT'S GREAT TO HEAR, MS. DEERING. PLEASE LET ME KNOW IF THERE'S EVER ANYTHING YOU NEED FROM ME. AND WELCOME TO MIAMI.
LANG, WE'LL TALK LATER.
WOW...THANKS, DARLA. YOU, UH, YOU DIDN'T HAVE TO DO THAT.
EH, IT'S TRUE. YOU'RE DOING GOOD WORK, SCOTT. I'M IMPRESSED.
I, UH...I APPRECIATE THAT, THEN. GOTTA MAKE SURE YOU'RE SECURE. I MEAN, YOU HAVE A SUIT THAT TURNS YOU INTO THE THING, BUT--
I GET IT.
OH, AND HEY, I SAW ON E!--I MEAN, MY TEENAGE DAUGHTER SAW ON E!--THAT YOU AND THAT PAUL SCHEER GUY BROKE UP. SORRY TO HEAR THAT.
IT'S FINE. WE'RE STILL FRIENDS. ARE... WE?
SORRY?
FRIENDS, I MEAN. I KNOW IT'S BEEN A LITTLE WEIRD, I GUESS WHEN YOU THROW COSTUMES AND SUPER-POWERS ON TOP OF RELATIONSHIPS IT ALWAYS IS--AND OBVIOUSLY WE DIDN'T END ON THE BEST TERMS--
BUT MOVING DOWN HERE, NOT KNOWING ANYONE--IT'S ACTUALLY BEEN KIND OF NICE KNOWING YOU'RE AROUND. SO...
SO? OH! YEAH--YEAH, OF COURSE--
FRIENDS.
BEEP BEEP
SORRY, MY PHONE, IT'S-- PEGGY?!!
YOUR EX-WIFE?
SOMETHING HAPPENED-- WITH MY DAUGHTER. I--DARLA, I'M SORRY--I GOTTA GO--
YEAH, OF COURSE--

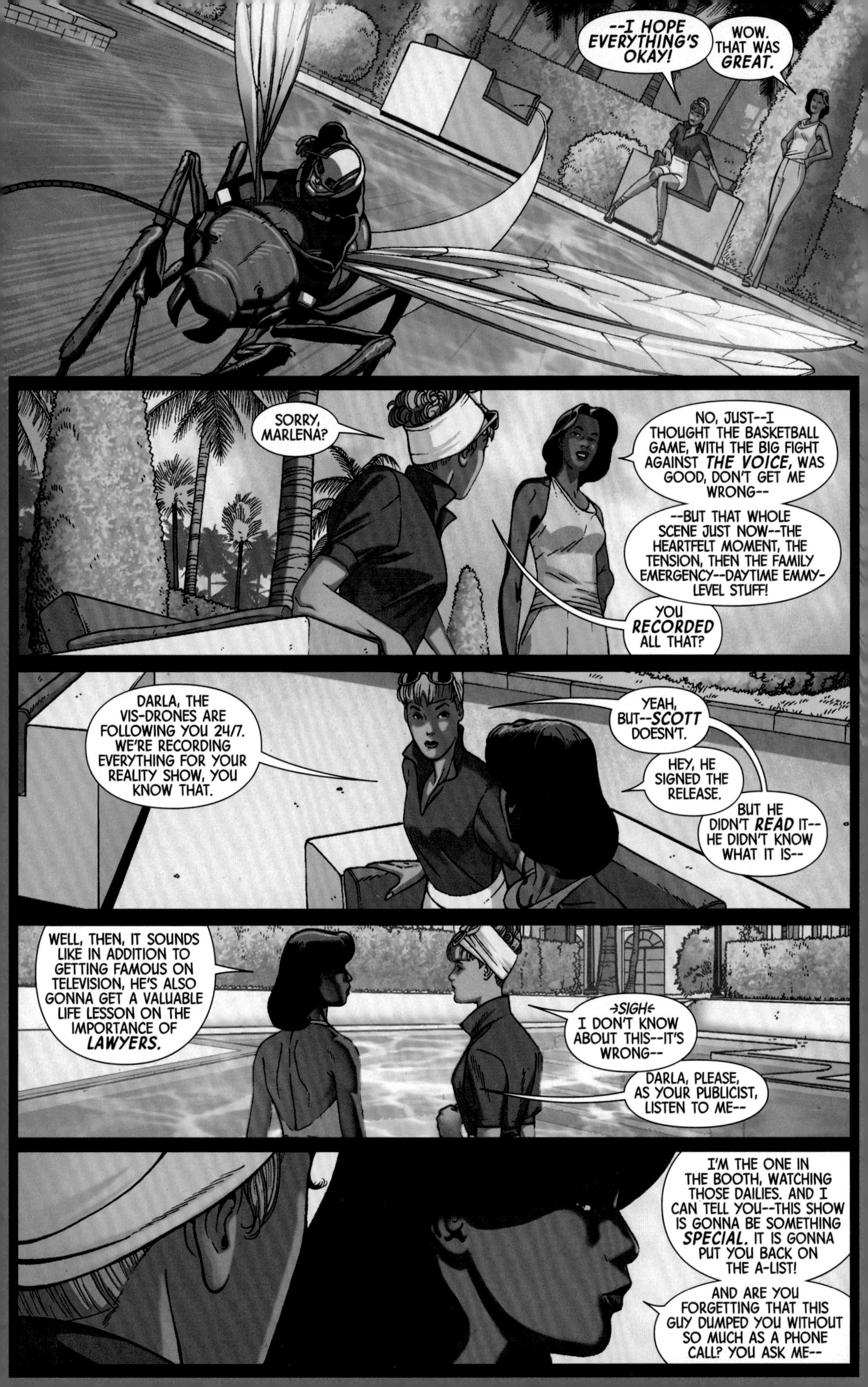

--I HOPE EVERYTHING'S OKAY!
WOW. THAT WAS GREAT.
SORRY, MARLENA?
NO, JUST--I THOUGHT THE BASKETBALL GAME, WITH THE BIG FIGHT AGAINST THE VOICE, WAS GOOD, DON'T GET ME WRONG--
--BUT THAT WHOLE SCENE JUST NOW--THE HEARTFELT MOMENT, THE TENSION, THEN THE FAMILY EMERGENCY--DAYTIME EMMY-LEVEL STUFF!
YOU RECORDED ALL THAT?
DARLA, THE VIS-DRONES ARE FOLLOWING YOU 24/7. WE'RE RECORDING EVERYTHING FOR YOUR REALITY SHOW, YOU KNOW THAT.
YEAH, BUT--SCOTT DOESN'T.
HEY, HE SIGNED THE RELEASE.
BUT HE DIDN'T READ IT--HE DIDN'T KNOW WHAT IT IS--
WELL, THEN, IT SOUNDS LIKE IN ADDITION TO GETTING FAMOUS ON TELEVISION, HE'S ALSO GONNA GET A VALUABLE LIFE LESSON ON THE IMPORTANCE OF LAWYERS.
→SIGH← I DON'T KNOW ABOUT THIS--IT'S WRONG--
DARLA, PLEASE, AS YOUR PUBLICIST, LISTEN TO ME--
I'M THE ONE IN THE BOOTH, WATCHING THOSE DAILIES. AND I CAN TELL YOU--THIS SHOW IS GONNA BE SOMETHING SPECIAL. IT IS GONNA PUT YOU BACK ON THE A-LIST!
AND ARE YOU FORGETTING THAT THIS GUY DUMPED YOU WITHOUT SO MUCH AS A PHONE CALL? YOU ASK ME--

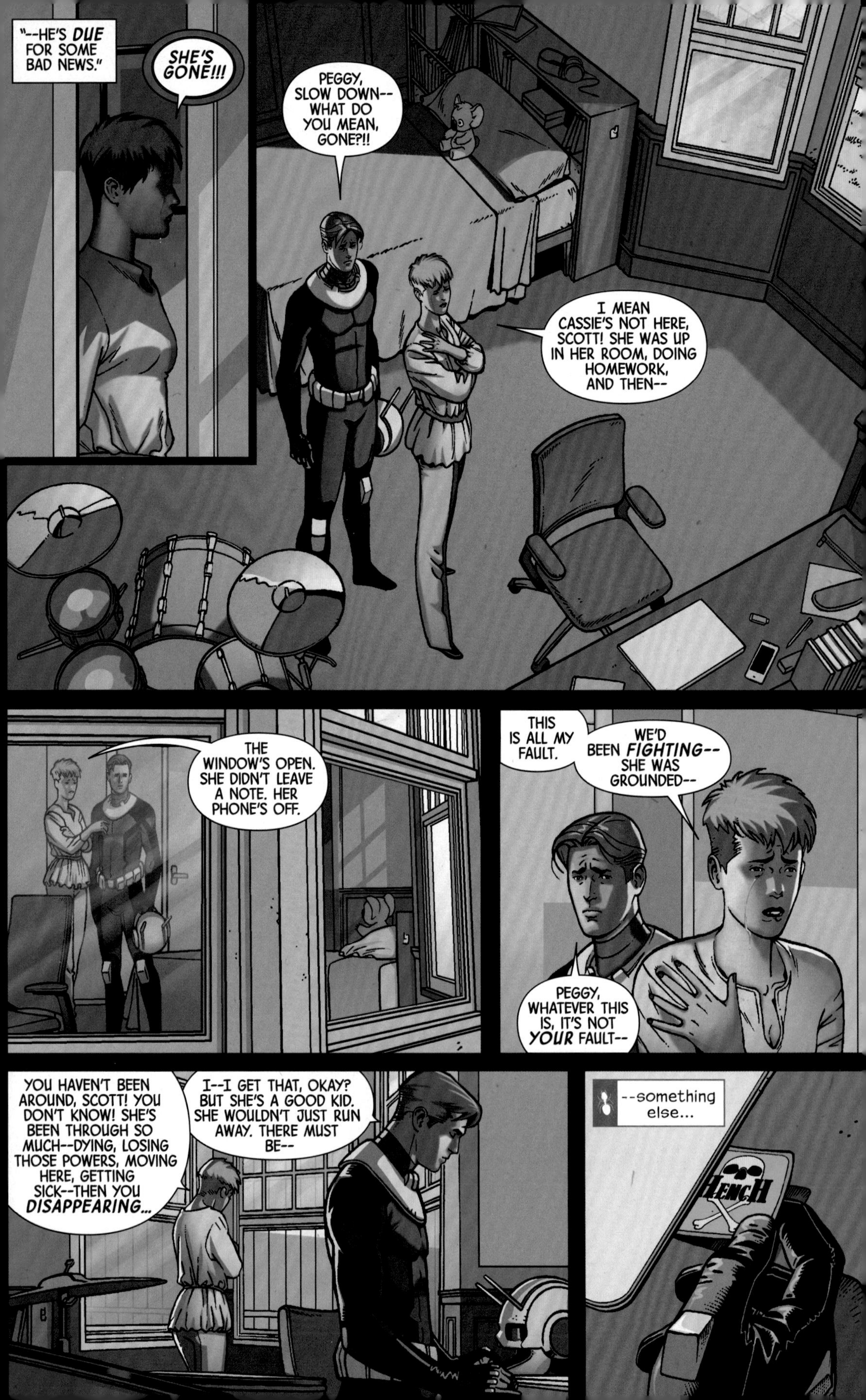
"--HE'S DUE FOR SOME BAD NEWS."
SHE'S GONE!!!
PEGGY, SLOW DOWN-- WHAT DO YOU MEAN, GONE?!!
I MEAN CASSIE'S NOT HERE, SCOTT! SHE WAS UP IN HER ROOM, DOING HOMEWORK, AND THEN--
THE WINDOW'S OPEN. SHE DIDN'T LEAVE A NOTE. HER PHONE'S OFF.
THIS IS ALL MY FAULT.
WE'D BEEN FIGHTING-- SHE WAS GROUNDED--
PEGGY, WHATEVER THIS IS, IT'S NOT YOUR FAULT--
YOU HAVEN'T BEEN AROUND, SCOTT! YOU DON'T KNOW! SHE'S BEEN THROUGH SO MUCH--DYING, LOSING THOSE POWERS, MOVING HERE, GETTING SICK--THEN YOU DISAPPEARING...
I--I GET THAT, OKAY? BUT SHE'S A GOOD KID. SHE WOULDN'T JUST RUN AWAY. THERE MUST BE--
--something else...
HENCH

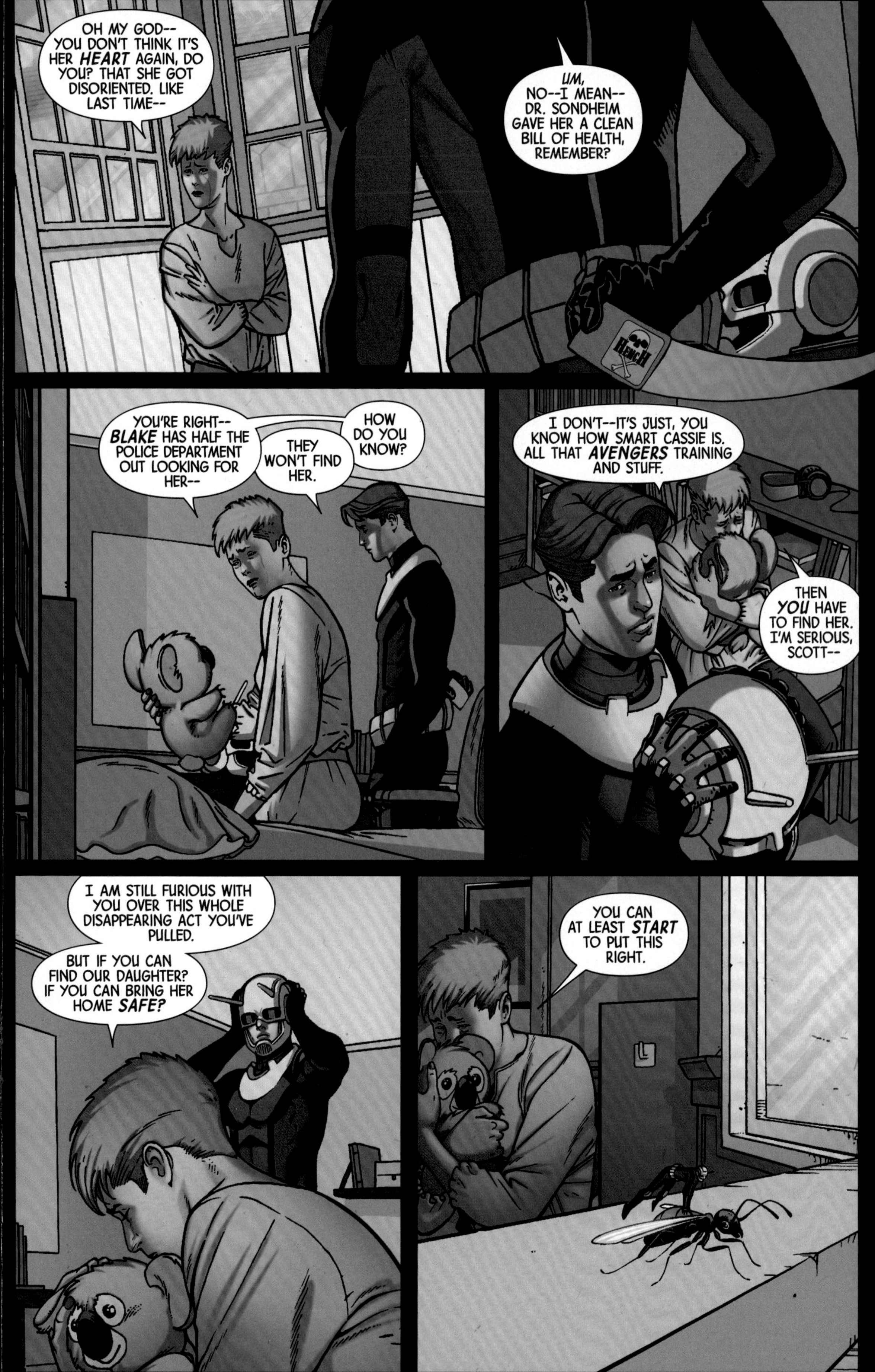
OH MY GOD-- YOU DON'T THINK IT'S HER HEART AGAIN, DO YOU? THAT SHE GOT DISORIENTED. LIKE LAST TIME--
UM, NO--I MEAN-- DR. SONDHEIM GAVE HER A CLEAN BILL OF HEALTH, REMEMBER?
HENCH
YOU'RE RIGHT-- BLAKE HAS HALF THE POLICE DEPARTMENT OUT LOOKING FOR HER--
THEY WON'T FIND HER.
HOW DO YOU KNOW?
I DON'T--IT'S JUST, YOU KNOW HOW SMART CASSIE IS. ALL THAT AVENGERS TRAINING AND STUFF.
THEN YOU HAVE TO FIND HER. I'M SERIOUS, SCOTT--
I AM STILL FURIOUS WITH YOU OVER THIS WHOLE DISAPPEARING ACT YOU'VE PULLED.
BUT IF YOU CAN FIND OUR DAUGHTER? IF YOU CAN BRING HER HOME SAFE?
YOU CAN AT LEAST START TO PUT THIS RIGHT.

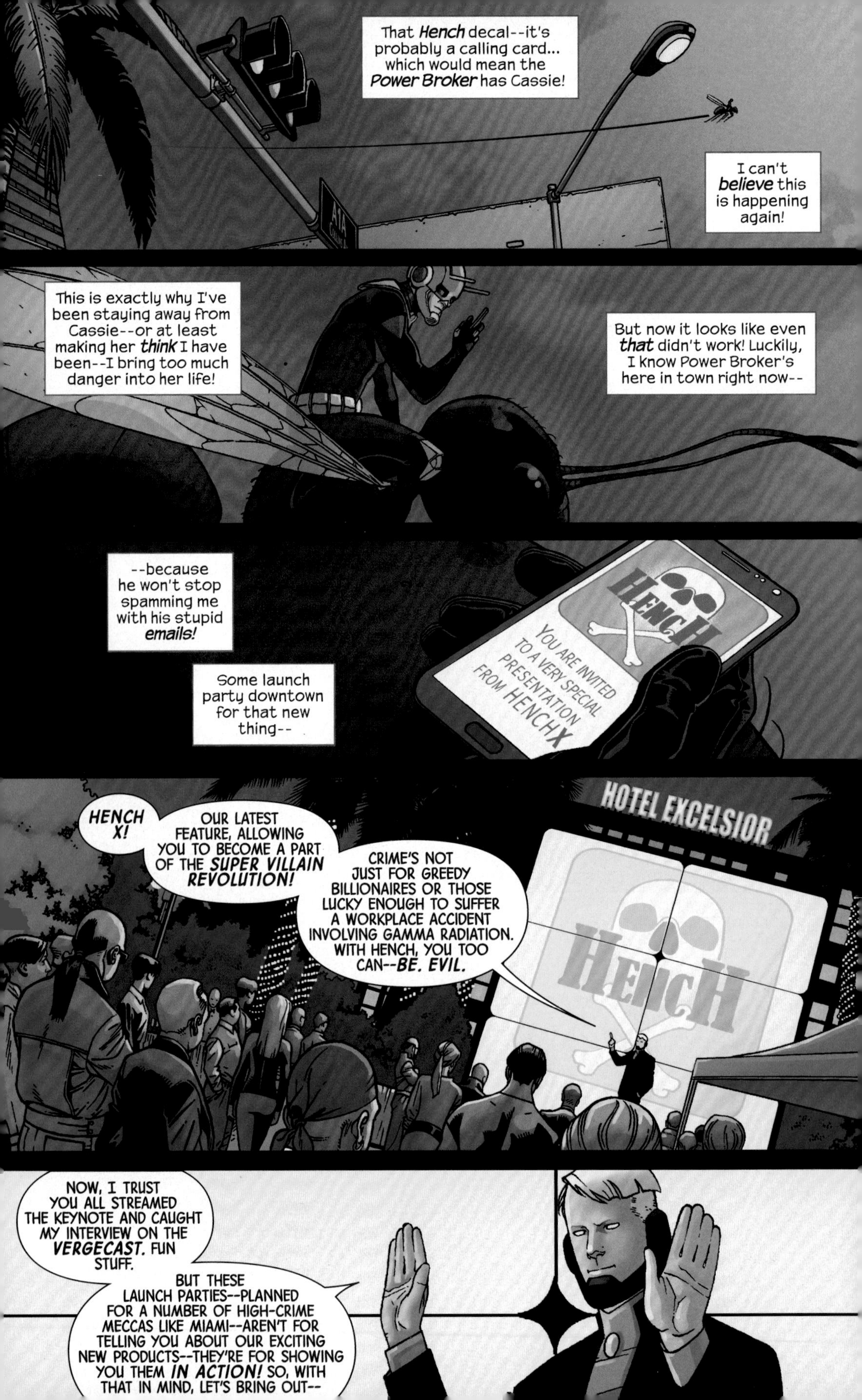
That Hench decal--it's probably a calling card... which would mean the Power Broker has Cassie!
I can't believe this is happening again!
This is exactly why I've been staying away from Cassie--or at least making her think I have been--I bring too much danger into her life!
But now it looks like even that didn't work! Luckily, I know Power Broker's here in town right now--
--because he won't stop spamming me with his stupid emails!
Some launch party downtown for that new thing--
HENCH
YOU ARE INVITED TO A VERY SPECIAL PRESENTATION FROM HENCHX
HOTEL EXCELSIOR
HENCH X!
OUR LATEST FEATURE, ALLOWING YOU TO BECOME A PART OF THE SUPER VILLAIN REVOLUTION!
CRIME'S NOT JUST FOR GREEDY BILLIONAIRES OR THOSE LUCKY ENOUGH TO SUFFER A WORKPLACE ACCIDENT INVOLVING GAMMA RADIATION. WITH HENCH, YOU TOO CAN--BE. EVIL.
HENCH
NOW, I TRUST YOU ALL STREAMED THE KEYNOTE AND CAUGHT MY INTERVIEW ON THE VERGECAST. FUN STUFF.
BUT THESE LAUNCH PARTIES--PLANNED FOR A NUMBER OF HIGH-CRIME MECCAS LIKE MIAMI--AREN'T FOR TELLING YOU ABOUT OUR EXCITING NEW PRODUCTS--THEY'RE FOR SHOWING YOU THEM IN ACTION! SO, WITH THAT IN MIND, LET'S BRING OUT--

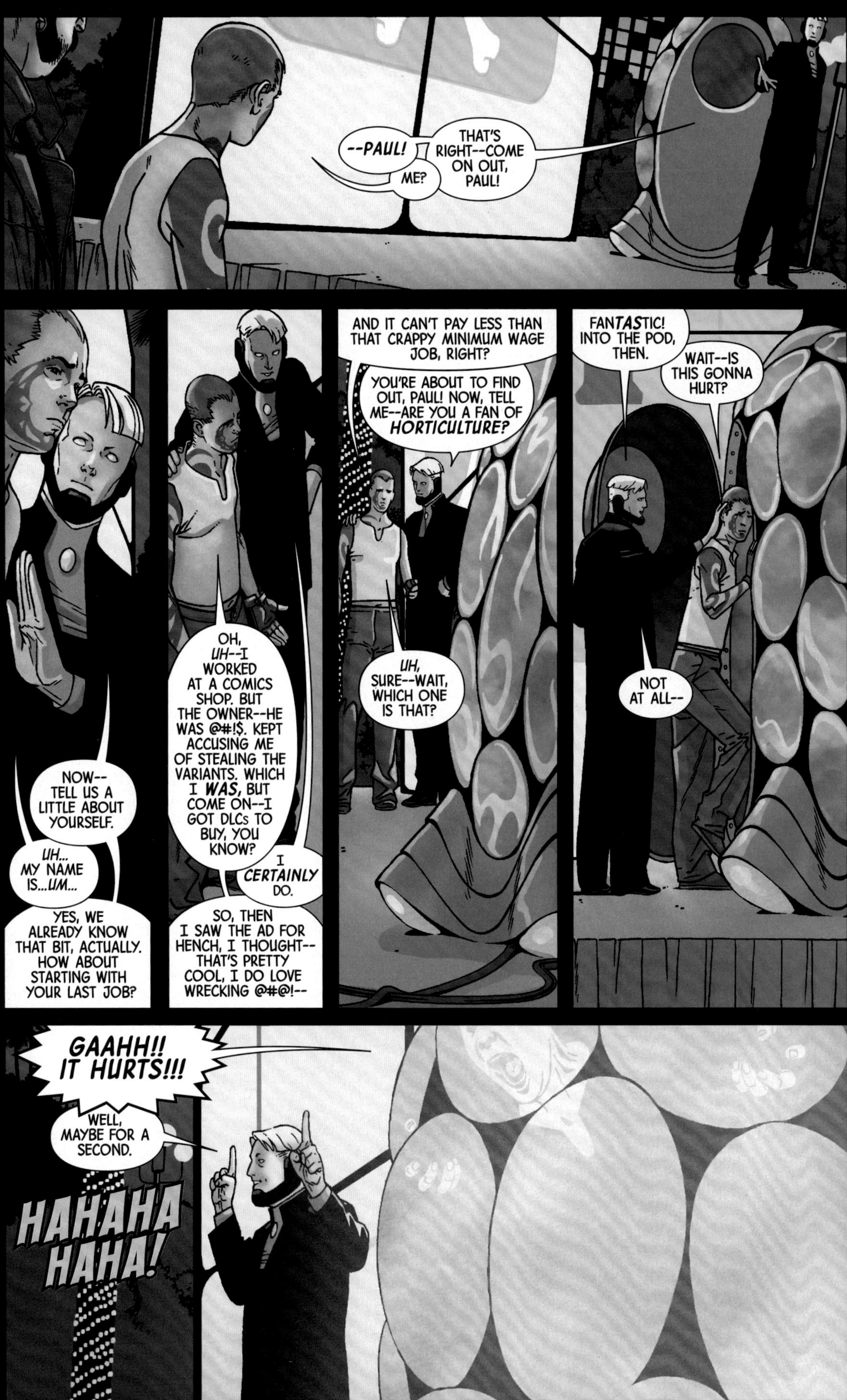
--PAUL!
ME?
THAT'S RIGHT--COME ON OUT, PAUL!
NOW--TELL US A LITTLE ABOUT YOURSELF.
UH... MY NAME IS...UM...
YES, WE ALREADY KNOW THAT BIT, ACTUALLY. HOW ABOUT STARTING WITH YOUR LAST JOB?
OH, UH--I WORKED AT A COMICS SHOP. BUT THE OWNER--HE WAS @#!$. KEPT ACCUSING ME OF STEALING THE VARIANTS. WHICH I WAS, BUT COME ON--I GOT DLCs TO BUY, YOU KNOW?
I CERTAINLY DO.
SO, THEN I SAW THE AD FOR HENCH, I THOUGHT--THAT'S PRETTY COOL, I DO LOVE WRECKING @#@!--
AND IT CAN'T PAY LESS THAN THAT CRAPPY MINIMUM WAGE JOB, RIGHT?
YOU'RE ABOUT TO FIND OUT, PAUL! NOW, TELL ME--ARE YOU A FAN OF HORTICULTURE?
UH, SURE--WAIT, WHICH ONE IS THAT?
FANTASTIC! INTO THE POD, THEN.
WAIT--IS THIS GONNA HURT?
NOT AT ALL--
GAAHH!! IT HURTS!!!
WELL, MAYBE FOR A SECOND.
HAHAHA HAHA!

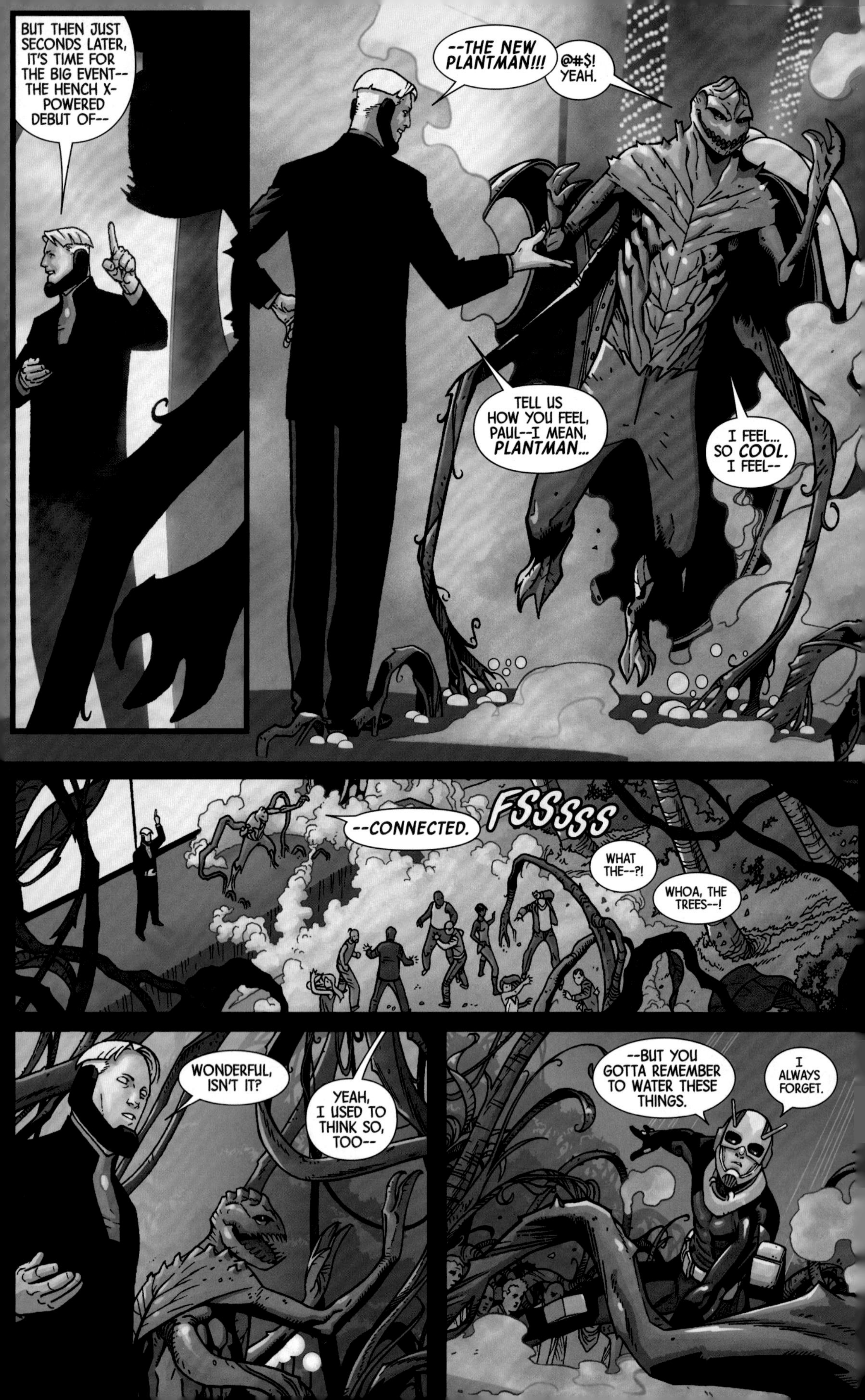
BUT THEN JUST SECONDS LATER, IT'S TIME FOR THE BIG EVENT--THE HENCH X-POWERED DEBUT OF--
--THE NEW PLANTMAN!!!
@#$! YEAH.
TELL US HOW YOU FEEL, PAUL--I MEAN, PLANTMAN...
I FEEL... SO COOL. I FEEL--
--CONNECTED.
FSSSSS
WHAT THE--?!
WHOA, THE TREES--!
WONDERFUL, ISN'T IT?
YEAH, I USED TO THINK SO, TOO--
--BUT YOU GOTTA REMEMBER TO WATER THESE THINGS.
I ALWAYS FORGET.

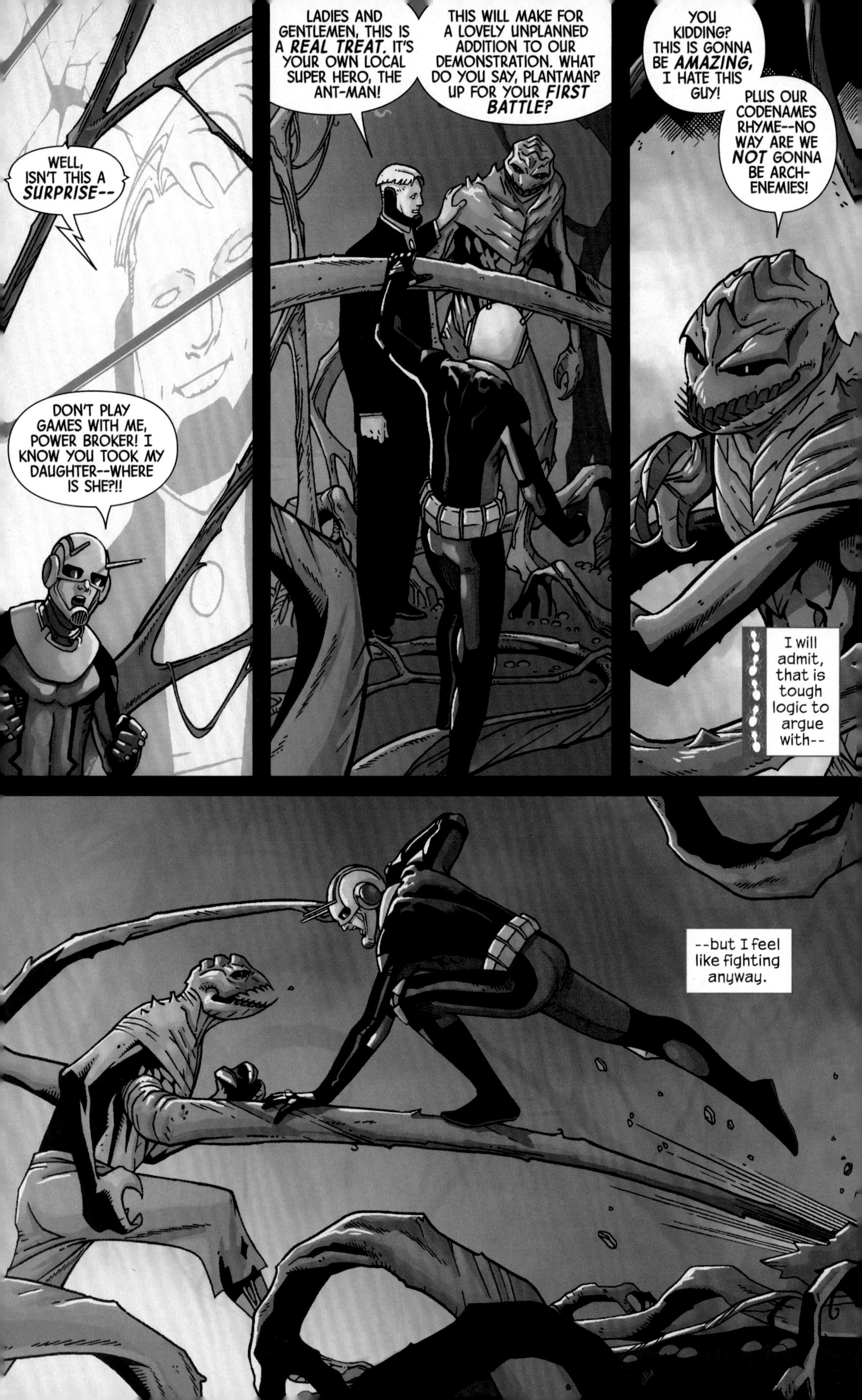
WELL, ISN'T THIS A SURPRISE--
DON'T PLAY GAMES WITH ME, POWER BROKER! I KNOW YOU TOOK MY DAUGHTER--WHERE IS SHE?!!
LADIES AND GENTLEMEN, THIS IS A REAL TREAT. IT'S YOUR OWN LOCAL SUPER HERO, THE ANT-MAN!
THIS WILL MAKE FOR A LOVELY UNPLANNED ADDITION TO OUR DEMONSTRATION. WHAT DO YOU SAY, PLANTMAN? UP FOR YOUR FIRST BATTLE?
YOU KIDDING? THIS IS GONNA BE AMAZING, I HATE THIS GUY!
PLUS OUR CODENAMES RHYME--NO WAY ARE WE NOT GONNA BE ARCH-ENEMIES!
I will admit, that is tough logic to argue with--
--but I feel like fighting anyway.

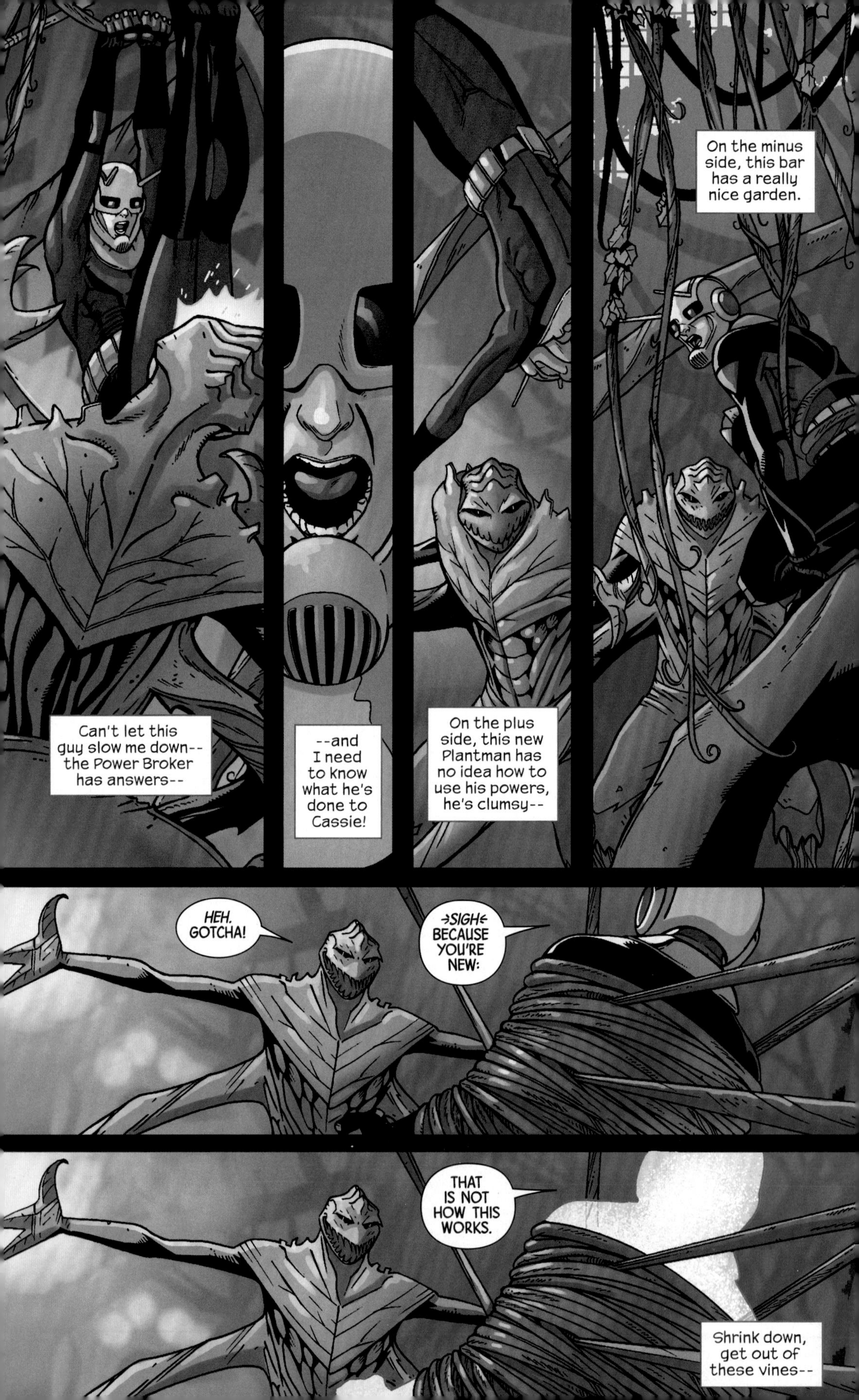

Can't let this guy slow me down-- the Power Broker has answers--
--and I need to know what he's done to Cassie!
On the plus side, this new Plantman has no idea how to use his powers, he's clumsy--
On the minus side, this bar has a really nice garden.
HEH. GOTCHA!
➔SIGH➔ BECAUSE YOU'RE NEW:
THAT IS NOT HOW THIS WORKS.
Shrink down, get out of these vines--

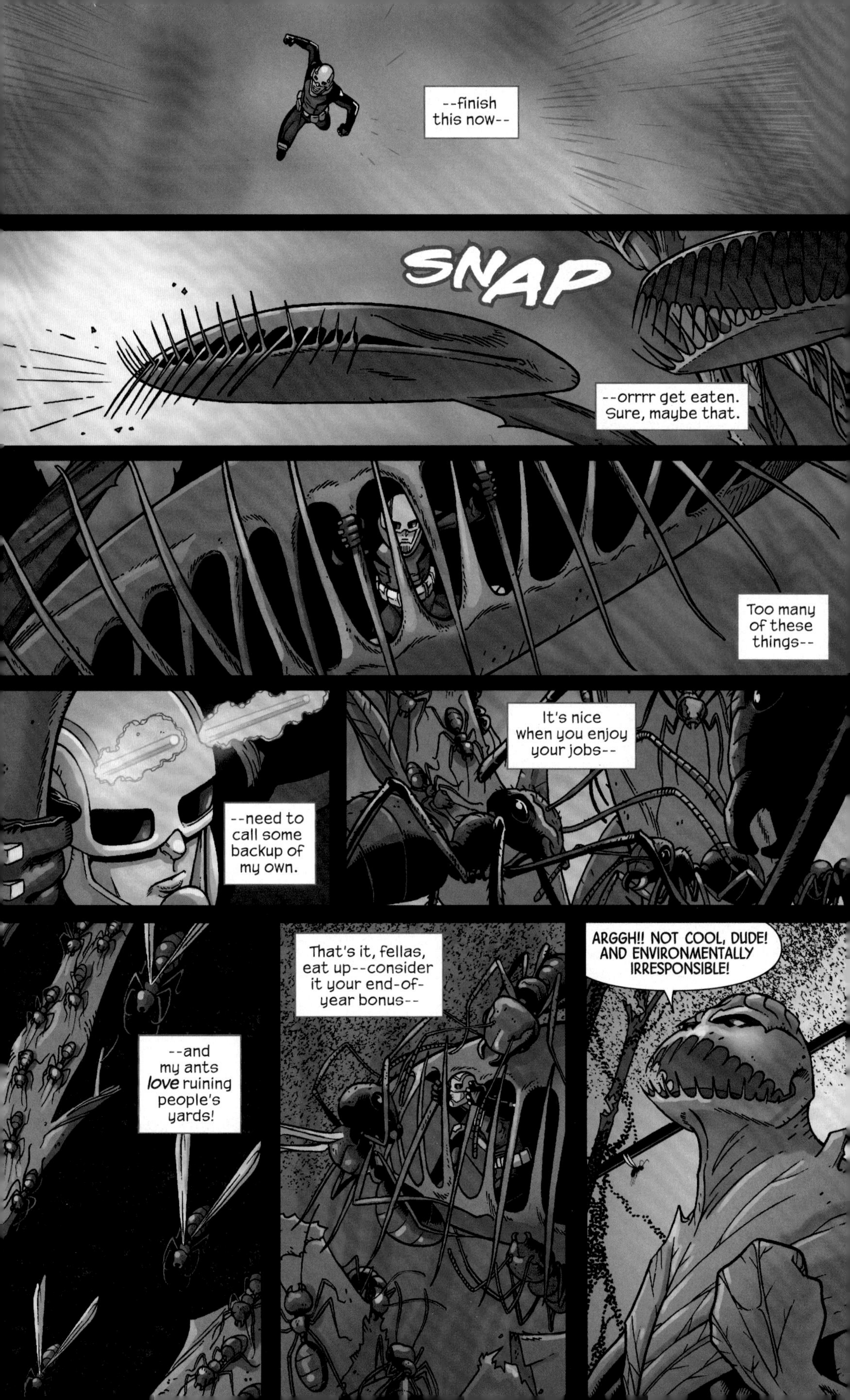
--finish this now--
SNAP
--orrrr get eaten. Sure, maybe that.
Too many of these things--
--need to call some backup of my own.
It's nice when you enjoy your jobs--
--and my ants *love* ruining people's yards!
That's it, fellas, eat up--consider it your end-of-year bonus--
ARGGH!! NOT COOL, DUDE! AND ENVIRONMENTALLY IRRESPONSIBLE!

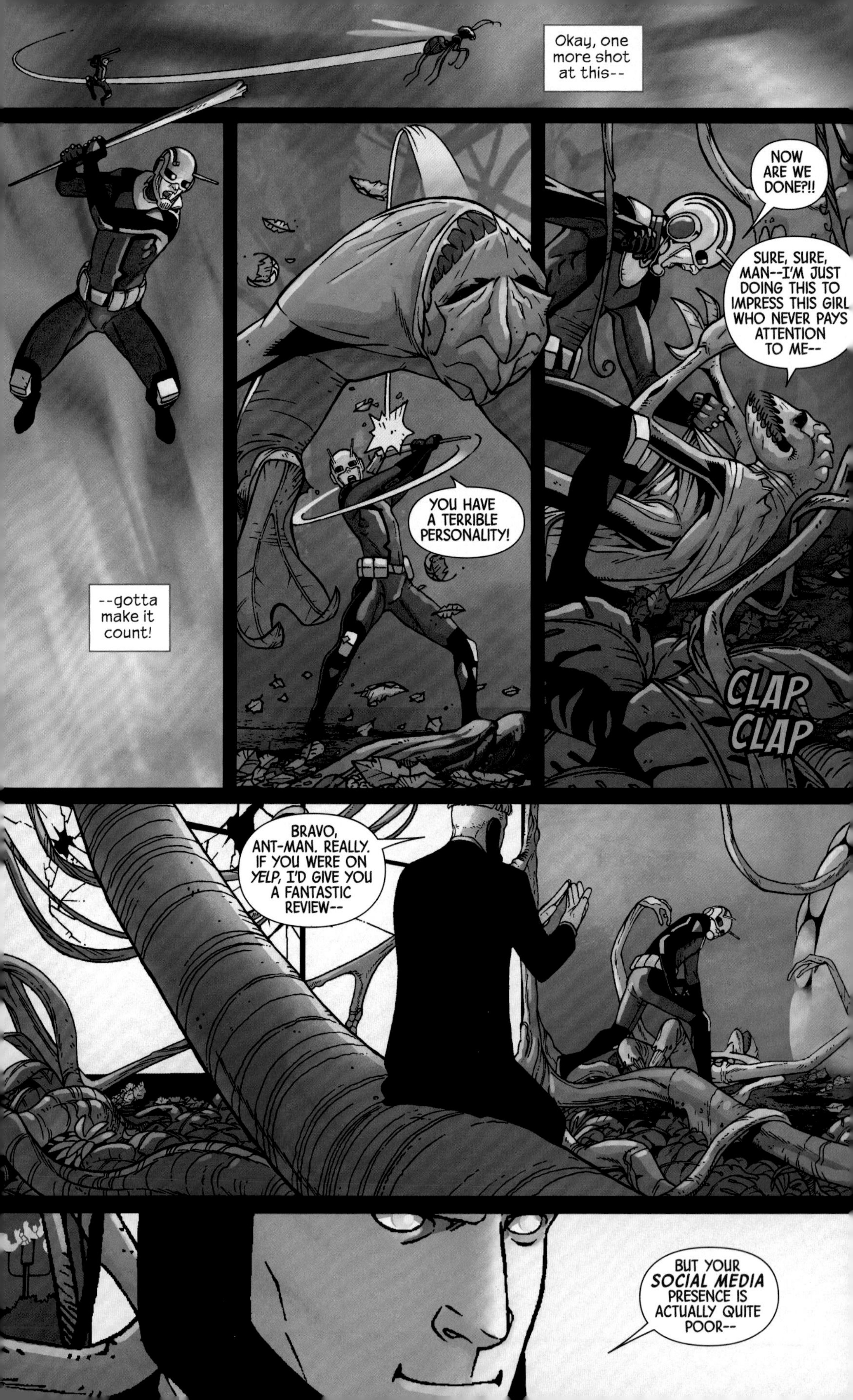
Okay, one more shot at this--
--gotta make it count!
YOU HAVE A TERRIBLE PERSONALITY!
NOW ARE WE DONE?!!
SURE, SURE, MAN--I'M JUST DOING THIS TO IMPRESS THIS GIRL WHO NEVER PAYS ATTENTION TO ME--
CLAP CLAP
BRAVO, ANT-MAN. REALLY. IF YOU WERE ON YELP, I'D GIVE YOU A FANTASTIC REVIEW--
BUT YOUR SOCIAL MEDIA PRESENCE IS ACTUALLY QUITE POOR--

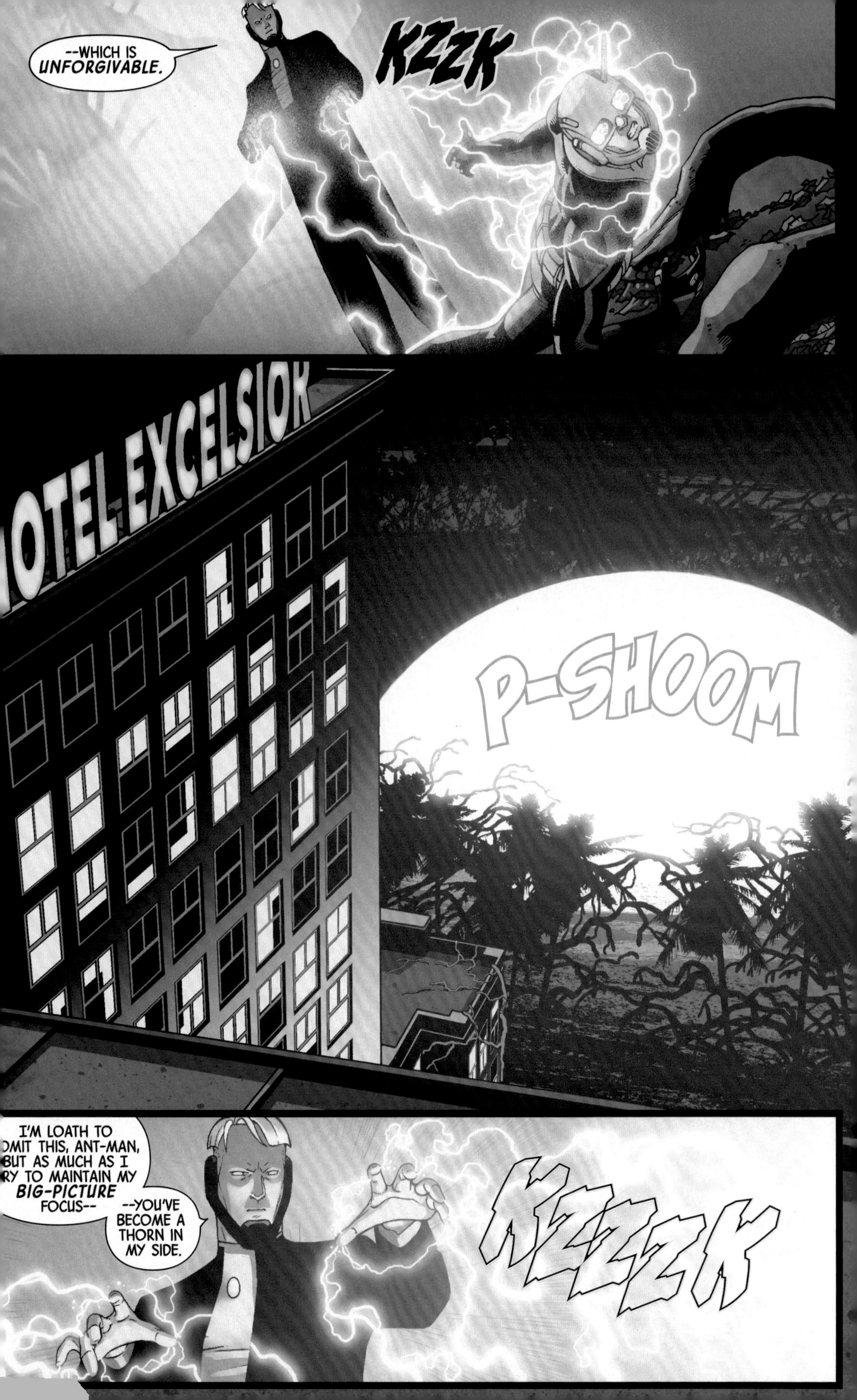

--WHICH IS UNFORGIVABLE.
KZZK
HOTEL EXCELSIOR
P-SHOOM
I'M LOATH TO
DMIT THIS, ANT-MAN,
BUT AS MUCH AS I
RY TO MAINTAIN MY
BIG-PICTURE
FOCUS--
--YOU'VE BECOME A THORN IN MY SIDE.
KZZZK

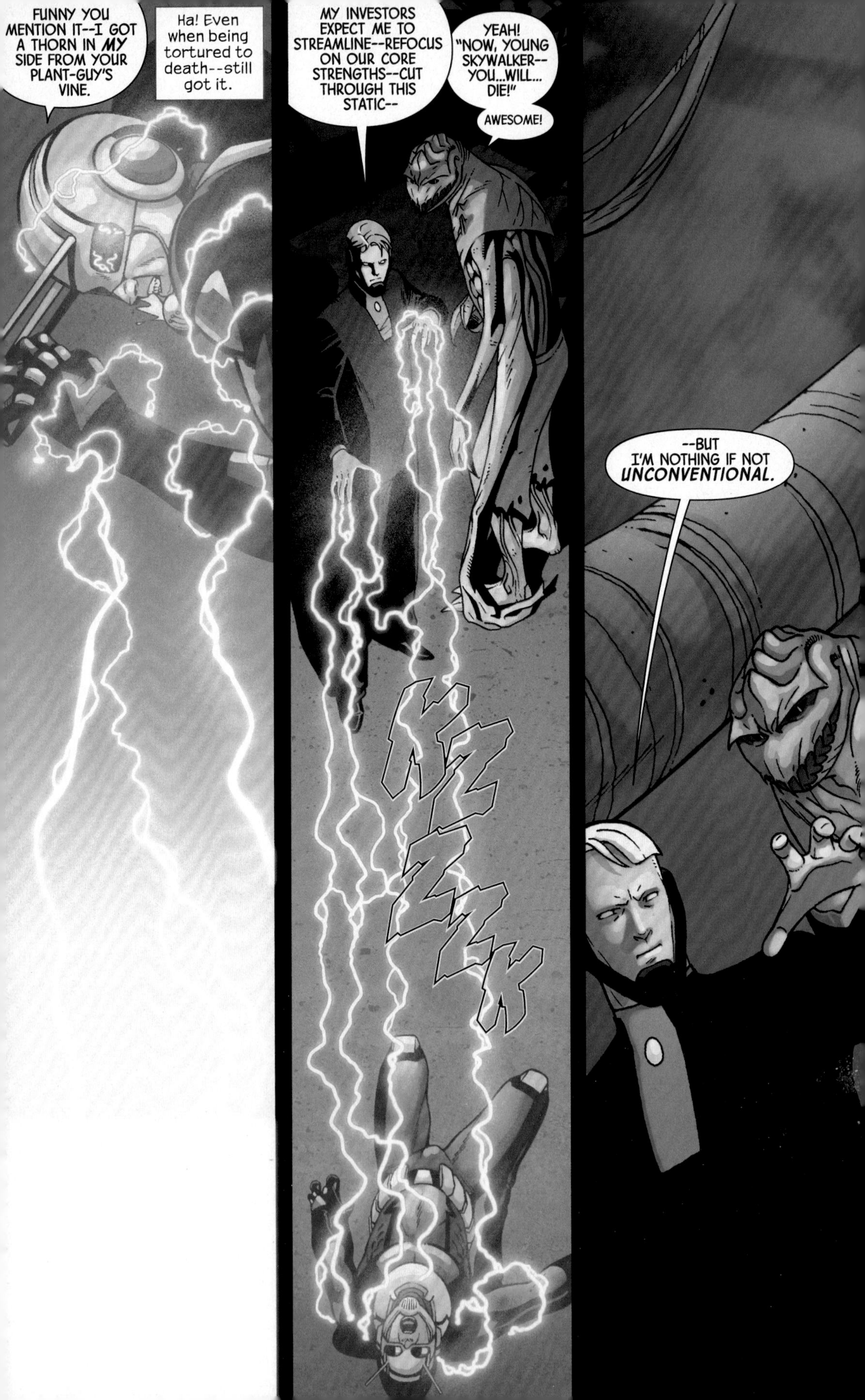
FUNNY YOU MENTION IT--I GOT A THORN IN *MY* SIDE FROM YOUR PLANT-GUY'S VINE.
Ha! Even when being tortured to death--still got it.
MY INVESTORS EXPECT ME TO STREAMLINE--REFOCUS ON OUR CORE STRENGTHS--CUT THROUGH THIS STATIC--
YEAH! "NOW, YOUNG SKYWALKER--YOU...WILL... DIE!"
AWESOME!
KZZZK
--BUT I'M NOTHING IF NOT *UNCONVENTIONAL.*

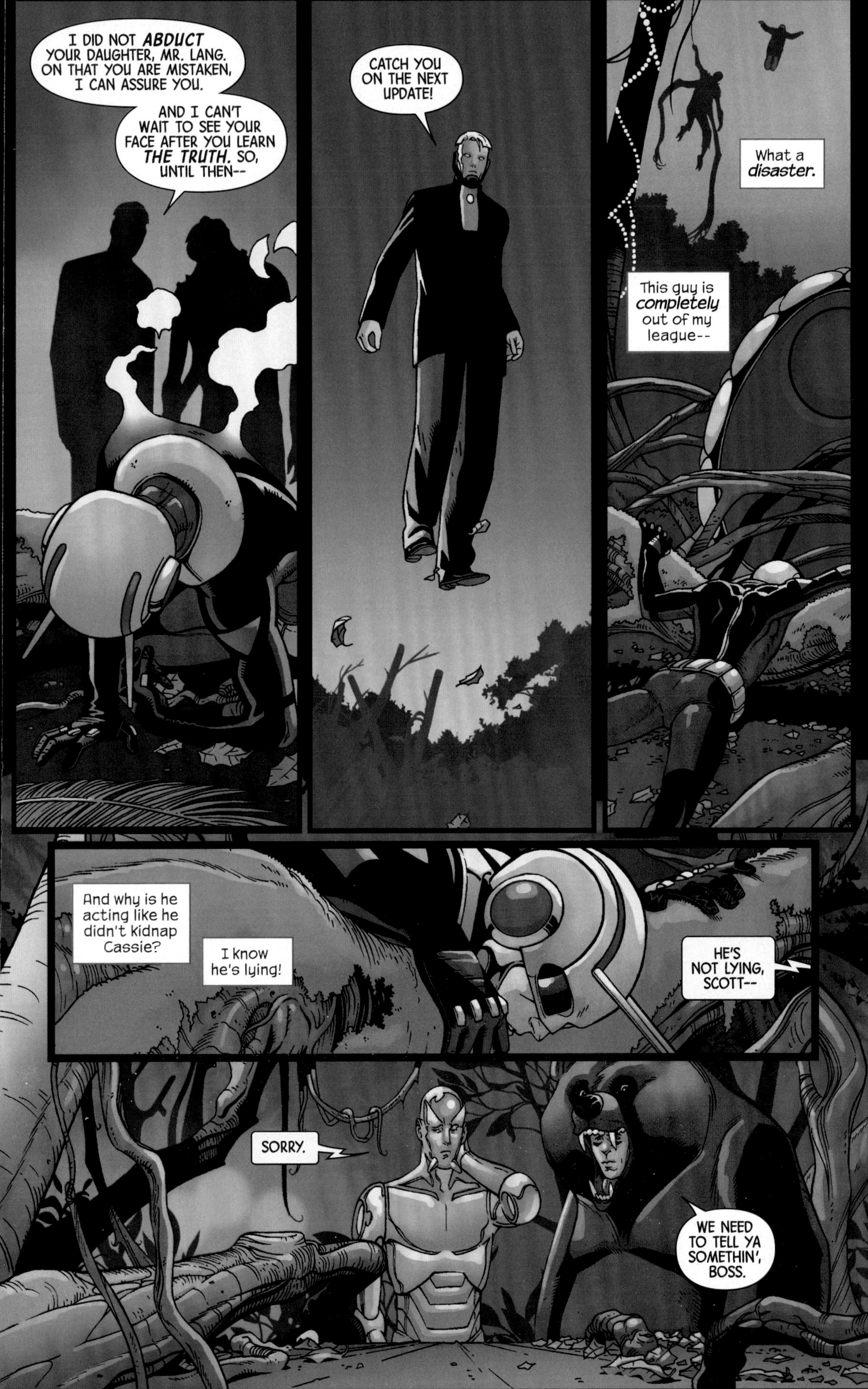
I DID NOT ABDUCT YOUR DAUGHTER, MR. LANG. ON THAT YOU ARE MISTAKEN, I CAN ASSURE YOU.
AND I CAN'T WAIT TO SEE YOUR FACE AFTER YOU LEARN THE TRUTH. SO, UNTIL THEN--
CATCH YOU ON THE NEXT UPDATE!
What a disaster.
This guy is completely out of my league--
And why is he acting like he didn't kidnap Cassie?
I know he's lying!
HE'S NOT LYING, SCOTT--
SORRY.
WE NEED TO TELL YA SOMETHIN', BOSS.

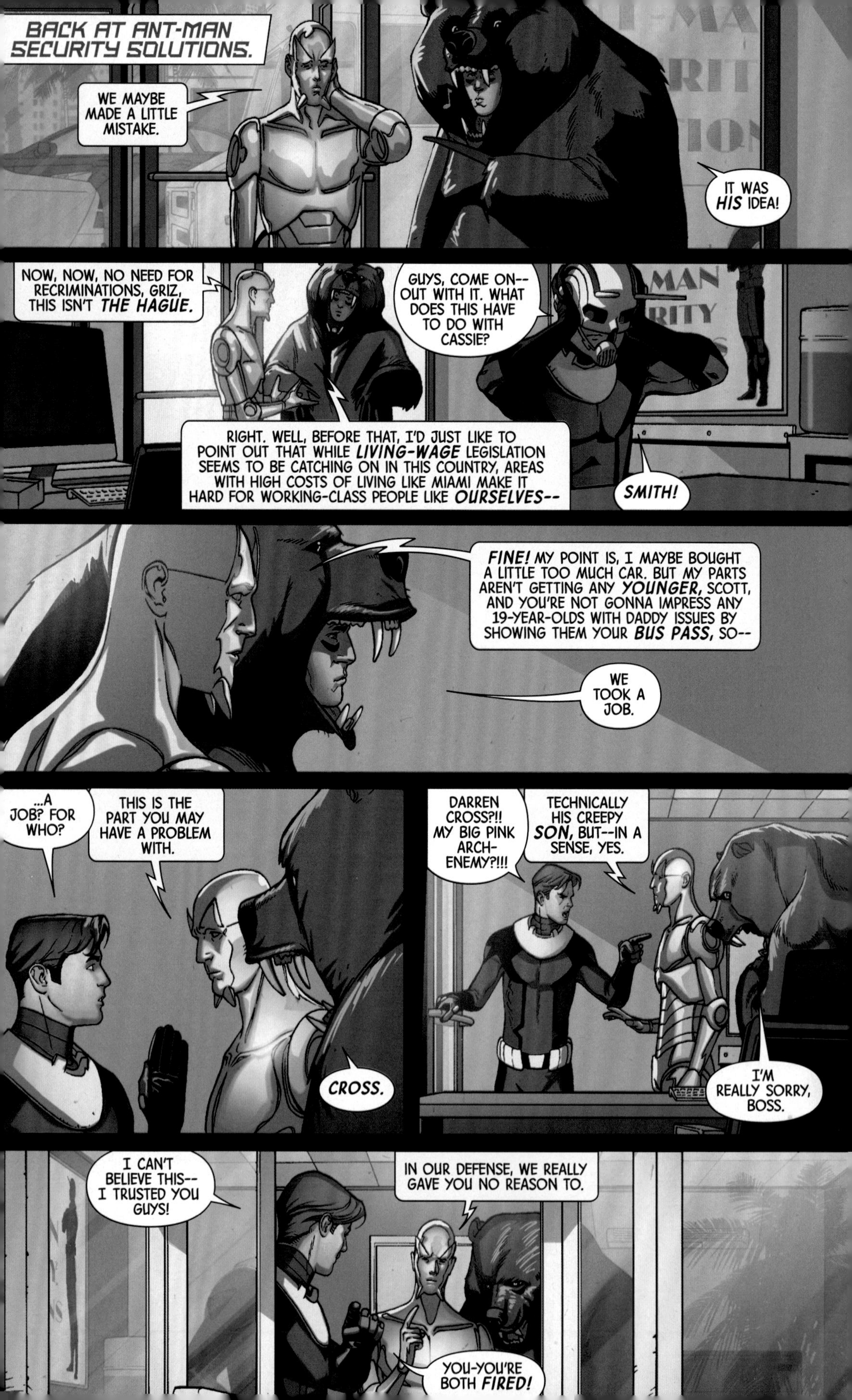
BACK AT ANT-MAN SECURITY SOLUTIONS.
WE MAYBE MADE A LITTLE MISTAKE.
IT WAS HIS IDEA!
NOW, NOW, NO NEED FOR RECRIMINATIONS, GRIZ, THIS ISN'T THE HAGUE.
GUYS, COME ON-- OUT WITH IT. WHAT DOES THIS HAVE TO DO WITH CASSIE?
RIGHT. WELL, BEFORE THAT, I'D JUST LIKE TO POINT OUT THAT WHILE LIVING-WAGE LEGISLATION SEEMS TO BE CATCHING ON IN THIS COUNTRY, AREAS WITH HIGH COSTS OF LIVING LIKE MIAMI MAKE IT HARD FOR WORKING-CLASS PEOPLE LIKE OURSELVES--
SMITH!
FINE! MY POINT IS, I MAYBE BOUGHT A LITTLE TOO MUCH CAR. BUT MY PARTS AREN'T GETTING ANY YOUNGER, SCOTT, AND YOU'RE NOT GONNA IMPRESS ANY 19-YEAR-OLDS WITH DADDY ISSUES BY SHOWING THEM YOUR BUS PASS, SO--
WE TOOK A JOB.
...A JOB? FOR WHO?
THIS IS THE PART YOU MAY HAVE A PROBLEM WITH.
CROSS.
DARREN CROSS?!! MY BIG PINK ARCH-ENEMY?!!!
TECHNICALLY HIS CREEPY SON, BUT--IN A SENSE, YES.
I'M REALLY SORRY, BOSS.
I CAN'T BELIEVE THIS-- I TRUSTED YOU GUYS!
IN OUR DEFENSE, WE REALLY GAVE YOU NO REASON TO.
YOU-YOU'RE BOTH FIRED!

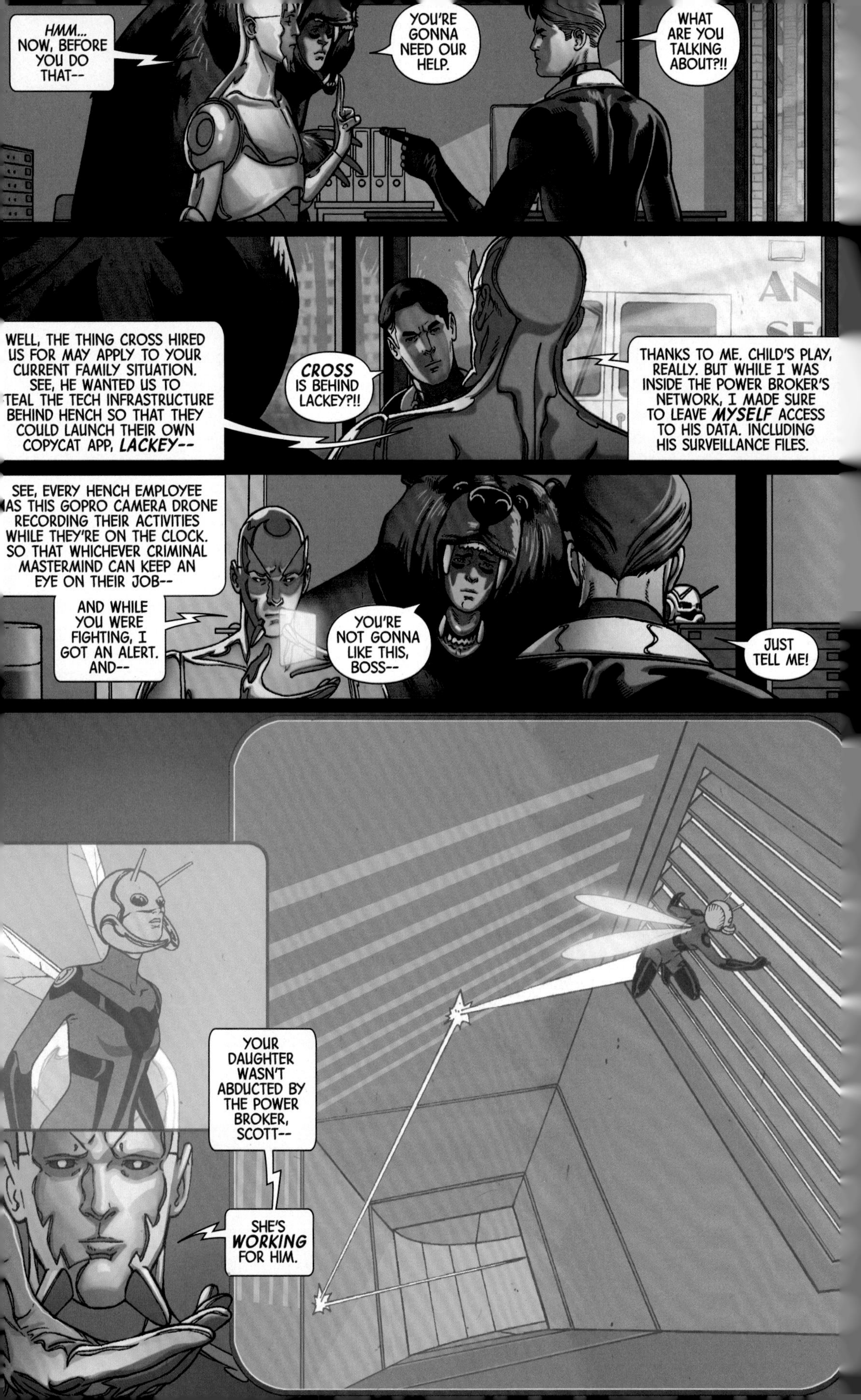
HMM... NOW, BEFORE YOU DO THAT--
YOU'RE GONNA NEED OUR HELP.
WHAT ARE YOU TALKING ABOUT?!!
WELL, THE THING CROSS HIRED US FOR MAY APPLY TO YOUR CURRENT FAMILY SITUATION. SEE, HE WANTED US TO TEAL THE TECH INFRASTRUCTURE BEHIND HENCH SO THAT THEY COULD LAUNCH THEIR OWN COPYCAT APP, LACKEY--
CROSS IS BEHIND LACKEY?!!
THANKS TO ME. CHILD'S PLAY, REALLY. BUT WHILE I WAS INSIDE THE POWER BROKER'S NETWORK, I MADE SURE TO LEAVE MYSELF ACCESS TO HIS DATA. INCLUDING HIS SURVEILLANCE FILES.
SEE, EVERY HENCH EMPLOYEE AS THIS GOPRO CAMERA DRONE RECORDING THEIR ACTIVITIES WHILE THEY'RE ON THE CLOCK. SO THAT WHICHEVER CRIMINAL MASTERMIND CAN KEEP AN EYE ON THEIR JOB--
AND WHILE YOU WERE FIGHTING, I GOT AN ALERT. AND--
YOU'RE NOT GONNA LIKE THIS, BOSS--
JUST TELL ME!
YOUR DAUGHTER WASN'T ABDUCTED BY THE POWER BROKER, SCOTT--
SHE'S WORKING FOR HIM.

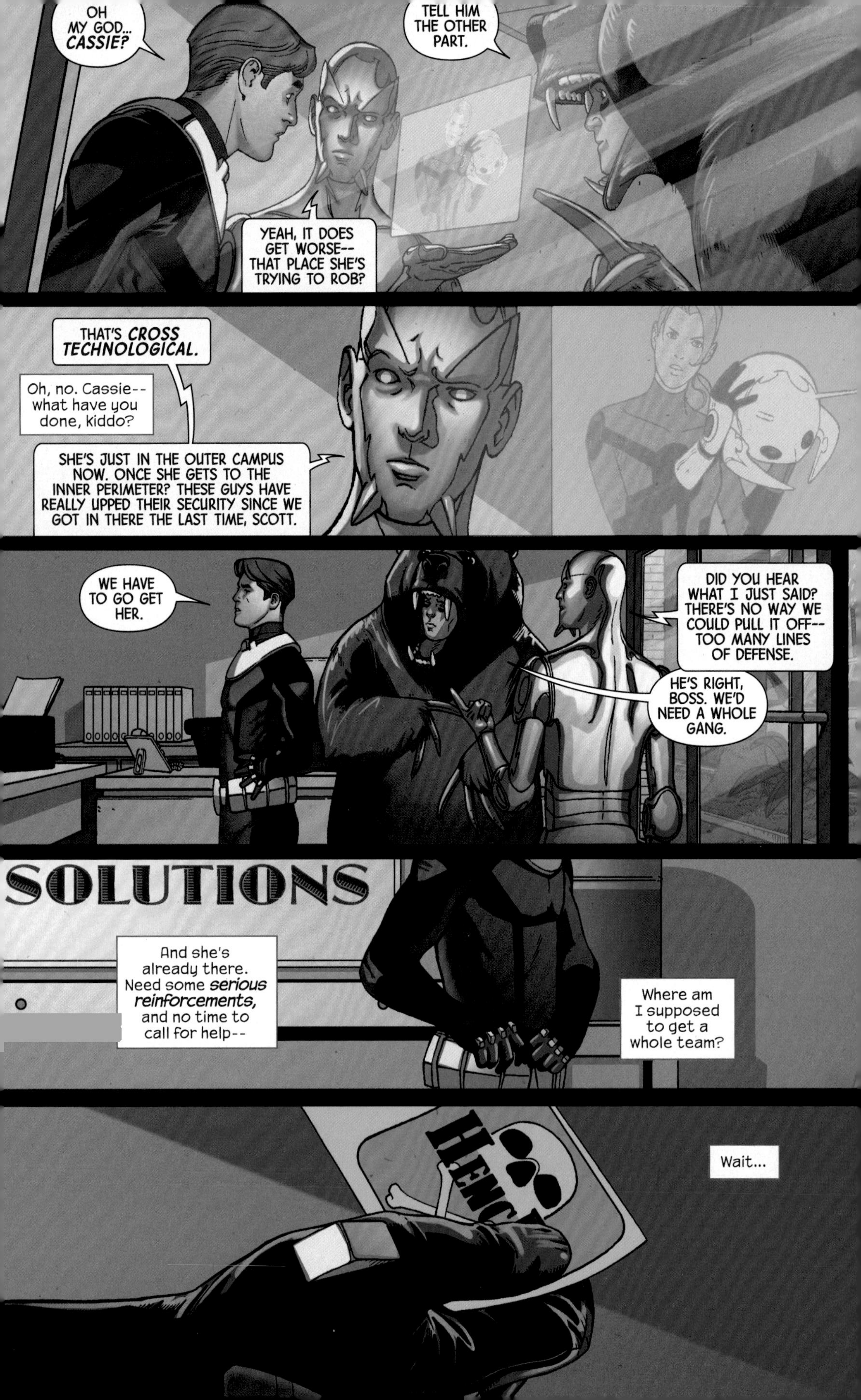

OH MY GOD... CASSIE?
TELL HIM THE OTHER PART.
YEAH, IT DOES GET WORSE-- THAT PLACE SHE'S TRYING TO ROB?
THAT'S CROSS TECHNOLOGICAL.
Oh, no. Cassie-- what have you done, kiddo?
SHE'S JUST IN THE OUTER CAMPUS NOW. ONCE SHE GETS TO THE INNER PERIMETER? THESE GUYS HAVE REALLY UPPED THEIR SECURITY SINCE WE GOT IN THERE THE LAST TIME, SCOTT.
WE HAVE TO GO GET HER.
DID YOU HEAR WHAT I JUST SAID? THERE'S NO WAY WE COULD PULL IT OFF-- TOO MANY LINES OF DEFENSE.
HE'S RIGHT, BOSS. WE'D NEED A WHOLE GANG.
SOLUTIONS
And she's already there. Need some serious reinforcements, and no time to call for help--
Where am I supposed to get a whole team?
HENC
Wait...

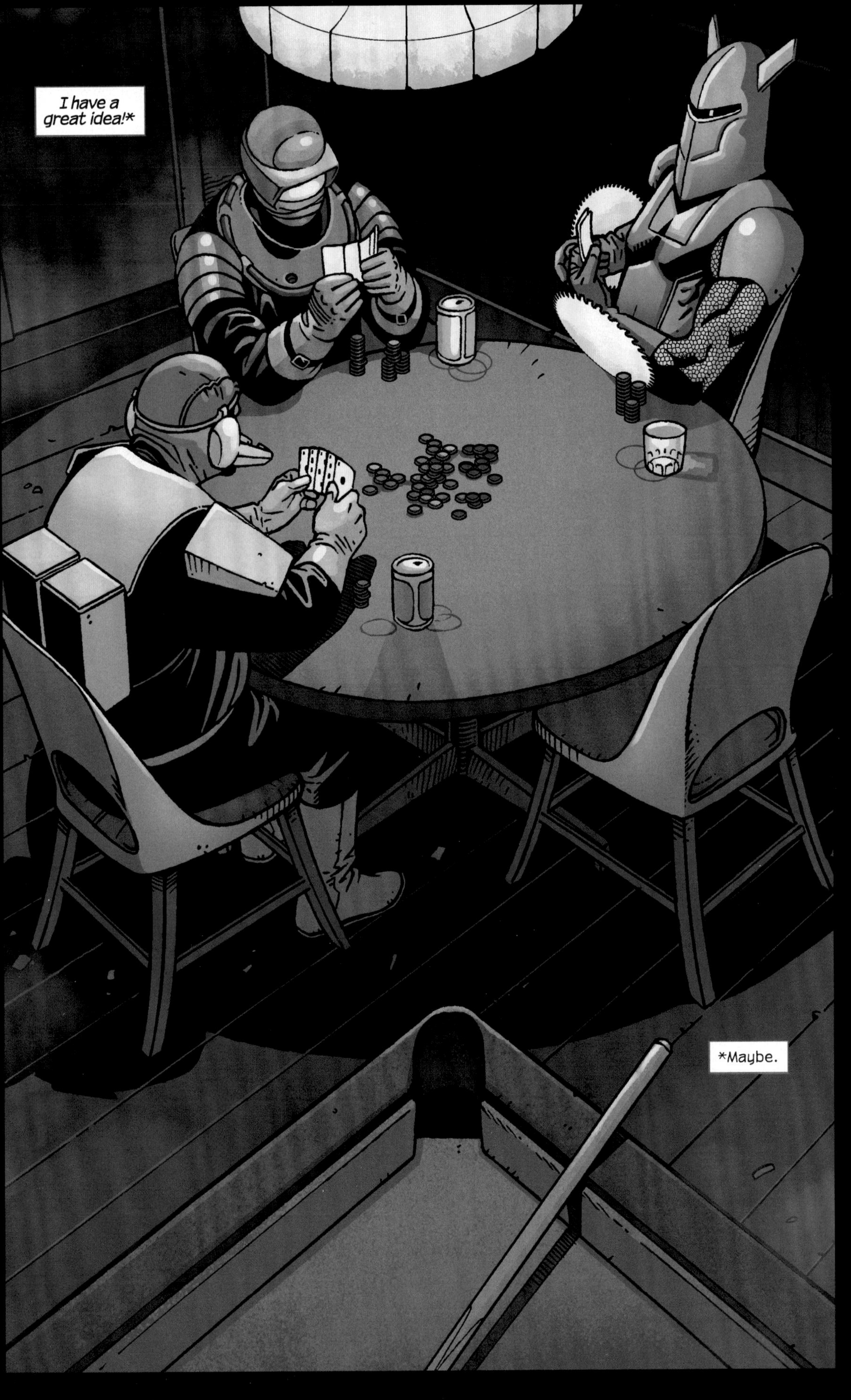

I have a great idea!*
*Maybe.

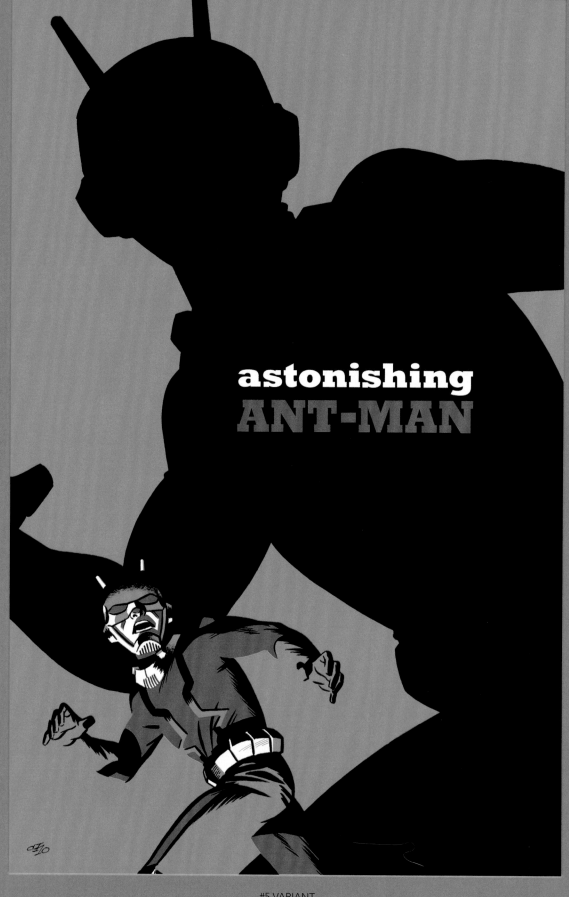

astonishing
ANT-MAN

#5 VARIANT
BY MICHAEL CHO

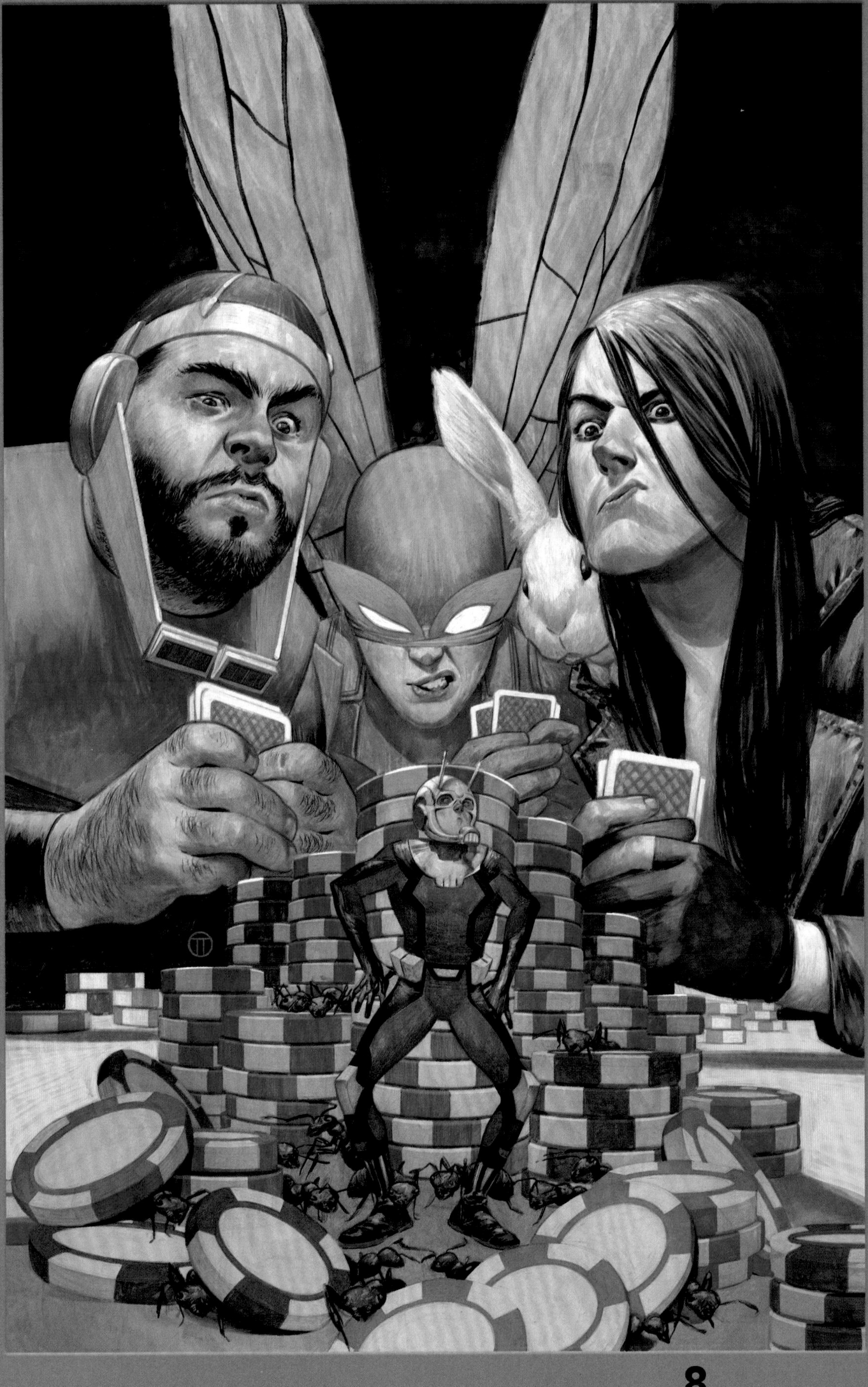

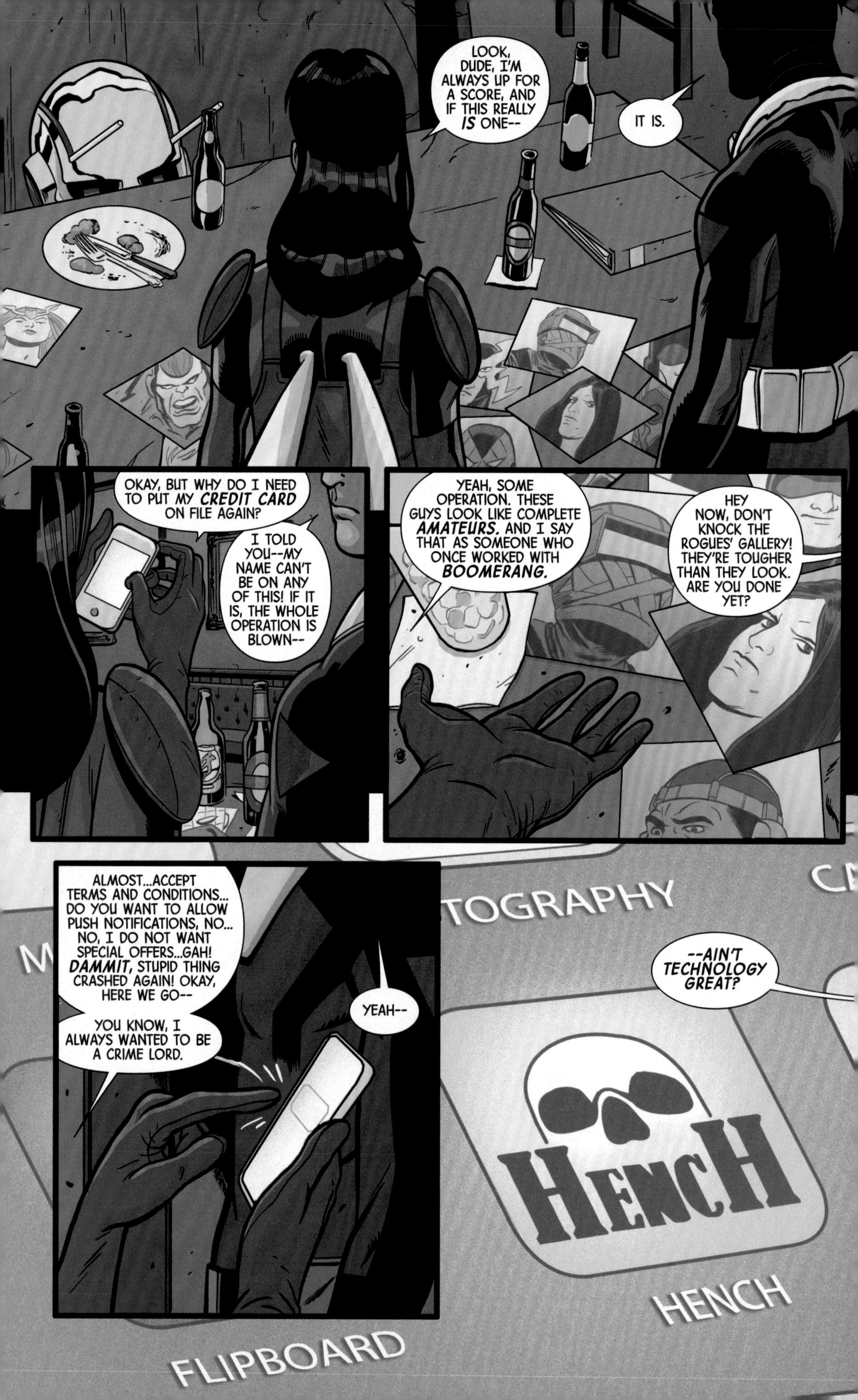
LOOK, DUDE, I'M ALWAYS UP FOR A SCORE, AND IF THIS REALLY IS ONE--
IT IS.
OKAY, BUT WHY DO I NEED TO PUT MY CREDIT CARD ON FILE AGAIN?
I TOLD YOU--MY NAME CAN'T BE ON ANY OF THIS! IF IT IS, THE WHOLE OPERATION IS BLOWN--
YEAH, SOME OPERATION. THESE GUYS LOOK LIKE COMPLETE AMATEURS. AND I SAY THAT AS SOMEONE WHO ONCE WORKED WITH BOOMERANG.
HEY NOW, DON'T KNOCK THE ROGUES' GALLERY! THEY'RE TOUGHER THAN THEY LOOK. ARE YOU DONE YET?
ALMOST...ACCEPT TERMS AND CONDITIONS... DO YOU WANT TO ALLOW PUSH NOTIFICATIONS, NO... NO, I DO NOT WANT SPECIAL OFFERS...GAH! DAMMIT, STUPID THING CRASHED AGAIN! OKAY, HERE WE GO--
YEAH--
YOU KNOW, I ALWAYS WANTED TO BE A CRIME LORD.
--AIN'T TECHNOLOGY GREAT?
TOGRAPHY
HENCH
HENCH
FLIPBOARD

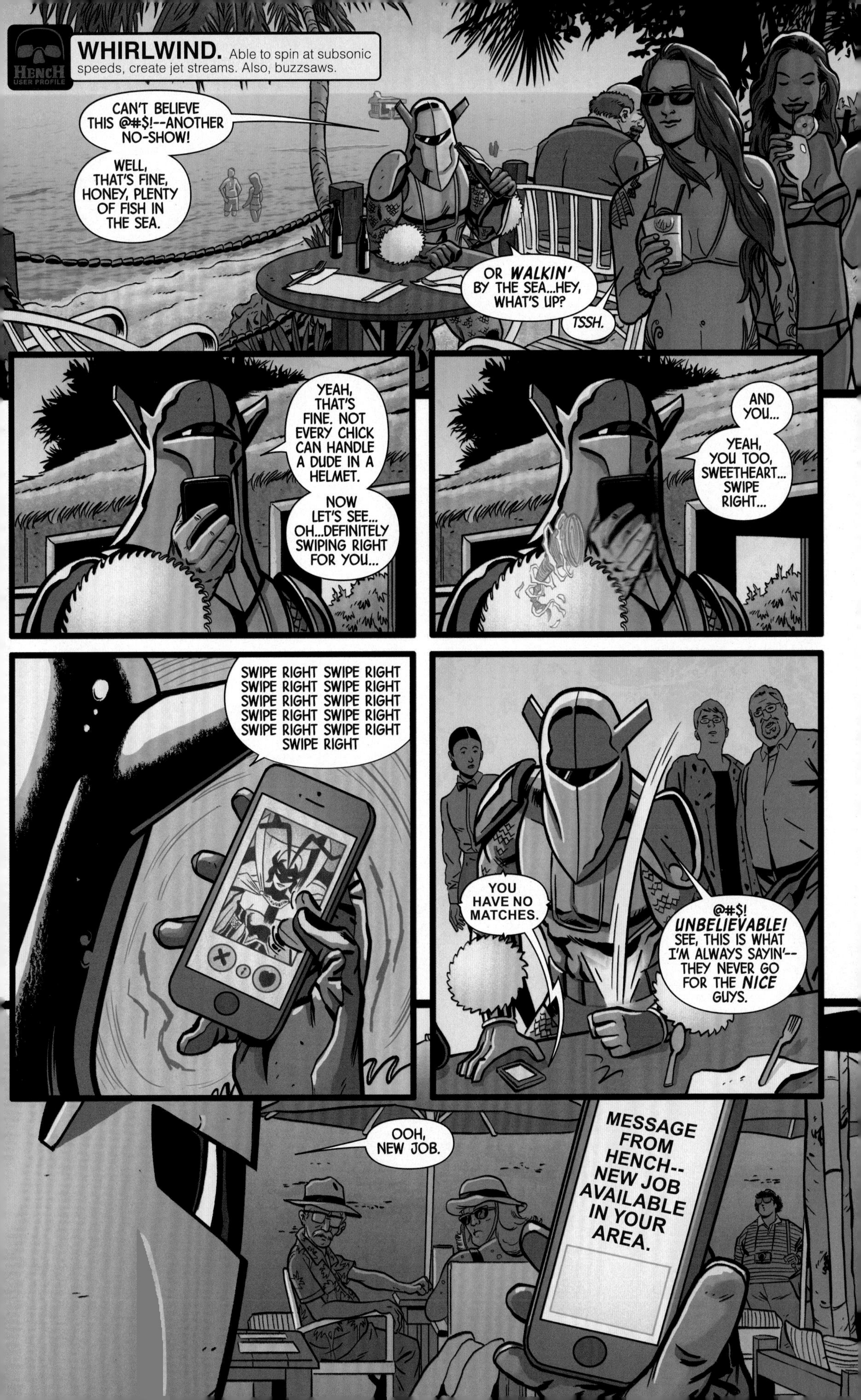
WHIRLWIND. Able to spin at subsonic speeds, create jet streams. Also, buzzsaws.
HENCH USER PROFILE
CAN'T BELIEVE THIS @#$!--ANOTHER NO-SHOW!
WELL, THAT'S FINE, HONEY, PLENTY OF FISH IN THE SEA.
OR WALKIN' BY THE SEA...HEY, WHAT'S UP?
TSSH.
YEAH, THAT'S FINE. NOT EVERY CHICK CAN HANDLE A DUDE IN A HELMET.
NOW LET'S SEE... OH...DEFINITELY SWIPING RIGHT FOR YOU...
AND YOU...
YEAH, YOU TOO, SWEETHEART... SWIPE RIGHT...
SWIPE RIGHT SWIPE RIGHT SWIPE RIGHT SWIPE RIGHT SWIPE RIGHT SWIPE RIGHT SWIPE RIGHT SWIPE RIGHT SWIPE RIGHT SWIPE RIGHT SWIPE RIGHT
YOU HAVE NO MATCHES.
@#$! UNBELIEVABLE! SEE, THIS IS WHAT I'M ALWAYS SAYIN'-- THEY NEVER GO FOR THE NICE GUYS.
OOH, NEW JOB.
MESSAGE FROM HENCH-- NEW JOB AVAILABLE IN YOUR AREA.

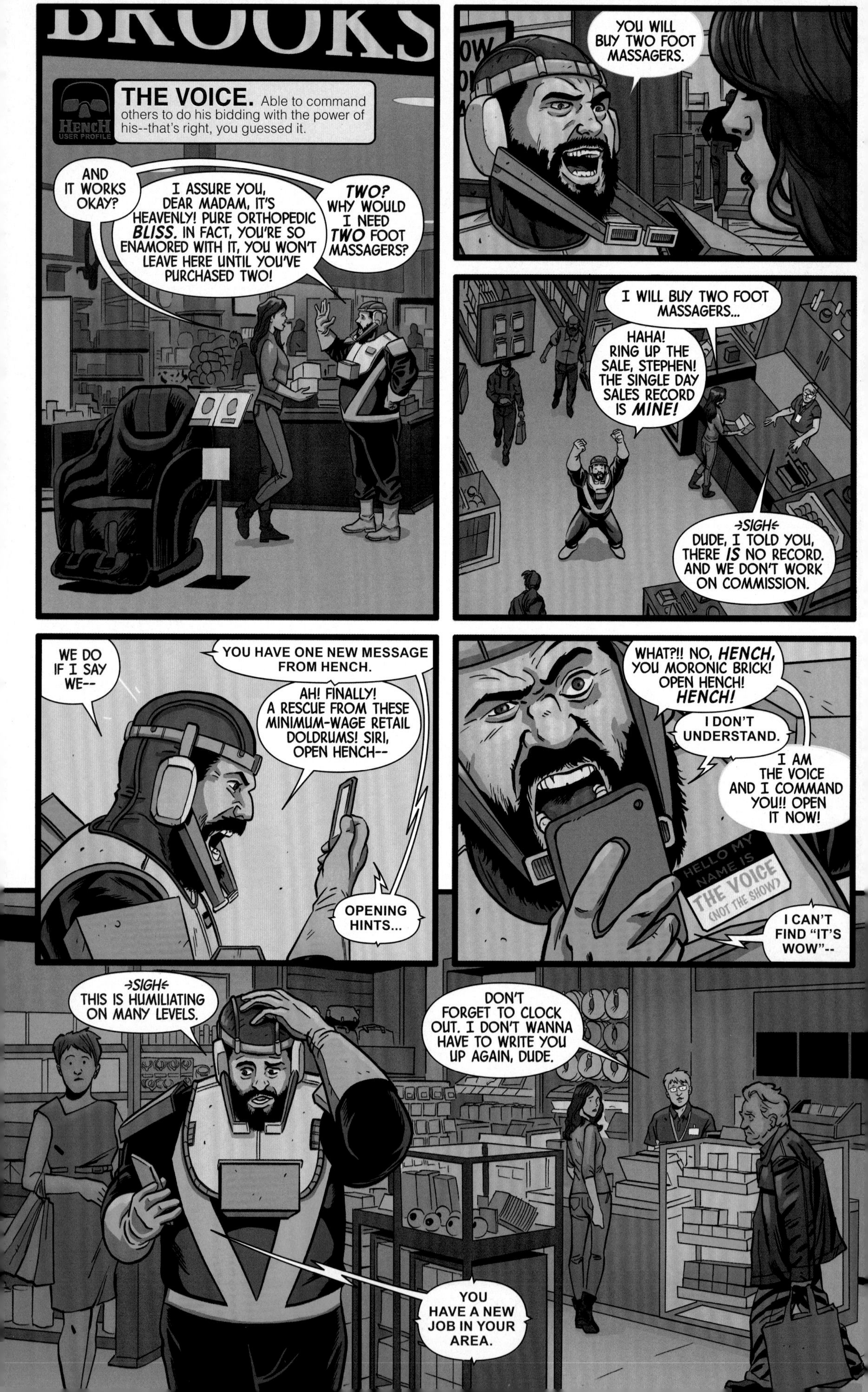
BROOKS
HENCH USER PROFILE
THE VOICE. Able to command others to do his bidding with the power of his--that's right, you guessed it.
AND IT WORKS OKAY?
I ASSURE YOU, DEAR MADAM, IT'S HEAVENLY! PURE ORTHOPEDIC BLISS. IN FACT, YOU'RE SO ENAMORED WITH IT, YOU WON'T LEAVE HERE UNTIL YOU'VE PURCHASED TWO!
TWO? WHY WOULD I NEED TWO FOOT MASSAGERS?
YOU WILL BUY TWO FOOT MASSAGERS.
I WILL BUY TWO FOOT MASSAGERS...
HAHA! RING UP THE SALE, STEPHEN! THE SINGLE DAY SALES RECORD IS MINE!
SIGH
DUDE, I TOLD YOU, THERE IS NO RECORD. AND WE DON'T WORK ON COMMISSION.
WE DO IF I SAY WE--
YOU HAVE ONE NEW MESSAGE FROM HENCH.
AH! FINALLY! A RESCUE FROM THESE MINIMUM-WAGE RETAIL DOLDRUMS! SIRI, OPEN HENCH--
OPENING HINTS...
WHAT?!! NO, HENCH, YOU MORONIC BRICK! OPEN HENCH! HENCH!
I DON'T UNDERSTAND.
I AM THE VOICE AND I COMMAND YOU!! OPEN IT NOW!
HELLO MY NAME IS THE VOICE (NOT THE SHOW)
I CAN'T FIND "IT'S WOW"--
SIGH
THIS IS HUMILIATING ON MANY LEVELS.
DON'T FORGET TO CLOCK OUT. I DON'T WANNA HAVE TO WRITE YOU UP AGAIN, DUDE.
YOU HAVE A NEW JOB IN YOUR AREA.

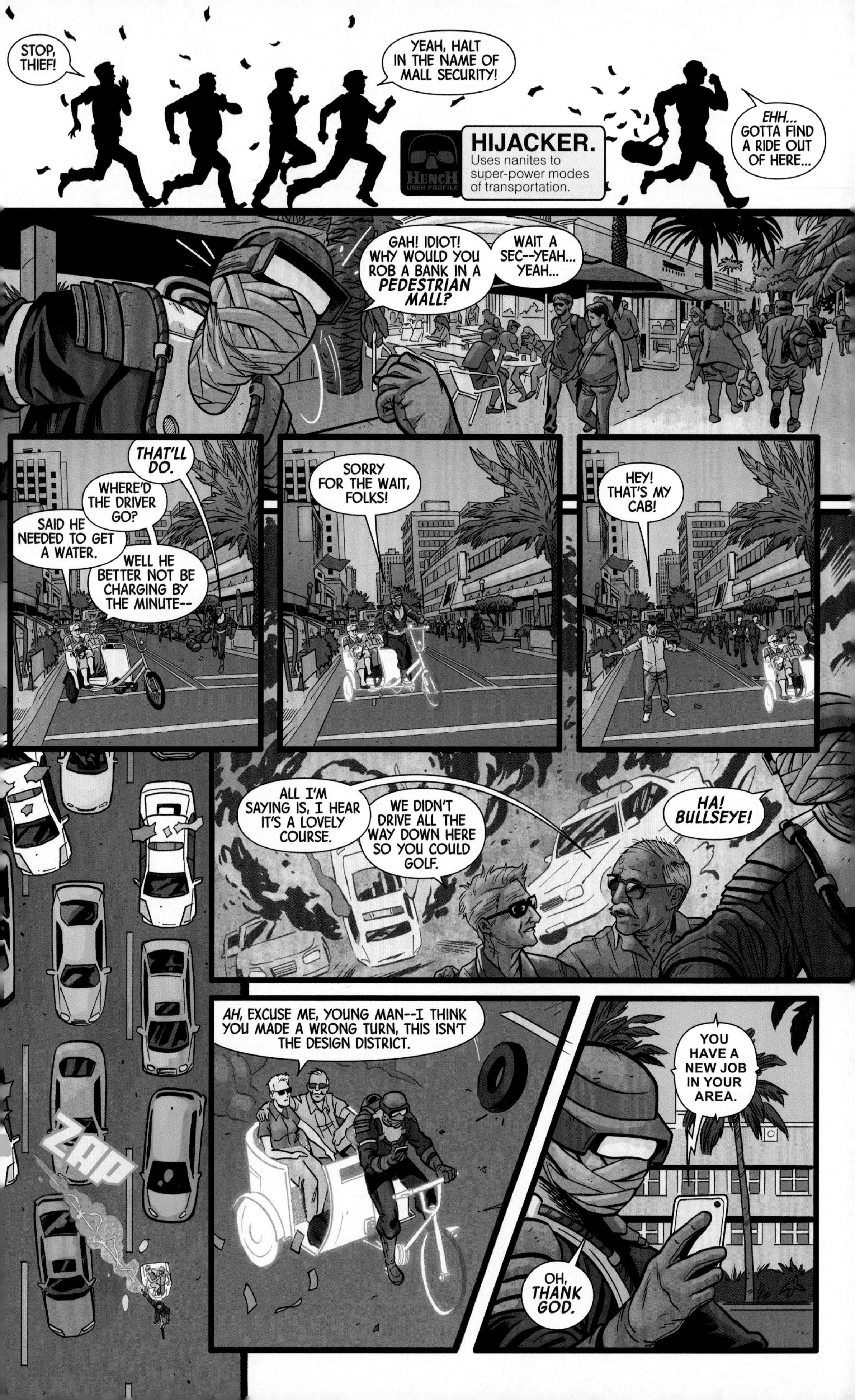
STOP, THIEF!
YEAH, HALT IN THE NAME OF MALL SECURITY!
HENCH USER PROFILE
HIJACKER.
Uses nanites to super-power modes of transportation.
EHH... GOTTA FIND A RIDE OUT OF HERE...
GAH! IDIOT! WHY WOULD YOU ROB A BANK IN A PEDESTRIAN MALL?
WAIT A SEC--YEAH... YEAH...
THAT'LL DO.
WHERE'D THE DRIVER GO?
SAID HE NEEDED TO GET A WATER.
WELL HE BETTER NOT BE CHARGING BY THE MINUTE--
SORRY FOR THE WAIT, FOLKS!
HEY! THAT'S MY CAB!
ZAP
ALL I'M SAYING IS, I HEAR IT'S A LOVELY COURSE.
WE DIDN'T DRIVE ALL THE WAY DOWN HERE SO YOU COULD GOLF.
HA! BULLSEYE!
AH, EXCUSE ME, YOUNG MAN--I THINK YOU MADE A WRONG TURN, THIS ISN'T THE DESIGN DISTRICT.
YOU HAVE A NEW JOB IN YOUR AREA.
OH, THANK GOD.

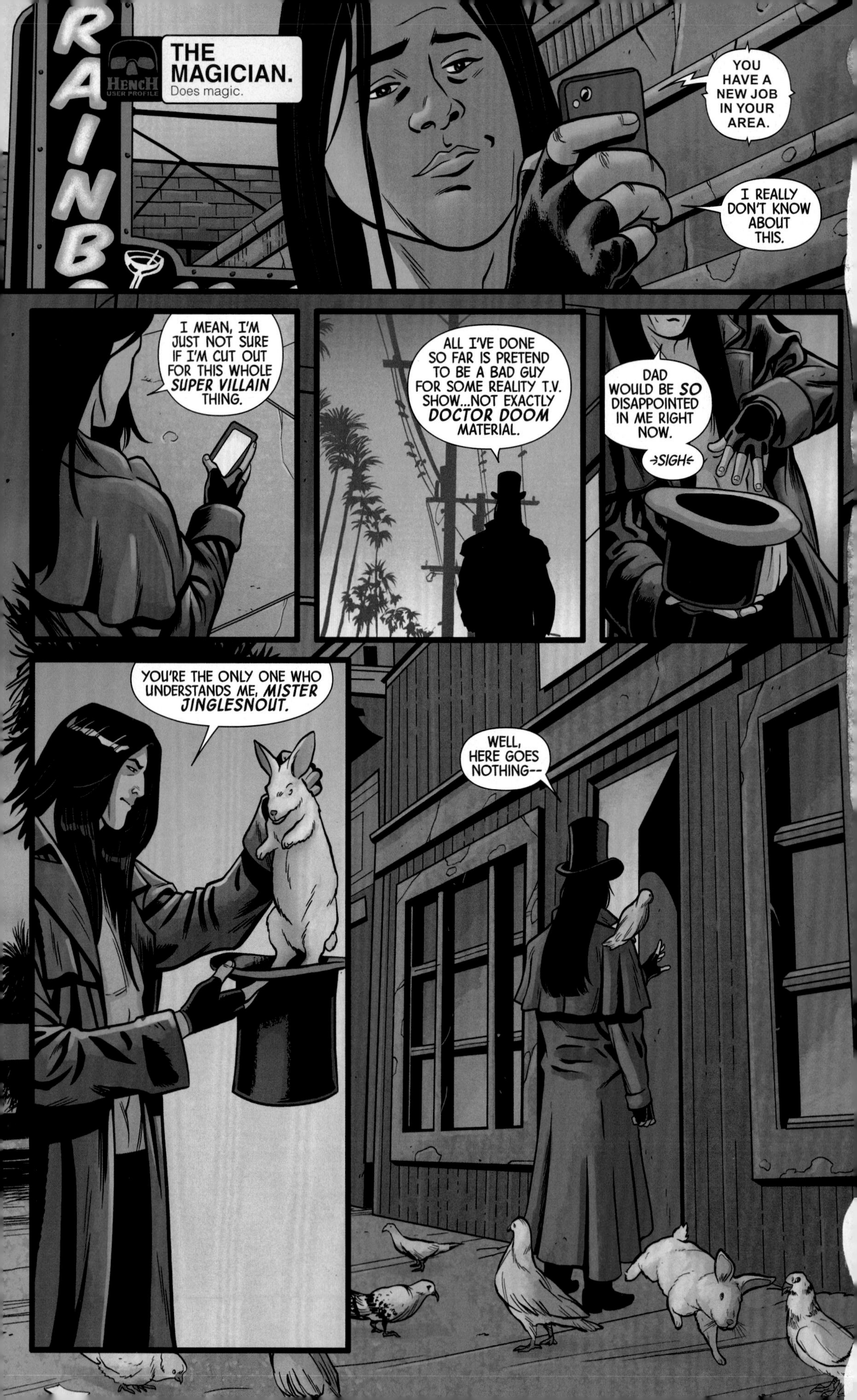
RAINB
HENCH USER PROFILE
THE MAGICIAN.
Does magic.
YOU HAVE A NEW JOB IN YOUR AREA.
I REALLY DON'T KNOW ABOUT THIS.
I MEAN, I'M JUST NOT SURE IF I'M CUT OUT FOR THIS WHOLE SUPER VILLAIN THING.
ALL I'VE DONE SO FAR IS PRETEND TO BE A BAD GUY FOR SOME REALITY T.V. SHOW...NOT EXACTLY DOCTOR DOOM MATERIAL.
DAD WOULD BE SO DISAPPOINTED IN ME RIGHT NOW.
SIGH
YOU'RE THE ONLY ONE WHO UNDERSTANDS ME, MISTER JINGLESNOUT.
WELL, HERE GOES NOTHING--

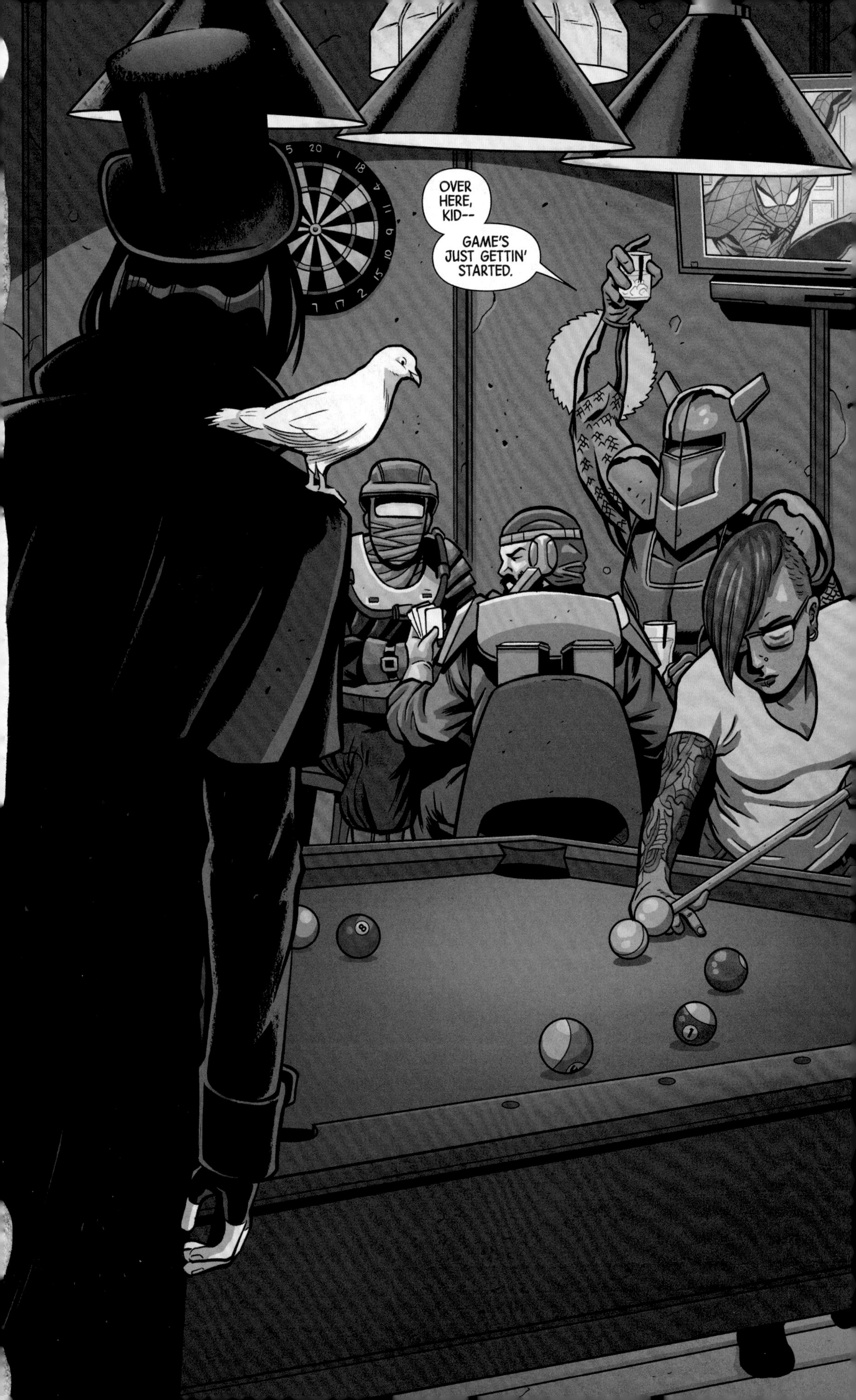
OVER HERE, KID--
GAME'S JUST GETTIN' STARTED.

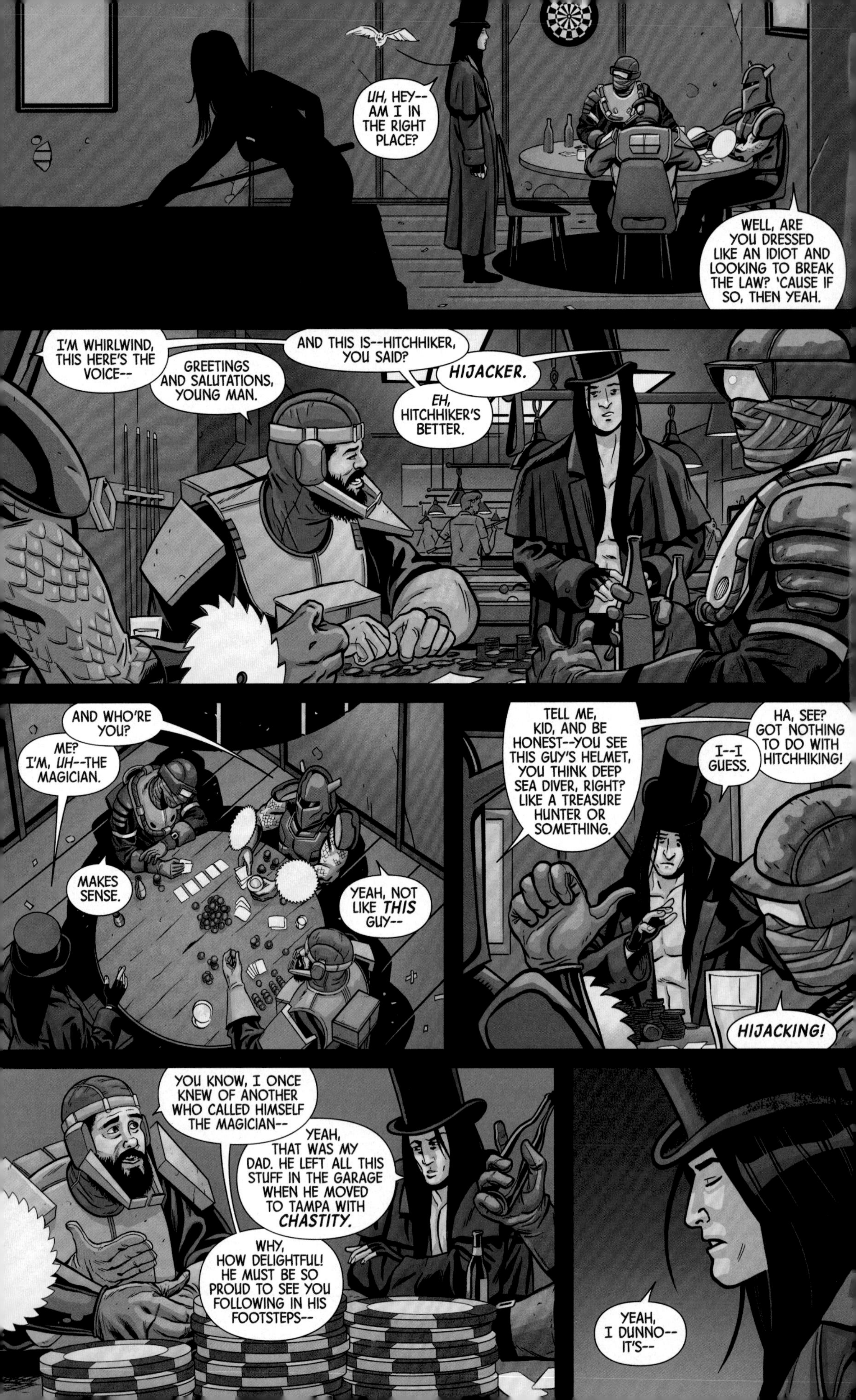
UH, HEY--AM I IN THE RIGHT PLACE?
WELL, ARE YOU DRESSED LIKE AN IDIOT AND LOOKING TO BREAK THE LAW? 'CAUSE IF SO, THEN YEAH.
I'M WHIRLWIND, THIS HERE'S THE VOICE--
GREETINGS AND SALUTATIONS, YOUNG MAN.
AND THIS IS--HITCHHIKER, YOU SAID?
HIJACKER.
EH, HITCHHIKER'S BETTER.
AND WHO'RE YOU?
ME? I'M, UH--THE MAGICIAN.
MAKES SENSE.
YEAH, NOT LIKE THIS GUY--
TELL ME, KID, AND BE HONEST--YOU SEE THIS GUY'S HELMET, YOU THINK DEEP SEA DIVER, RIGHT? LIKE A TREASURE HUNTER OR SOMETHING.
I--I GUESS.
HA, SEE? GOT NOTHING TO DO WITH HITCHHIKING!
HIJACKING!
YOU KNOW, I ONCE KNEW OF ANOTHER WHO CALLED HIMSELF THE MAGICIAN--
YEAH, THAT WAS MY DAD. HE LEFT ALL THIS STUFF IN THE GARAGE WHEN HE MOVED TO TAMPA WITH CHASTITY.
WHY, HOW DELIGHTFUL! HE MUST BE SO PROUD TO SEE YOU FOLLOWING IN HIS FOOTSTEPS--
YEAH, I DUNNO--IT'S--

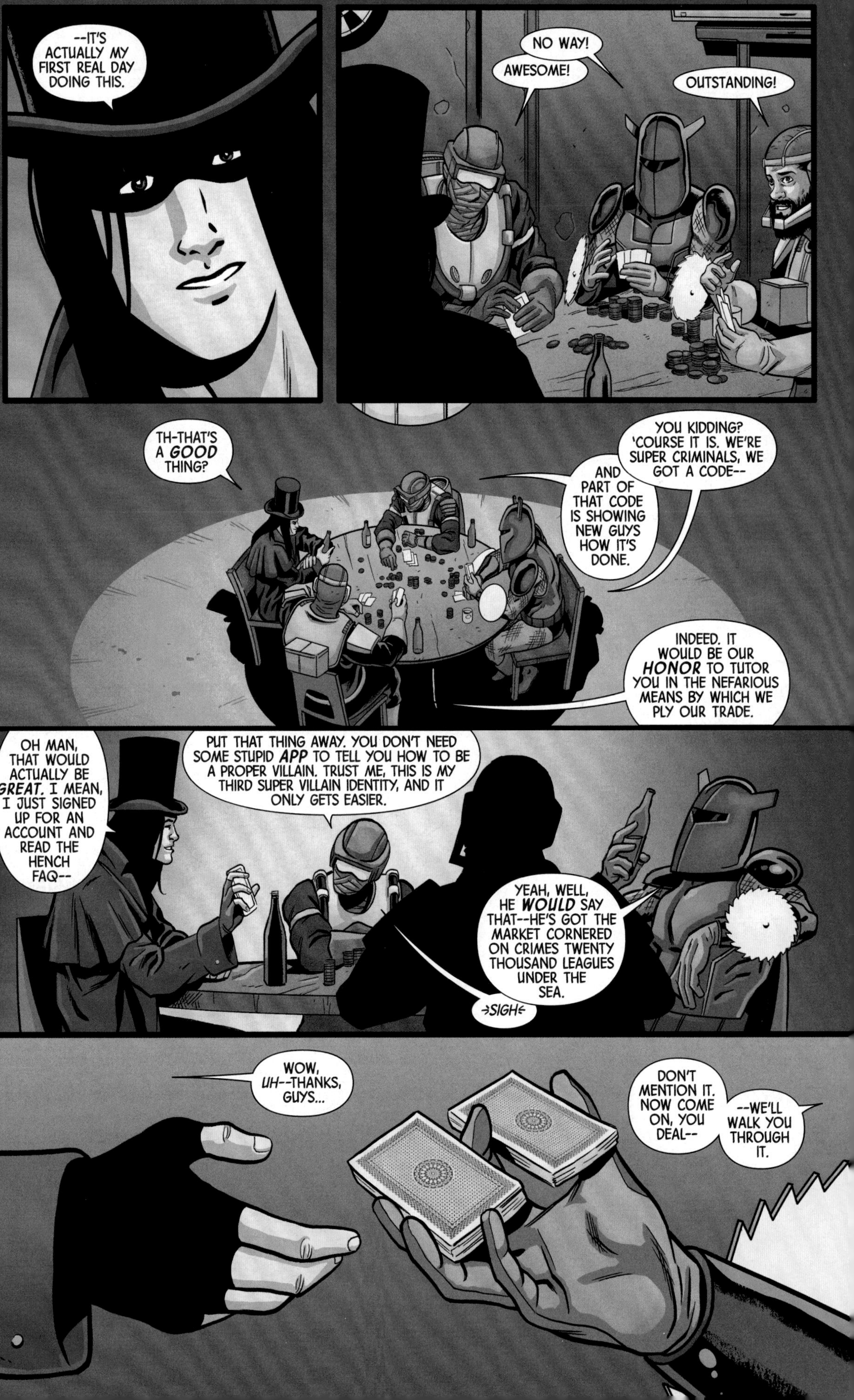
--IT'S ACTUALLY MY FIRST REAL DAY DOING THIS.
NO WAY!
AWESOME!
OUTSTANDING!
TH-THAT'S A GOOD THING?
YOU KIDDING? 'COURSE IT IS. WE'RE SUPER CRIMINALS, WE GOT A CODE--
AND PART OF THAT CODE IS SHOWING NEW GUYS HOW IT'S DONE.
INDEED. IT WOULD BE OUR HONOR TO TUTOR YOU IN THE NEFARIOUS MEANS BY WHICH WE PLY OUR TRADE.
OH MAN, THAT WOULD ACTUALLY BE GREAT. I MEAN, I JUST SIGNED UP FOR AN ACCOUNT AND READ THE HENCH FAQ--
PUT THAT THING AWAY. YOU DON'T NEED SOME STUPID APP TO TELL YOU HOW TO BE A PROPER VILLAIN. TRUST ME, THIS IS MY THIRD SUPER VILLAIN IDENTITY, AND IT ONLY GETS EASIER.
YEAH, WELL, HE WOULD SAY THAT--HE'S GOT THE MARKET CORNERED ON CRIMES TWENTY THOUSAND LEAGUES UNDER THE SEA.
SIGH
WOW, UH--THANKS, GUYS...
DON'T MENTION IT. NOW COME ON, YOU DEAL--
--WE'LL WALK YOU THROUGH IT.

OKAY, FIRST THINGS FIRST: BE CAREFUL WHO YOU TAKE JOBS WITH. SOMETIMES THE BEST PAYING GIGS ARE THE ONES YOU WANNA STEER THE CLEAREST FROM.

INDUBITABLY. LIKE THE NAZIS.

NAZIS?

OH YEAH, STAY AWAY FROM THEM--THE RED SKULL, BARON ZEMO, ARNIM ZOLA--YOU DON'T WANT ANY OF THAT.

YEAH, SEE, THEM FELLAS *LOVE* TO KILL THEIR HENCHMEN.

YOU WANNA PARTY LIKE INTERNATIONAL TERRORISTS, FINE, BUT DON'T BE SURPRISED WHEN THEY SWIVEL THE DEATH RAY IN YOUR DIRECTION.

AND THEY *ALL* GOT DEATH RAYS.

"THE PENALTY FOR FAILURE IS DEATH!" KER-POW! OR SOME SUCH MADNESS.

WHAT ABOUT *THEIR* ACCOUNTABILITY? IT WASN'T *MY* PLAN TO TRY TO TAKE OVER THE WORLD USING SUBLIMINAL ADS DURING CHILDREN'S PROGRAMMING!

HEY, WAIT-- THE NIGHT OF THE *RAGE-TODDLERS*? THAT WAS *YOU*?!!

→SIGH← I TRY NOT TO MENTION IT--

NO KIDDING--I DON'T LET MY NEPHEW WATCH *SESAME STREET* ANYMORE THANKS TO YOU!

POINT IS, YOU WANNA GET IN WITH A NICE, MID-LEVEL CRIME BOSS. NOTHING TOO FANCY. NONE OF THEM ARE GOOD--BUT A *TOMBSTONE* OR A *CRIME-MASTER* WILL DO YOU RIGHT MORE OFTEN THAN A *KINGPIN*--

AND SOME OF THEM HAVE VERY COMPETITIVE OFFERS. WHEN I WAS WITH *COUNT NEFARIA*, I EVEN RECEIVED DENTAL.

PAID FOR MY *INVISALIGN*.

WOW, I WOULD NOT HAVE GUESSED THAT...

YEAH, BUT THAT'S ASSUMING YOU WANNA EVEN GO THE HENCHMAN ROUTE--

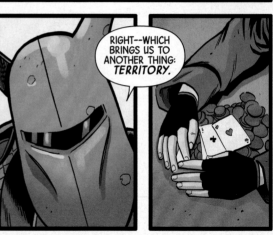

RIGHT--WHICH BRINGS US TO ANOTHER THING: *TERRITORY*.

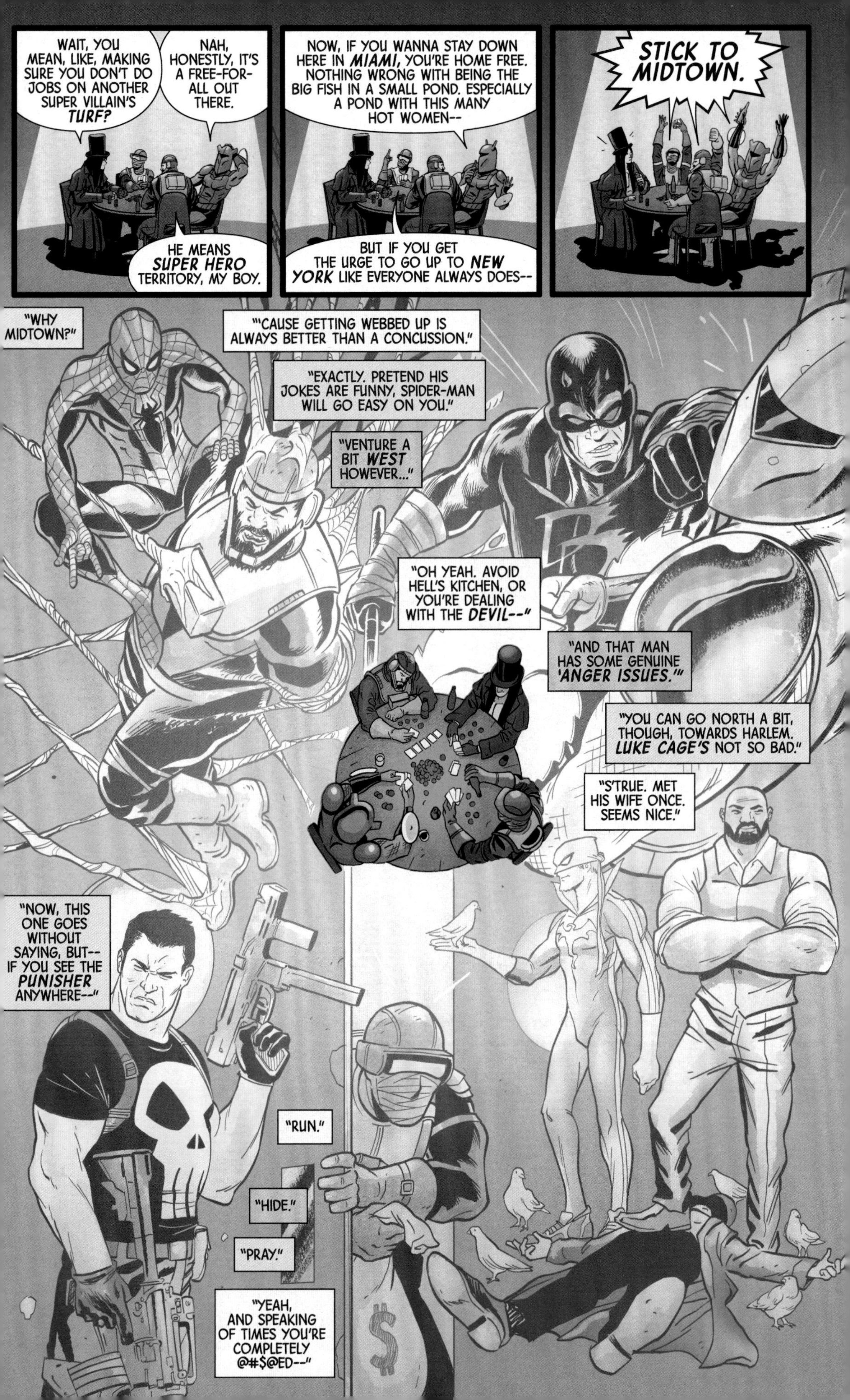
WAIT, YOU MEAN, LIKE, MAKING SURE YOU DON'T DO JOBS ON ANOTHER SUPER VILLAIN'S TURF?
NAH, HONESTLY, IT'S A FREE-FOR-ALL OUT THERE.
HE MEANS SUPER HERO TERRITORY, MY BOY.
NOW, IF YOU WANNA STAY DOWN HERE IN MIAMI, YOU'RE HOME FREE. NOTHING WRONG WITH BEING THE BIG FISH IN A SMALL POND. ESPECIALLY A POND WITH THIS MANY HOT WOMEN--
BUT IF YOU GET THE URGE TO GO UP TO NEW YORK LIKE EVERYONE ALWAYS DOES--
STICK TO MIDTOWN.
"WHY MIDTOWN?"
"'CAUSE GETTING WEBBED UP IS ALWAYS BETTER THAN A CONCUSSION."
"EXACTLY. PRETEND HIS JOKES ARE FUNNY, SPIDER-MAN WILL GO EASY ON YOU."
"VENTURE A BIT WEST HOWEVER..."
"OH YEAH. AVOID HELL'S KITCHEN, OR YOU'RE DEALING WITH THE DEVIL--"
"AND THAT MAN HAS SOME GENUINE 'ANGER ISSUES.'"
"YOU CAN GO NORTH A BIT, THOUGH, TOWARDS HARLEM. LUKE CAGE'S NOT SO BAD."
"S'TRUE. MET HIS WIFE ONCE. SEEMS NICE."
"NOW, THIS ONE GOES WITHOUT SAYING, BUT-- IF YOU SEE THE PUNISHER ANYWHERE--"
"RUN."
"HIDE."
"PRAY."
"YEAH, AND SPEAKING OF TIMES YOU'RE COMPLETELY @#$@ED--"

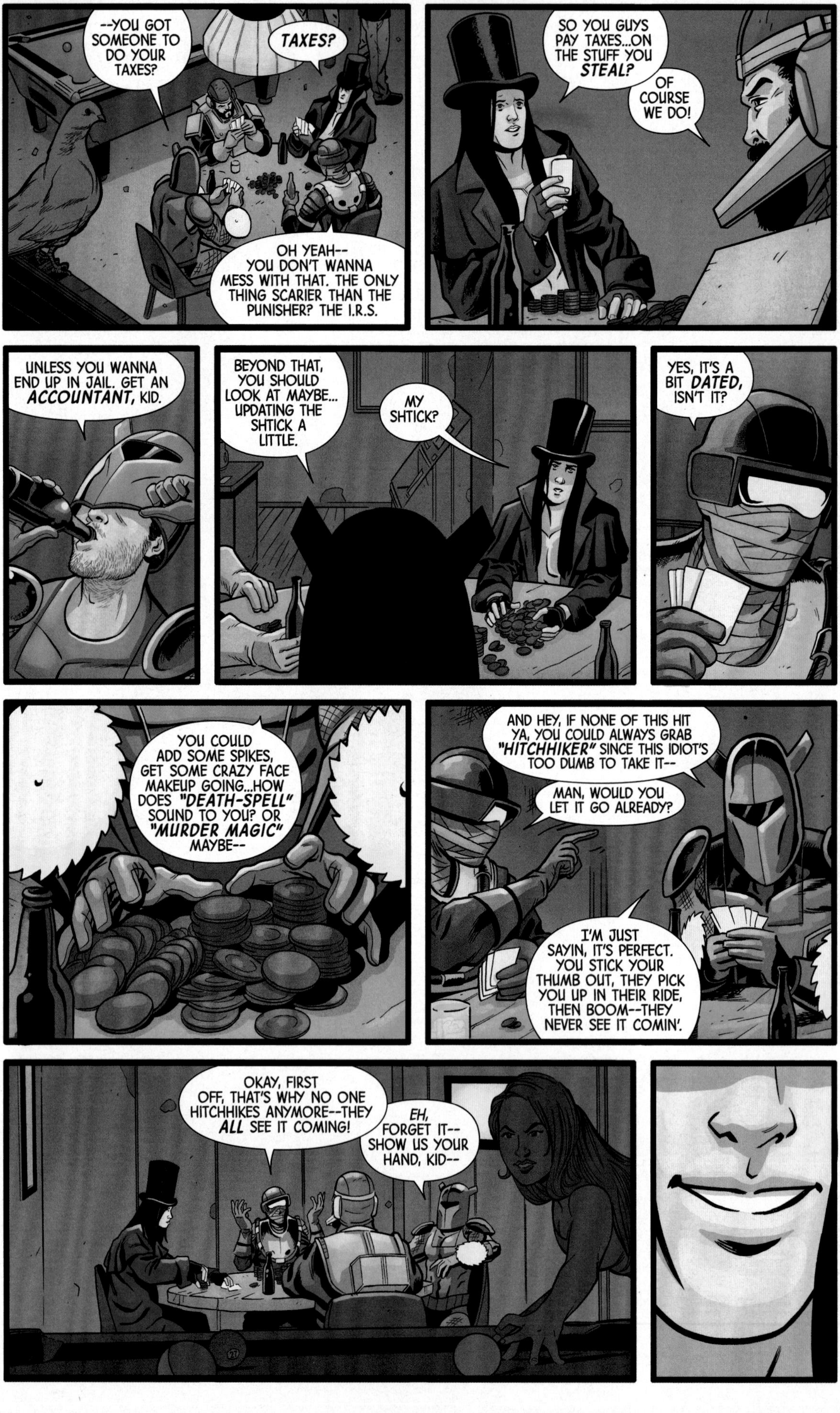
--YOU GOT SOMEONE TO DO YOUR TAXES?
TAXES?
OH YEAH-- YOU DON'T WANNA MESS WITH THAT. THE ONLY THING SCARIER THAN THE PUNISHER? THE I.R.S.
SO YOU GUYS PAY TAXES...ON THE STUFF YOU STEAL?
OF COURSE WE DO!
UNLESS YOU WANNA END UP IN JAIL. GET AN ACCOUNTANT, KID.
BEYOND THAT, YOU SHOULD LOOK AT MAYBE... UPDATING THE SHTICK A LITTLE.
MY SHTICK?
YES, IT'S A BIT DATED, ISN'T IT?
YOU COULD ADD SOME SPIKES, GET SOME CRAZY FACE MAKEUP GOING...HOW DOES "DEATH-SPELL" SOUND TO YOU? OR "MURDER MAGIC" MAYBE--
AND HEY, IF NONE OF THIS HIT YA, YOU COULD ALWAYS GRAB "HITCHHIKER" SINCE THIS IDIOT'S TOO DUMB TO TAKE IT--
MAN, WOULD YOU LET IT GO ALREADY?
I'M JUST SAYIN, IT'S PERFECT. YOU STICK YOUR THUMB OUT, THEY PICK YOU UP IN THEIR RIDE, THEN BOOM--THEY NEVER SEE IT COMIN'.
OKAY, FIRST OFF, THAT'S WHY NO ONE HITCHHIKES ANYMORE--THEY ALL SEE IT COMING!
EH, FORGET IT-- SHOW US YOUR HAND, KID--

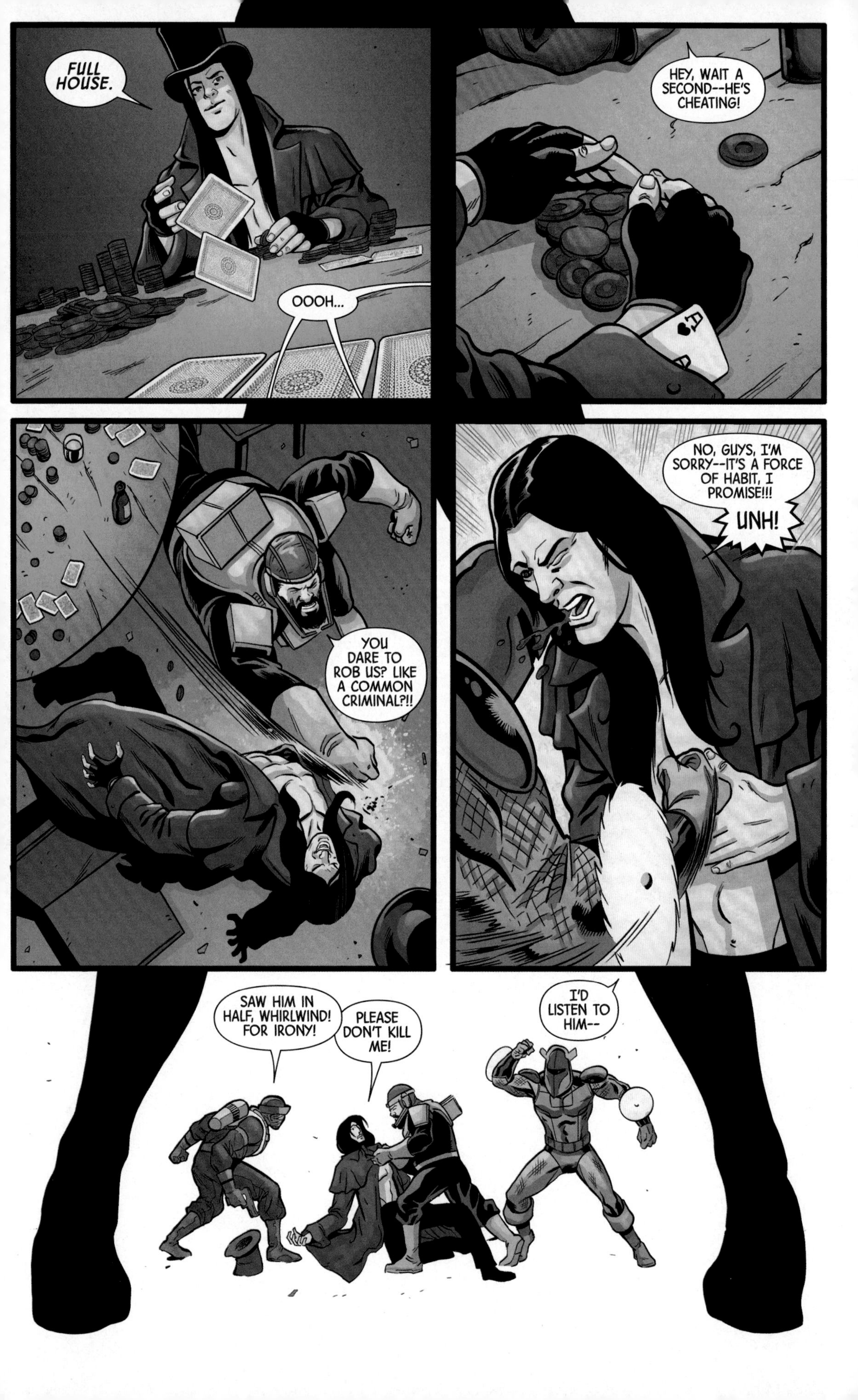
FULL HOUSE.
OOOH...
HEY, WAIT A SECOND--HE'S CHEATING!
YOU DARE TO ROB US? LIKE A COMMON CRIMINAL?!!
NO, GUYS, I'M SORRY--IT'S A FORCE OF HABIT, I PROMISE!!!
UNH!
SAW HIM IN HALF, WHIRLWIND! FOR IRONY!
PLEASE DON'T KILL ME!
I'D LISTEN TO HIM--

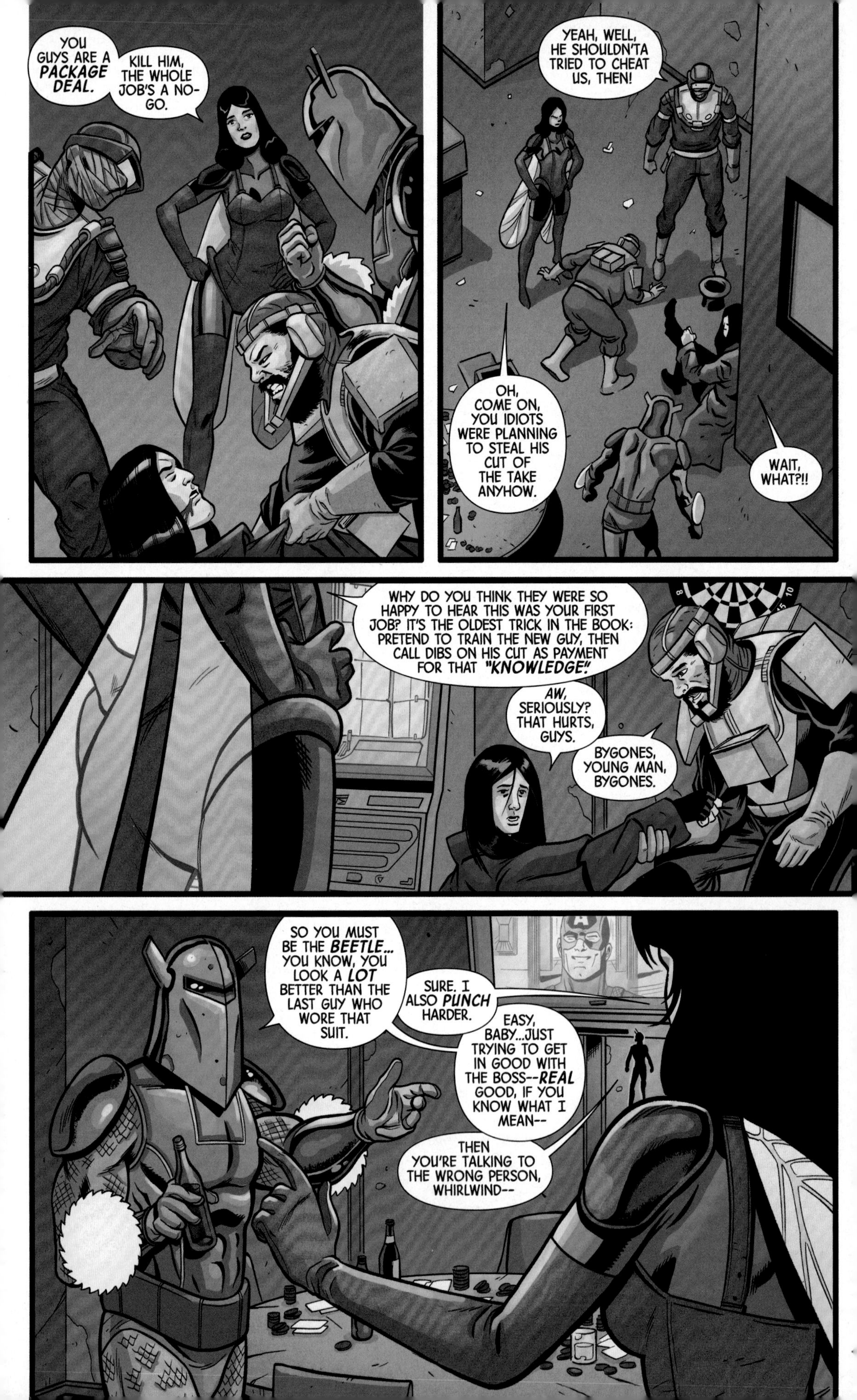
YOU GUYS ARE A *PACKAGE DEAL.*
KILL HIM, THE WHOLE JOB'S A NO-GO.
YEAH, WELL, HE SHOULDN'TA TRIED TO CHEAT US, THEN!
OH, COME ON, YOU IDIOTS WERE PLANNING TO STEAL HIS CUT OF THE TAKE ANYHOW.
WAIT, WHAT?!!
WHY DO YOU THINK THEY WERE SO HAPPY TO HEAR THIS WAS YOUR FIRST JOB? IT'S THE OLDEST TRICK IN THE BOOK: PRETEND TO TRAIN THE NEW GUY, THEN CALL DIBS ON HIS CUT AS PAYMENT FOR THAT *"KNOWLEDGE."*
AW, SERIOUSLY? THAT HURTS, GUYS.
BYGONES, YOUNG MAN, BYGONES.
SO YOU MUST BE THE *BEETLE*... YOU KNOW, YOU LOOK A *LOT* BETTER THAN THE LAST GUY WHO WORE THAT SUIT.
SURE. I ALSO *PUNCH* HARDER.
EASY, BABY...JUST TRYING TO GET IN GOOD WITH THE BOSS--*REAL* GOOD, IF YOU KNOW WHAT I MEAN--
THEN YOU'RE TALKING TO THE WRONG PERSON, WHIRLWIND--

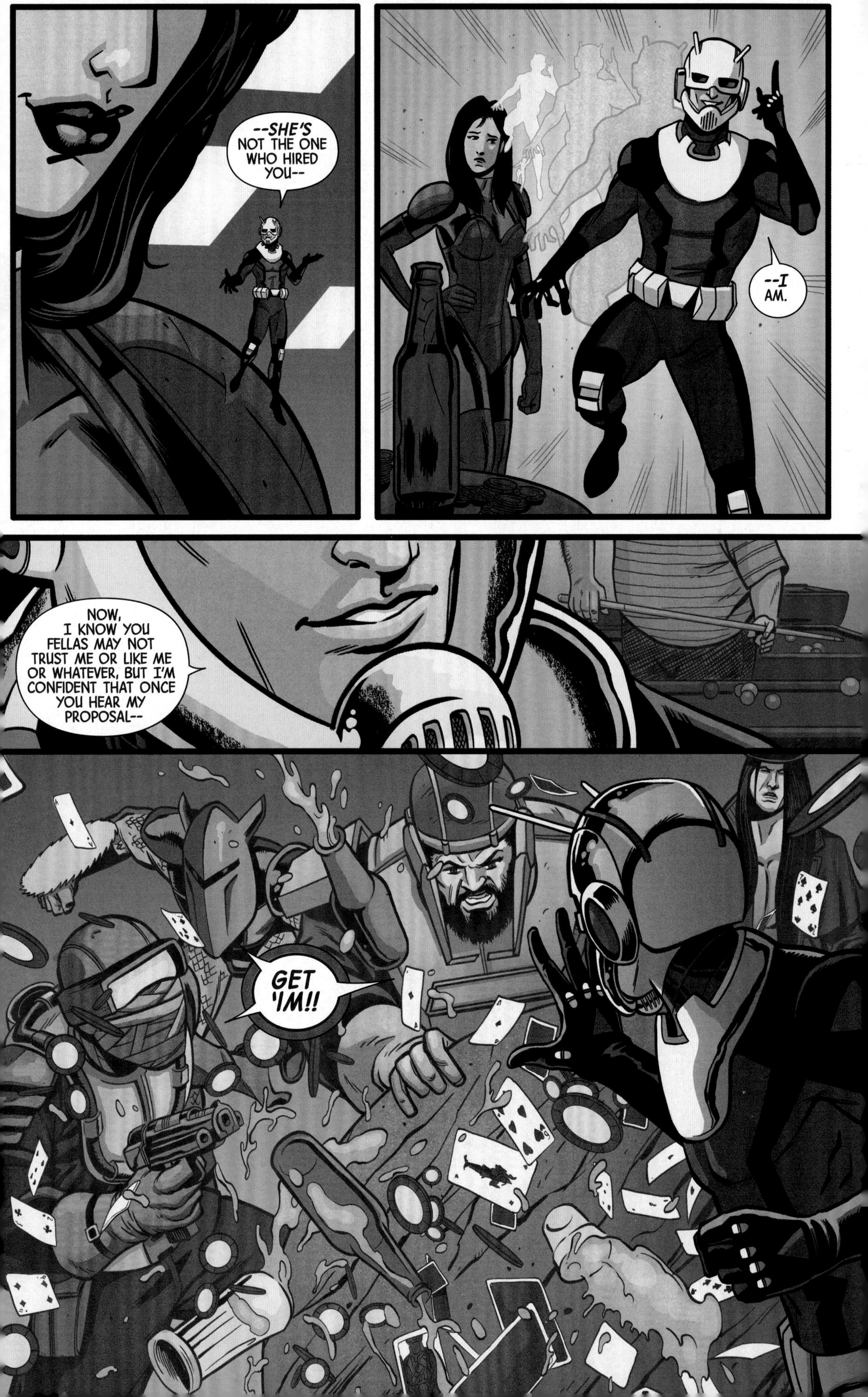
--SHE'S NOT THE ONE WHO HIRED YOU--
--I AM.
NOW, I KNOW YOU FELLAS MAY NOT TRUST ME OR LIKE ME OR WHATEVER, BUT I'M CONFIDENT THAT ONCE YOU HEAR MY PROPOSAL--
GET 'IM!!

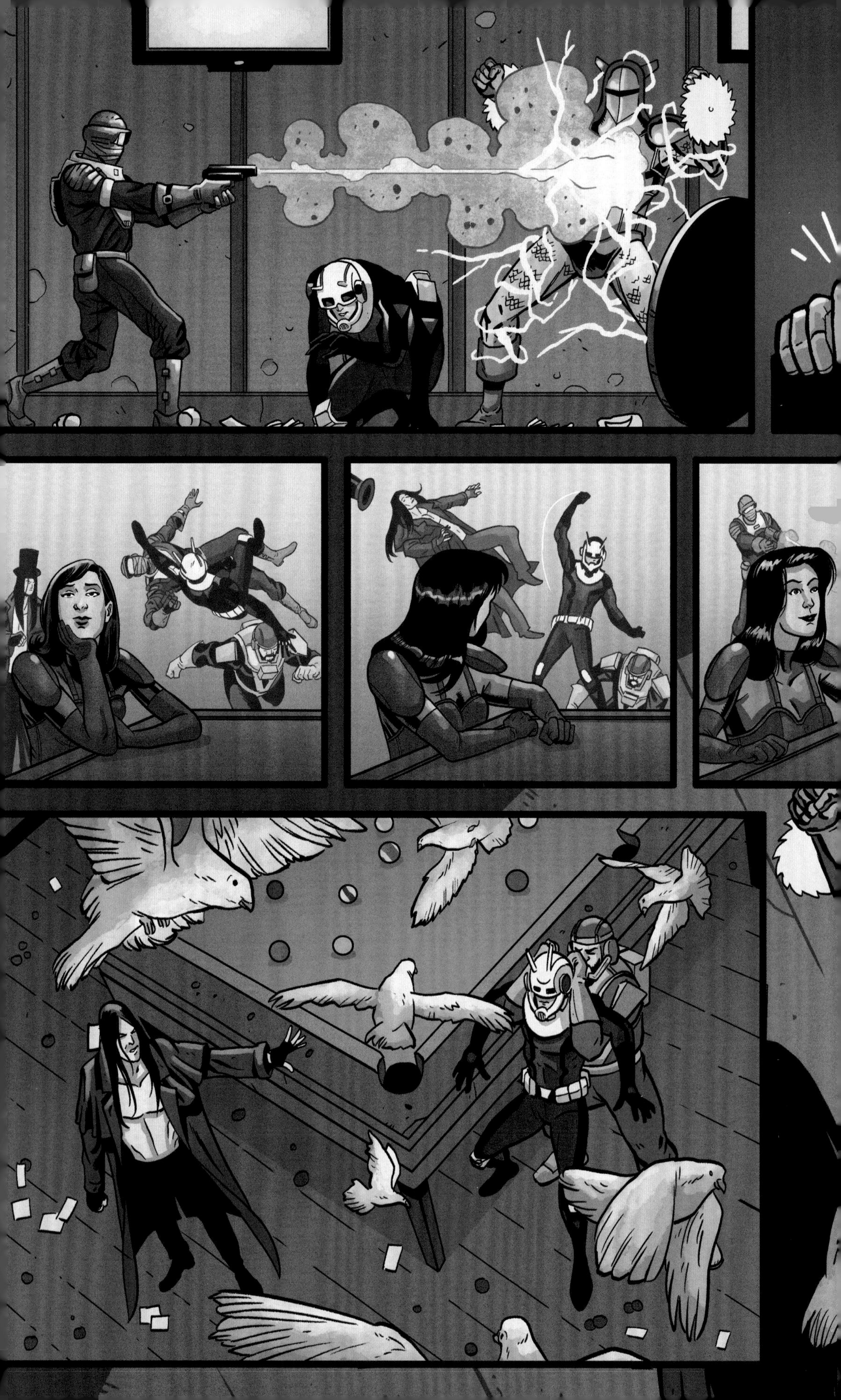

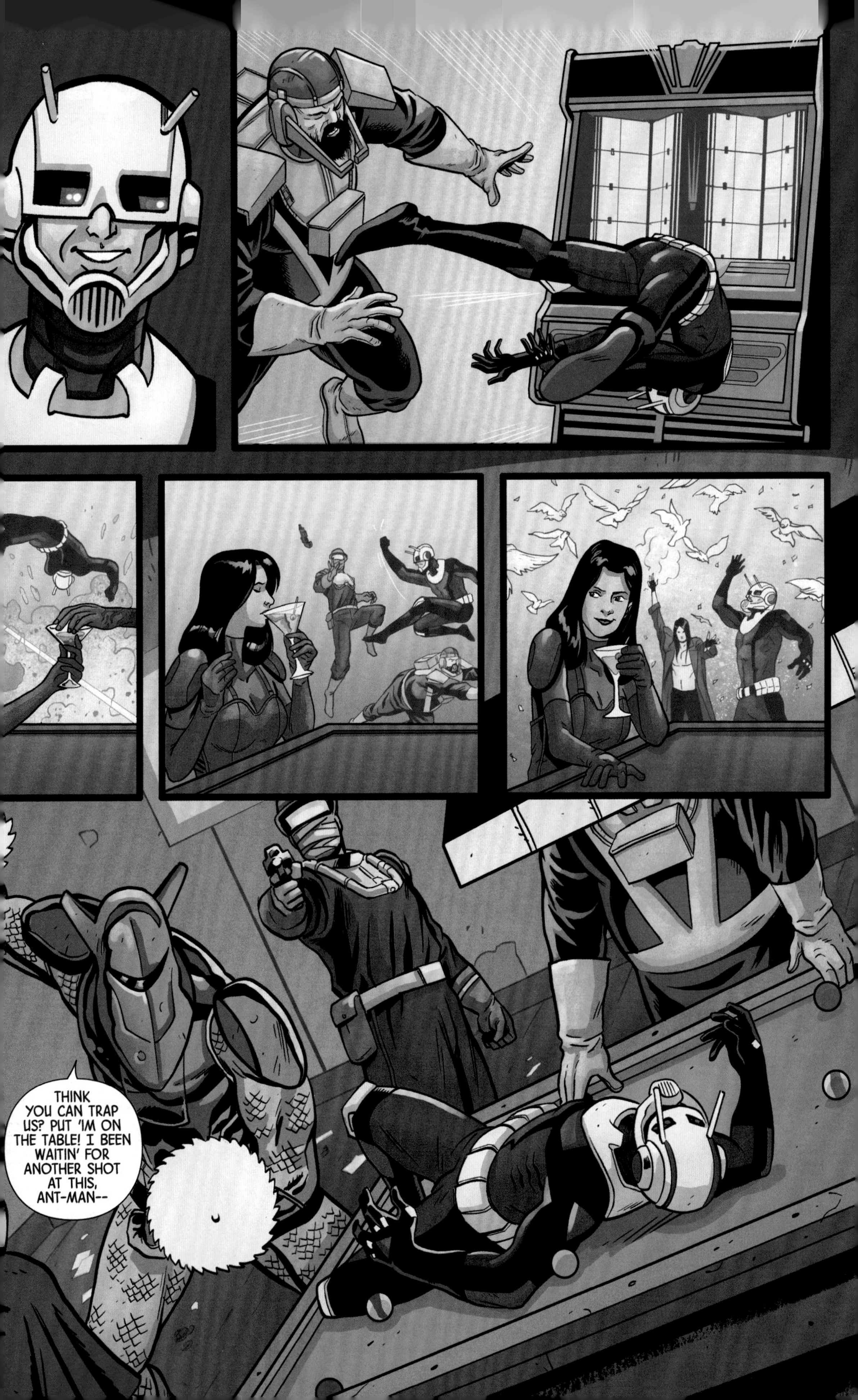
THINK YOU CAN TRAP US? PUT 'IM ON THE TABLE! I BEEN WAITIN' FOR ANOTHER SHOT AT THIS, ANT-MAN--

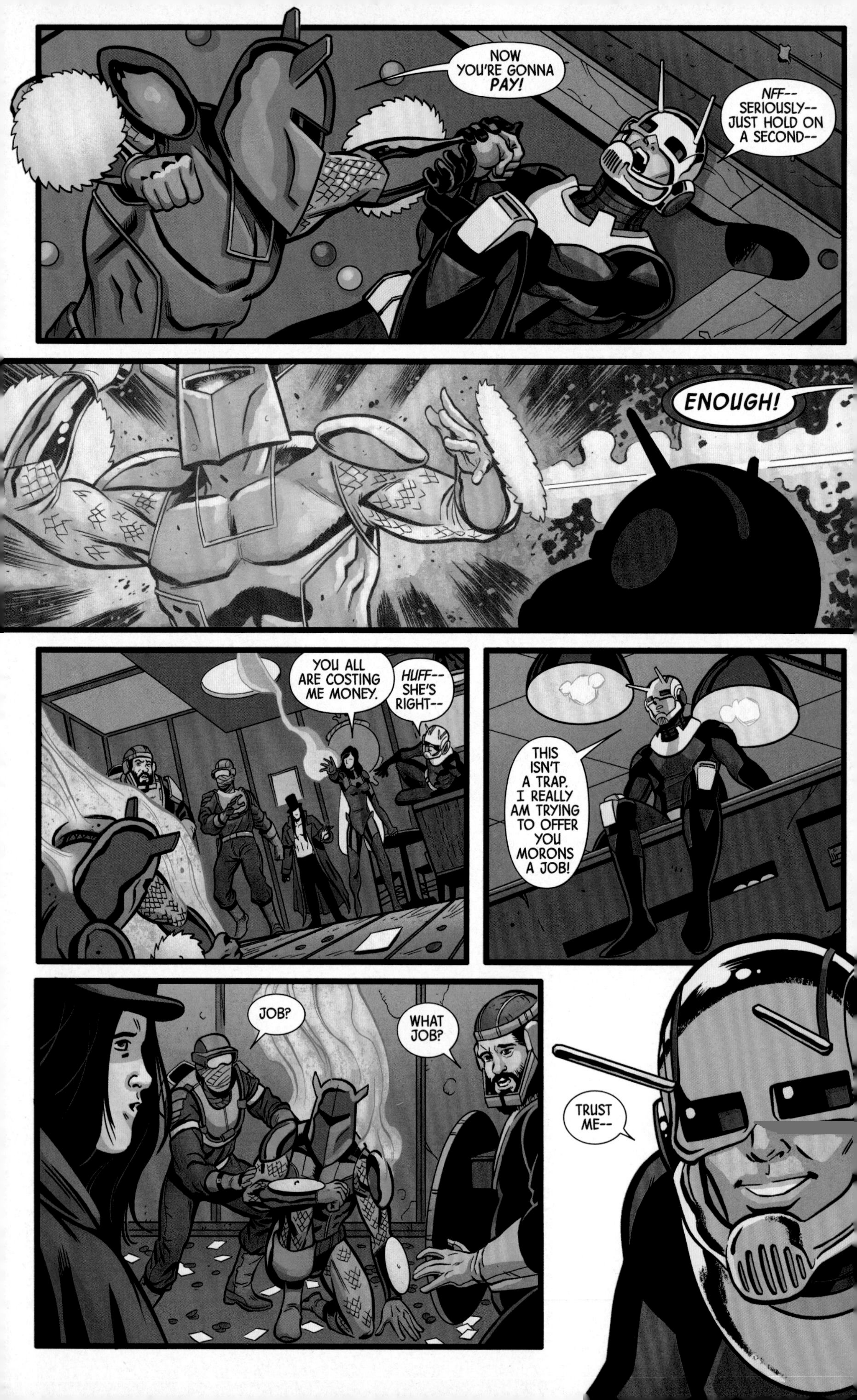
NOW YOU'RE GONNA PAY!
NFF-- SERIOUSLY-- JUST HOLD ON A SECOND--
ENOUGH!
YOU ALL ARE COSTING ME MONEY.
HUFF-- SHE'S RIGHT--
THIS ISN'T A TRAP. I REALLY AM TRYING TO OFFER YOU MORONS A JOB!
JOB?
WHAT JOB?
TRUST ME--

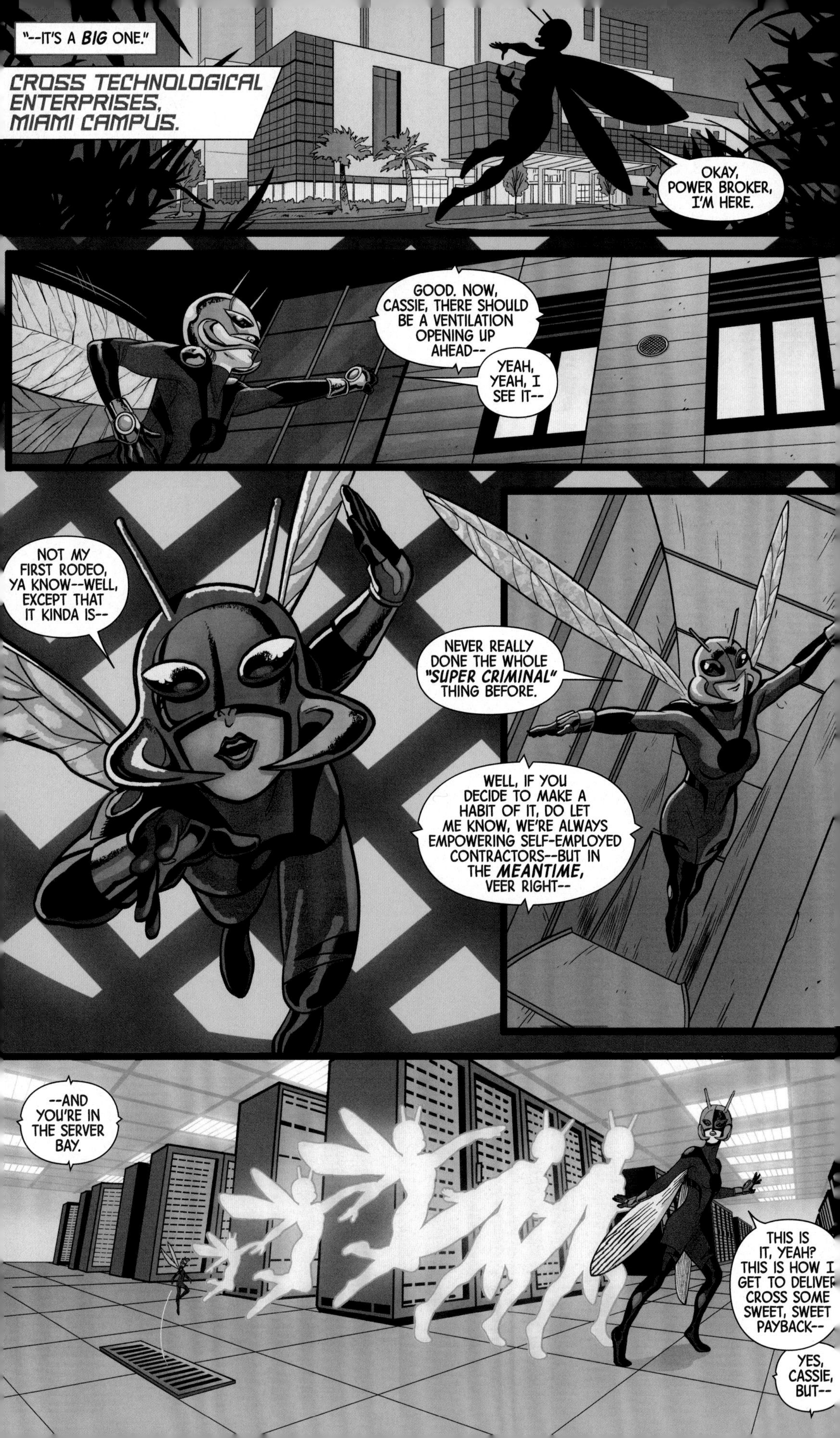
"--IT'S A BIG ONE."
CROSS TECHNOLOGICAL ENTERPRISES, MIAMI CAMPUS.
OKAY, POWER BROKER, I'M HERE.
GOOD. NOW, CASSIE, THERE SHOULD BE A VENTILATION OPENING UP AHEAD--
YEAH, YEAH, I SEE IT--
NOT MY FIRST RODEO, YA KNOW--WELL, EXCEPT THAT IT KINDA IS--
NEVER REALLY DONE THE WHOLE "SUPER CRIMINAL" THING BEFORE.
WELL, IF YOU DECIDE TO MAKE A HABIT OF IT, DO LET ME KNOW, WE'RE ALWAYS EMPOWERING SELF-EMPLOYED CONTRACTORS--BUT IN THE MEANTIME, VEER RIGHT--
--AND YOU'RE IN THE SERVER BAY.
THIS IS IT, YEAH? THIS IS HOW I GET TO DELIVER CROSS SOME SWEET, SWEET PAYBACK--
YES, CASSIE, BUT--

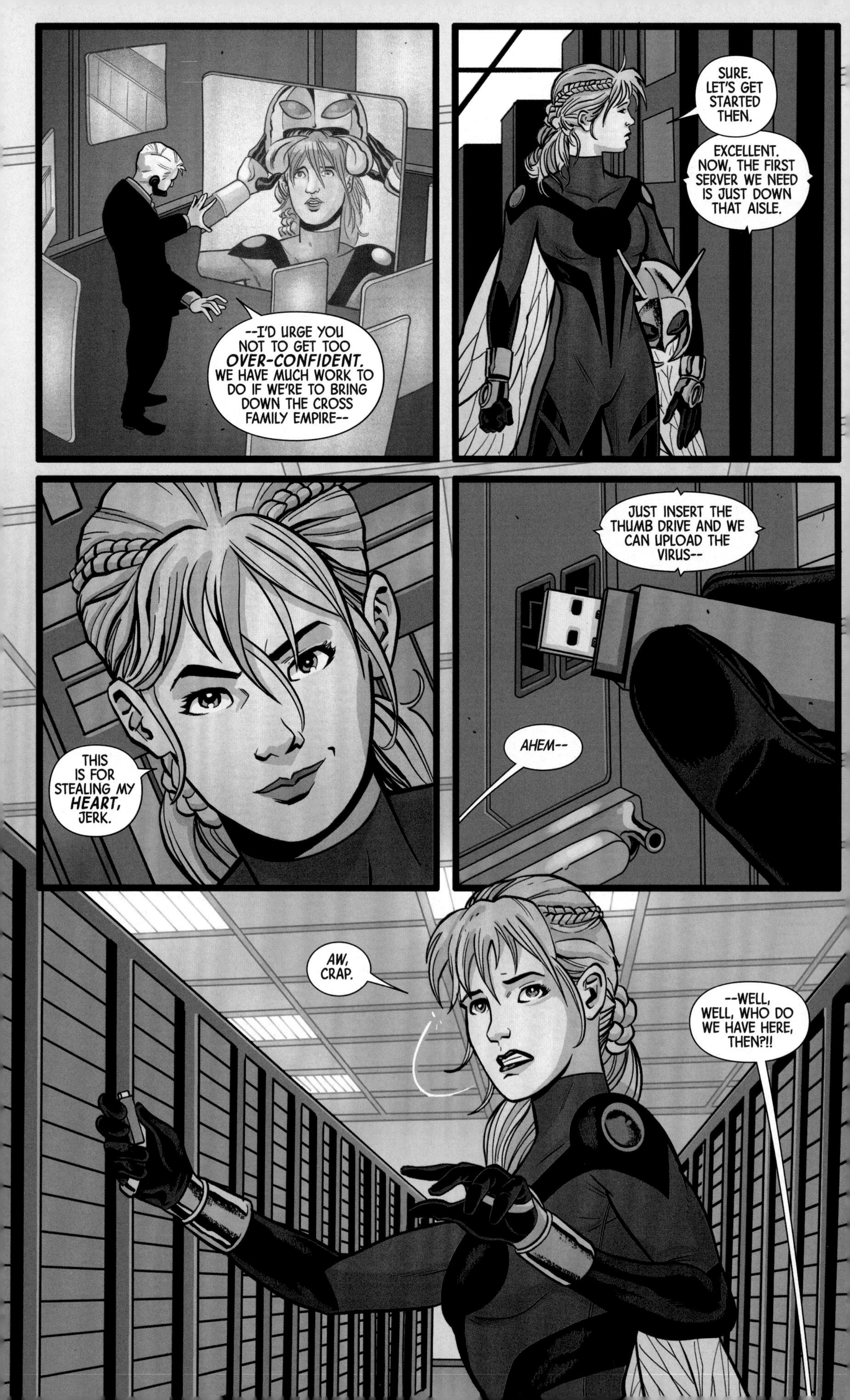
--I'D URGE YOU NOT TO GET TOO OVER-CONFIDENT. WE HAVE MUCH WORK TO DO IF WE'RE TO BRING DOWN THE CROSS FAMILY EMPIRE--
SURE. LET'S GET STARTED THEN.
EXCELLENT. NOW, THE FIRST SERVER WE NEED IS JUST DOWN THAT AISLE.
THIS IS FOR STEALING MY HEART, JERK.
JUST INSERT THE THUMB DRIVE AND WE CAN UPLOAD THE VIRUS--
AHEM--
AW, CRAP.
--WELL, WELL, WHO DO WE HAVE HERE, THEN?!!

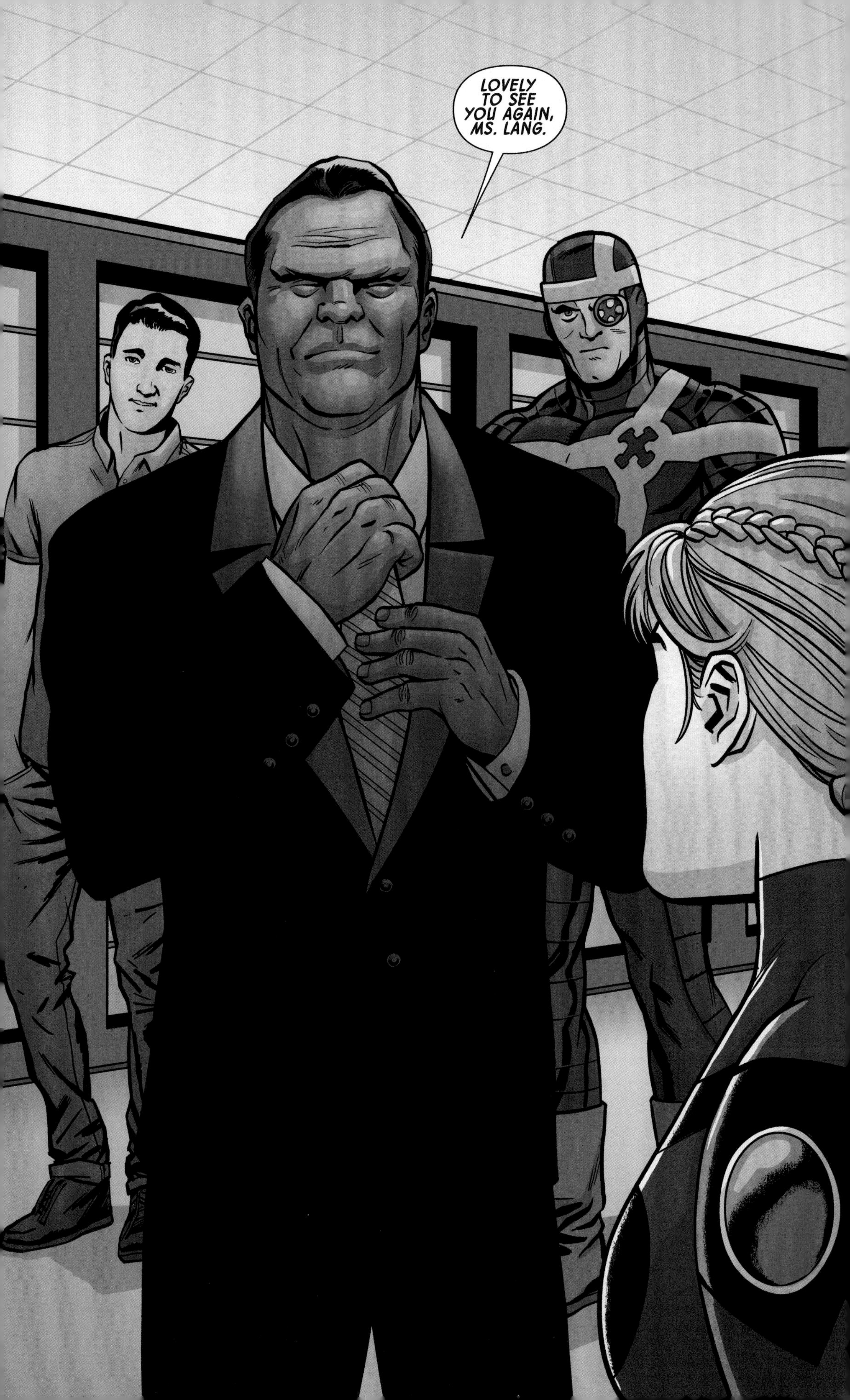
LOVELY TO SEE YOU AGAIN, MS. LANG.

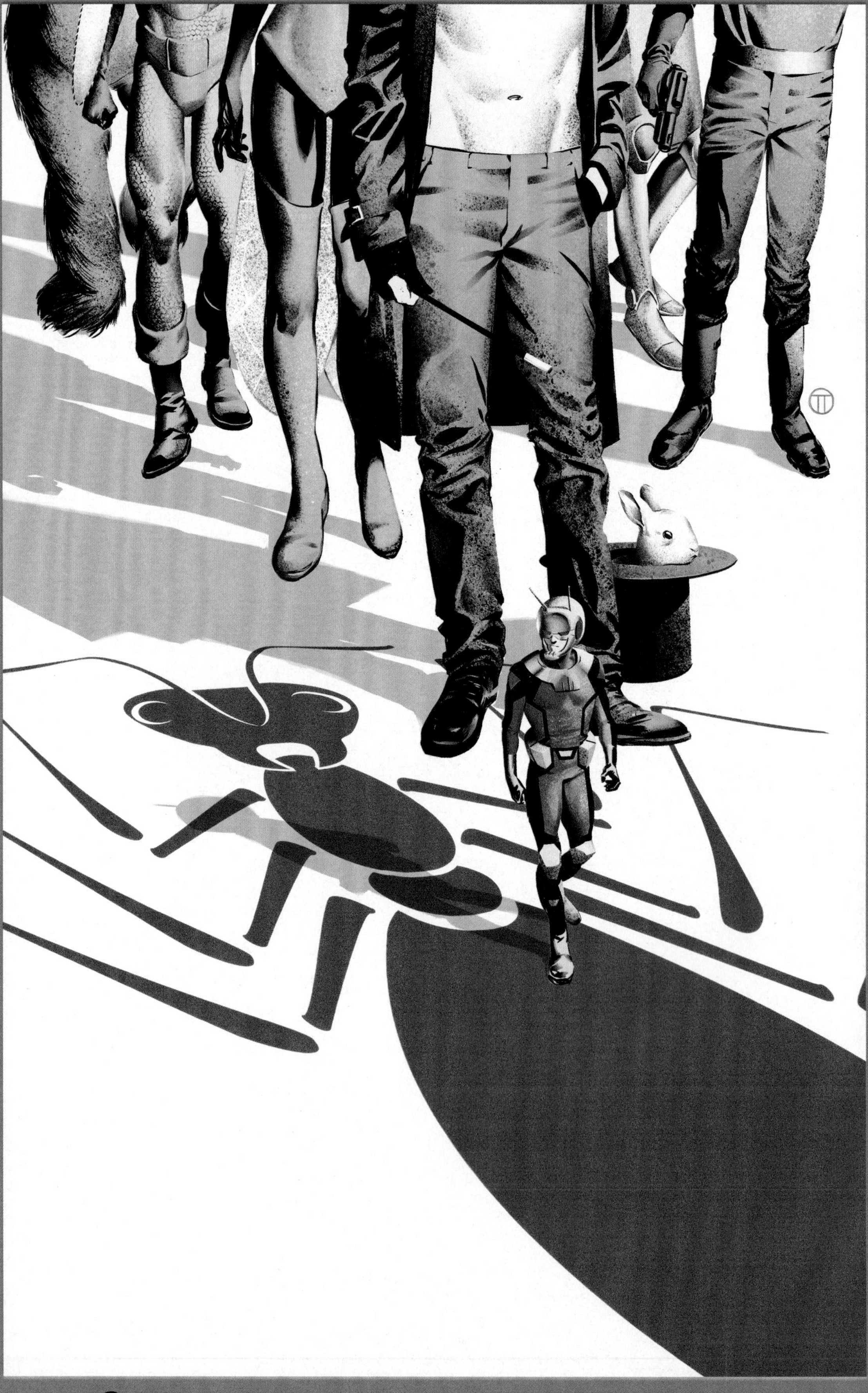

9

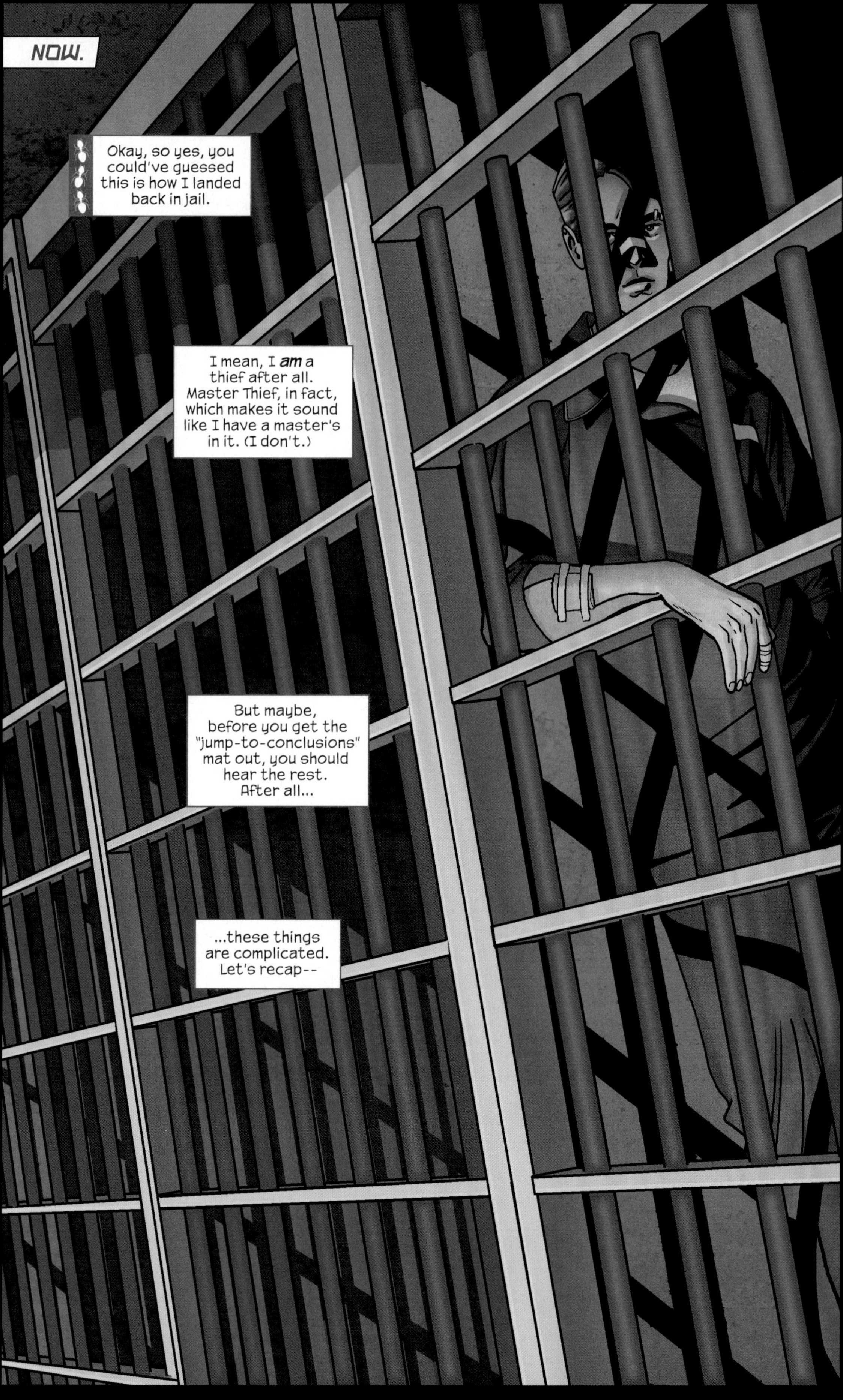
NOW.
Okay, so yes, you could've guessed this is how I landed back in jail.
I mean, I *am* a thief after all. Master Thief, in fact, which makes it sound like I have a master's in it. (I don't.)
But maybe, before you get the "jump-to-conclusions" mat out, you should hear the rest. After all...
...these things are complicated. Let's recap--

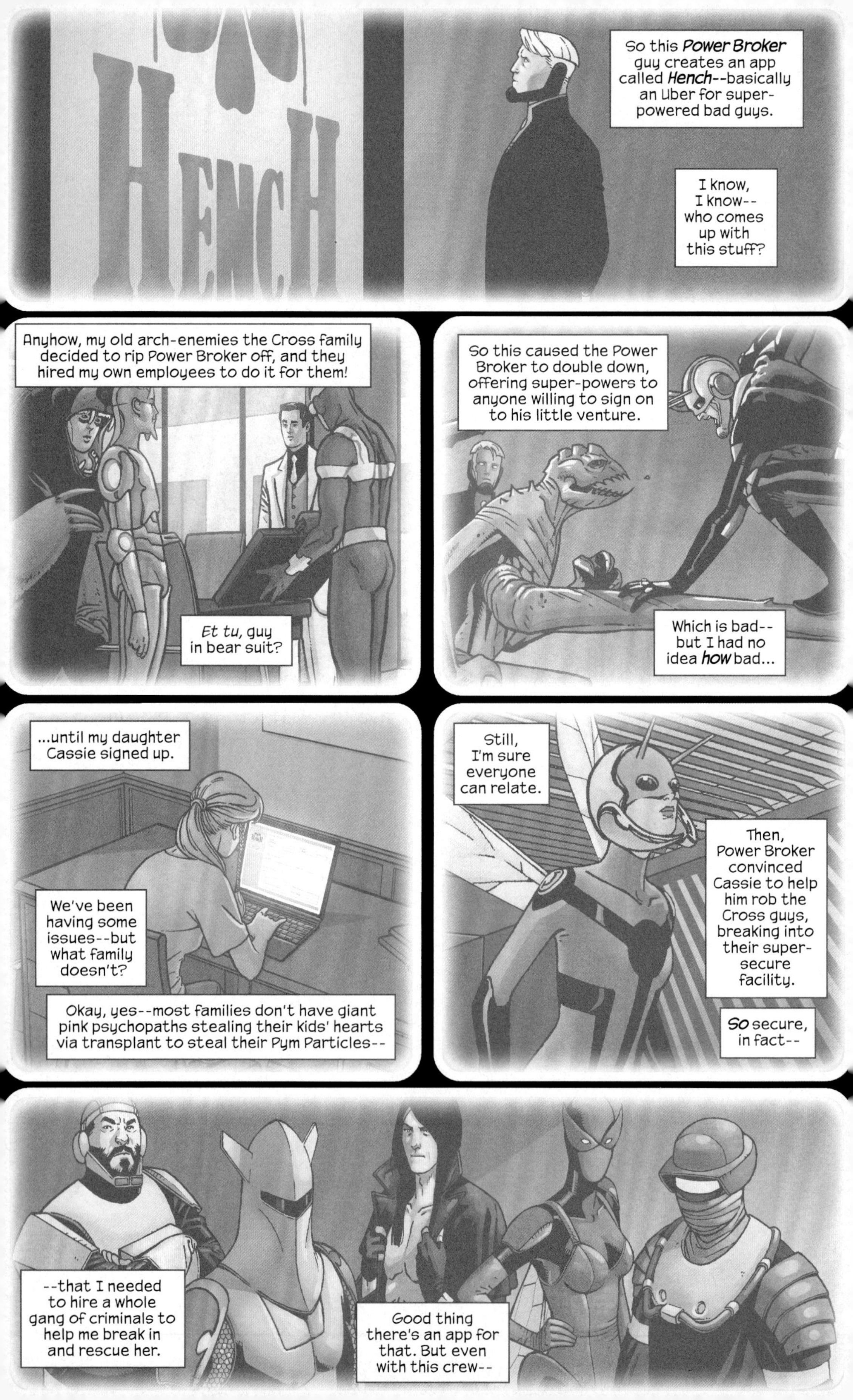
HENCH
So this *Power Broker* guy creates an app called *Hench*--basically an Uber for super-powered bad guys.
I know, I know--who comes up with this stuff?
Anyhow, my old arch-enemies the Cross family decided to rip Power Broker off, and they hired my own employees to do it for them!
Et tu, guy in bear suit?
So this caused the Power Broker to double down, offering super-powers to anyone willing to sign on to his little venture.
Which is bad--but I had no idea *how* bad...
...until my daughter Cassie signed up.
We've been having some issues--but what family doesn't?
Okay, yes--most families don't have giant pink psychopaths stealing their kids' hearts via transplant to steal their Pym Particles--
Still, I'm sure everyone can relate.
Then, Power Broker convinced Cassie to help him rob the Cross guys, breaking into their super-secure facility.
So secure, in fact--
--that I needed to hire a whole gang of criminals to help me break in and rescue her.
Good thing there's an app for that. But even with this crew--

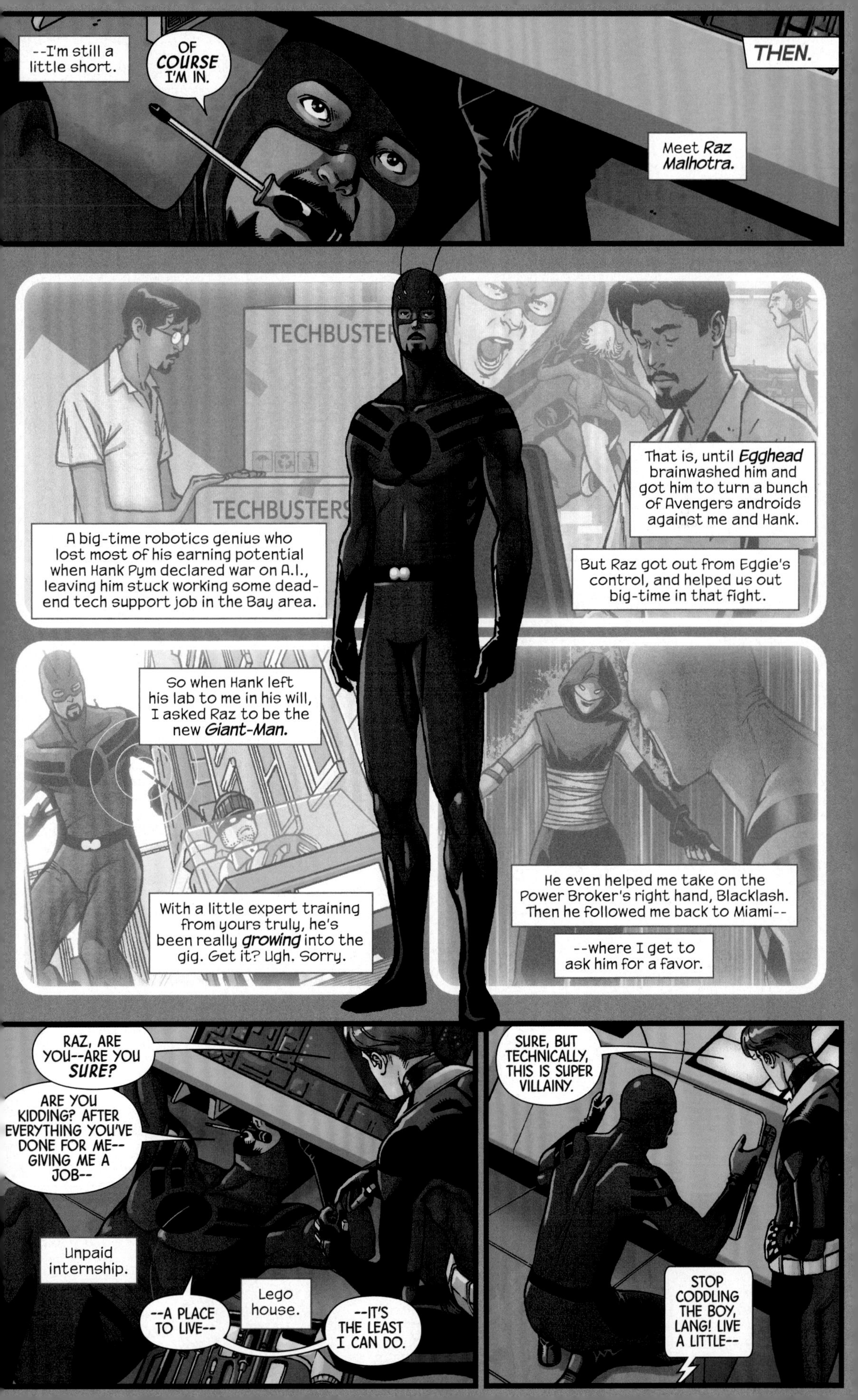
--I'm still a little short.
OF COURSE I'M IN.
THEN.
Meet Raz Malhotra.
A big-time robotics genius who lost most of his earning potential when Hank Pym declared war on A.I., leaving him stuck working some dead-end tech support job in the Bay area.
TECHBUSTERS
That is, until Egghead brainwashed him and got him to turn a bunch of Avengers androids against me and Hank.
But Raz got out from Eggie's control, and helped us out big-time in that fight.
So when Hank left his lab to me in his will, I asked Raz to be the new Giant-Man.
With a little expert training from yours truly, he's been really growing into the gig. Get it? Ugh. Sorry.
He even helped me take on the Power Broker's right hand, Blacklash. Then he followed me back to Miami--
--where I get to ask him for a favor.
RAZ, ARE YOU--ARE YOU SURE?
ARE YOU KIDDING? AFTER EVERYTHING YOU'VE DONE FOR ME--GIVING ME A JOB--
Unpaid internship.
--A PLACE TO LIVE--
Lego house.
--IT'S THE LEAST I CAN DO.
SURE, BUT TECHNICALLY, THIS IS SUPER VILLAINY.
STOP CODDLING THE BOY, LANG! LIVE A LITTLE--

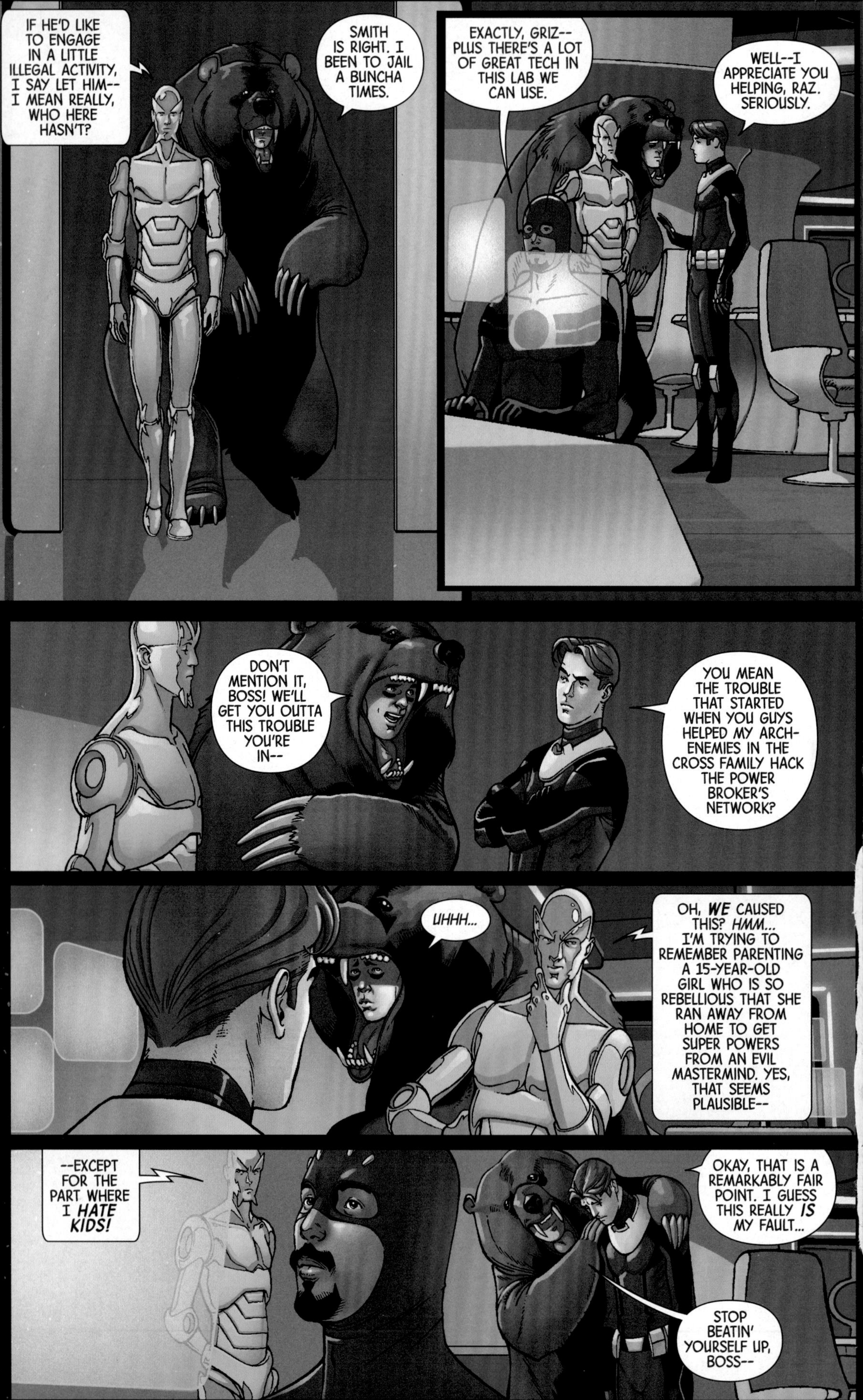
IF HE'D LIKE TO ENGAGE IN A LITTLE ILLEGAL ACTIVITY, I SAY LET HIM-- I MEAN REALLY, WHO HERE HASN'T?
SMITH IS RIGHT. I BEEN TO JAIL A BUNCHA TIMES.
EXACTLY, GRIZ-- PLUS THERE'S A LOT OF GREAT TECH IN THIS LAB WE CAN USE.
WELL--I APPRECIATE YOU HELPING, RAZ. SERIOUSLY.
DON'T MENTION IT, BOSS! WE'LL GET YOU OUTTA THIS TROUBLE YOU'RE IN--
YOU MEAN THE TROUBLE THAT STARTED WHEN YOU GUYS HELPED MY ARCH-ENEMIES IN THE CROSS FAMILY HACK THE POWER BROKER'S NETWORK?
UHHH...
OH, WE CAUSED THIS? HMM... I'M TRYING TO REMEMBER PARENTING A 15-YEAR-OLD GIRL WHO IS SO REBELLIOUS THAT SHE RAN AWAY FROM HOME TO GET SUPER POWERS FROM AN EVIL MASTERMIND. YES, THAT SEEMS PLAUSIBLE--
--EXCEPT FOR THE PART WHERE I HATE KIDS!
OKAY, THAT IS A REMARKABLY FAIR POINT. I GUESS THIS REALLY IS MY FAULT...
STOP BEATIN' YOURSELF UP, BOSS--

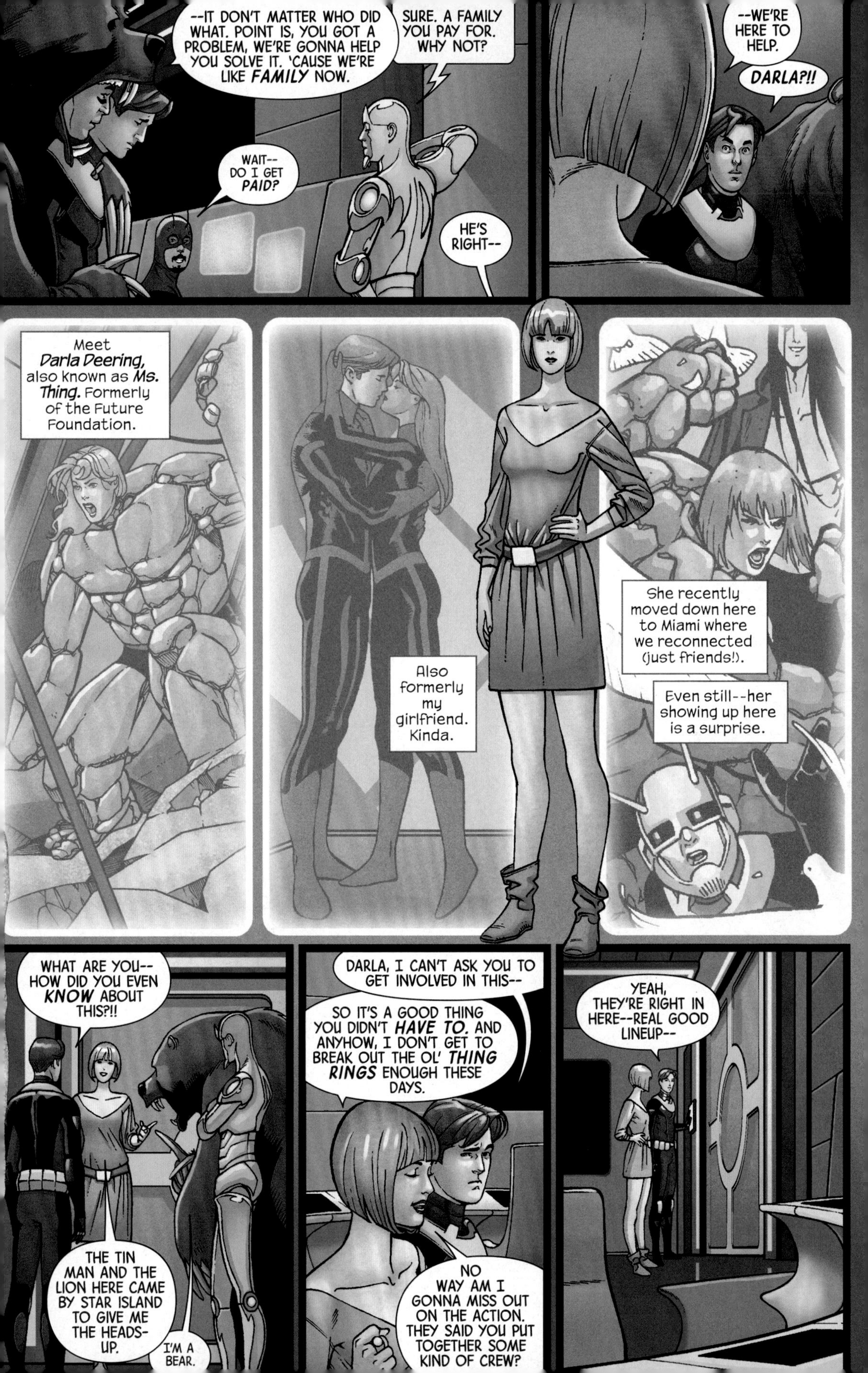
--IT DON'T MATTER WHO DID WHAT. POINT IS, YOU GOT A PROBLEM, WE'RE GONNA HELP YOU SOLVE IT. 'CAUSE WE'RE LIKE FAMILY NOW.
SURE. A FAMILY YOU PAY FOR. WHY NOT?
WAIT-- DO I GET PAID?
HE'S RIGHT--
--WE'RE HERE TO HELP.
DARLA?!!
Meet Darla Deering, also known as Ms. Thing. Formerly of the Future Foundation.
Also formerly my girlfriend. Kinda.
She recently moved down here to Miami where we reconnected (just friends!).
Even still--her showing up here is a surprise.
WHAT ARE YOU-- HOW DID YOU EVEN KNOW ABOUT THIS?!!
THE TIN MAN AND THE LION HERE CAME BY STAR ISLAND TO GIVE ME THE HEADS-UP.
I'M A BEAR.
DARLA, I CAN'T ASK YOU TO GET INVOLVED IN THIS--
SO IT'S A GOOD THING YOU DIDN'T HAVE TO. AND ANYHOW, I DON'T GET TO BREAK OUT THE OL' THING RINGS ENOUGH THESE DAYS.
NO WAY AM I GONNA MISS OUT ON THE ACTION. THEY SAID YOU PUT TOGETHER SOME KIND OF CREW?
YEAH, THEY'RE RIGHT IN HERE--REAL GOOD LINEUP--

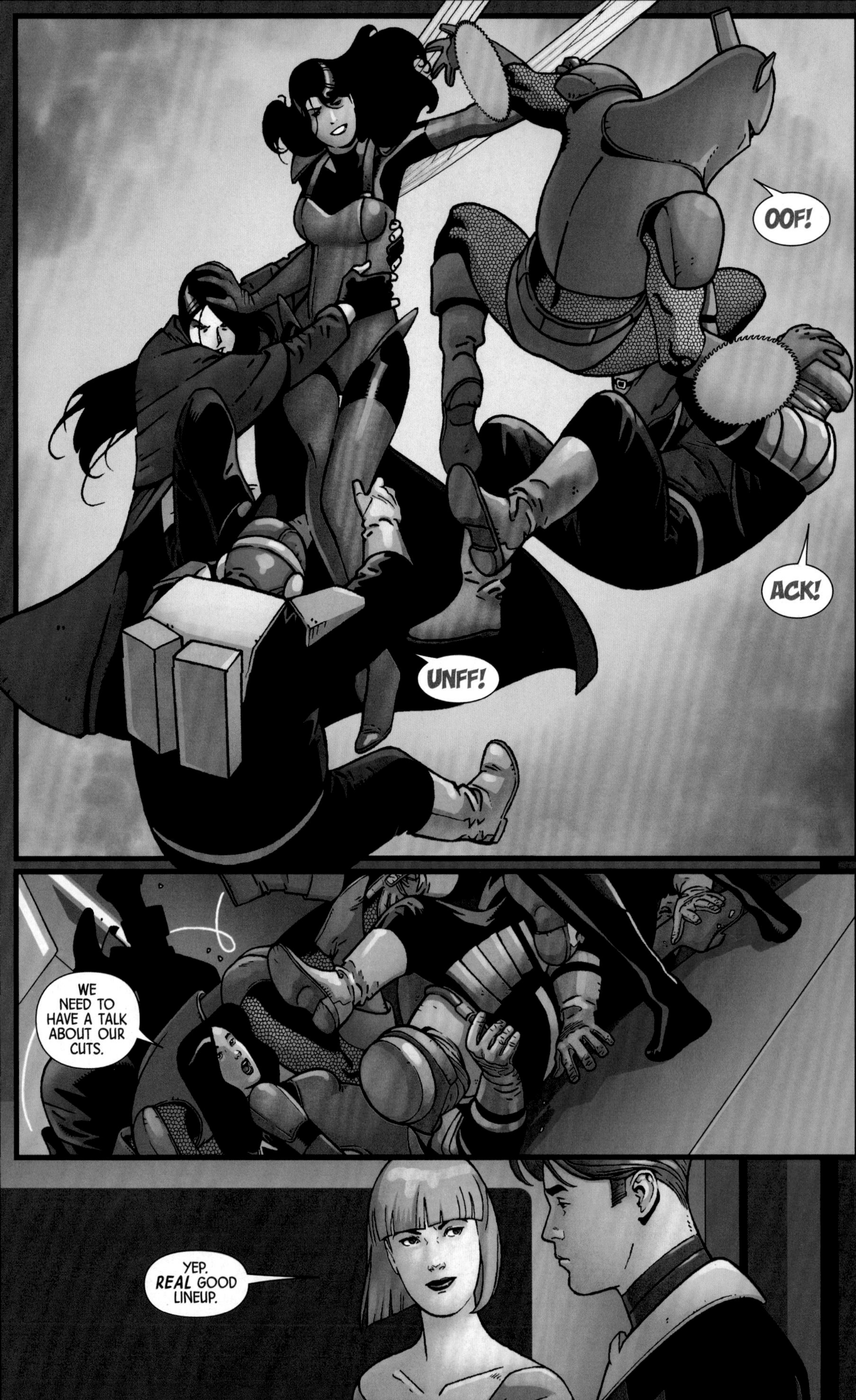
OOF!
ACK!
UNFF!
WE NEED TO HAVE A TALK ABOUT OUR CUTS.
YEP. *REAL* GOOD LINEUP.

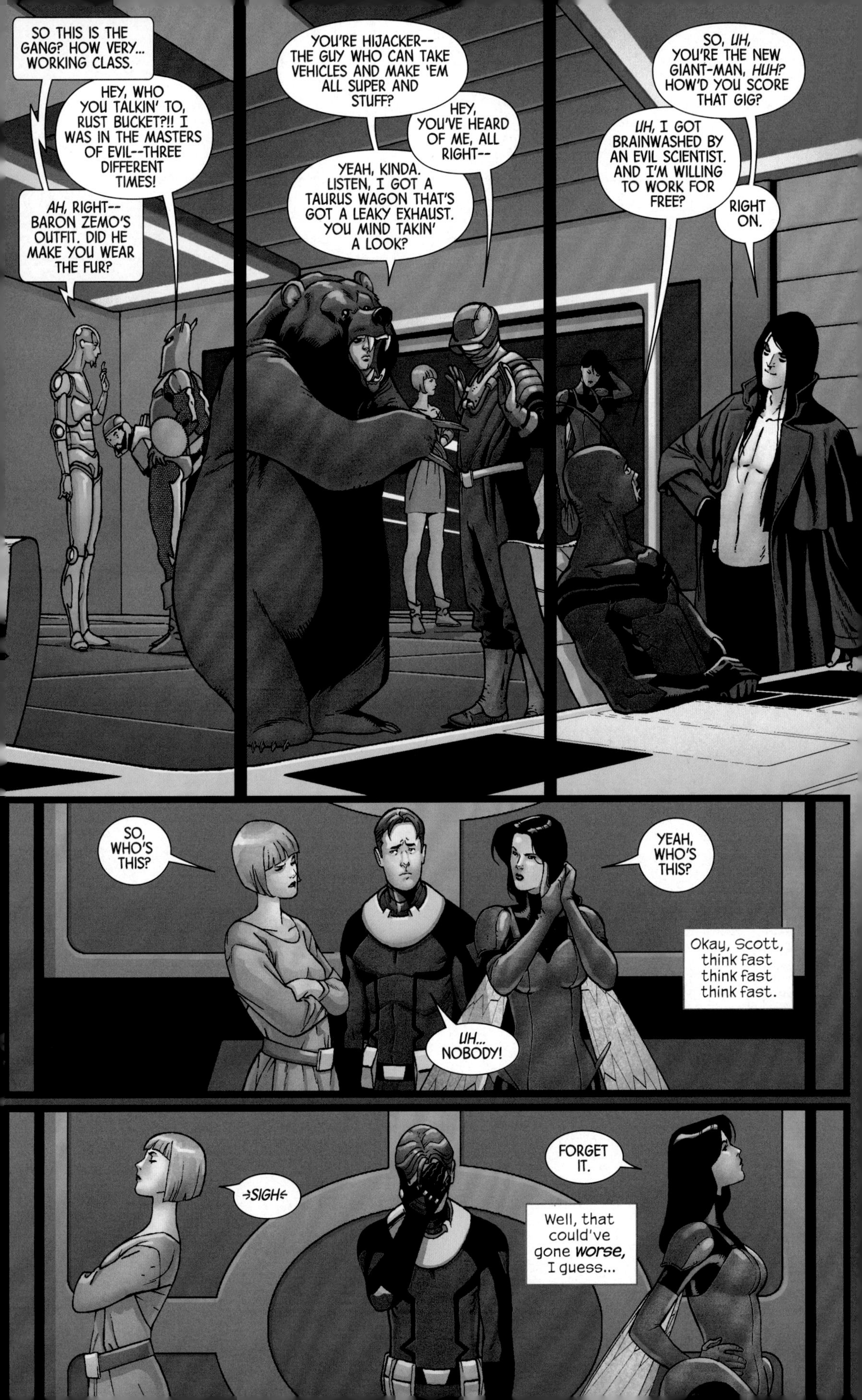
SO THIS IS THE GANG? HOW VERY... WORKING CLASS.
HEY, WHO YOU TALKIN' TO, RUST BUCKET?!! I WAS IN THE MASTERS OF EVIL--THREE DIFFERENT TIMES!
AH, RIGHT-- BARON ZEMO'S OUTFIT. DID HE MAKE YOU WEAR THE FUR?
YOU'RE HIJACKER-- THE GUY WHO CAN TAKE VEHICLES AND MAKE 'EM ALL SUPER AND STUFF?
HEY, YOU'VE HEARD OF ME, ALL RIGHT--
YEAH, KINDA. LISTEN, I GOT A TAURUS WAGON THAT'S GOT A LEAKY EXHAUST. YOU MIND TAKIN' A LOOK?
SO, UH, YOU'RE THE NEW GIANT-MAN, HUH? HOW'D YOU SCORE THAT GIG?
UH, I GOT BRAINWASHED BY AN EVIL SCIENTIST. AND I'M WILLING TO WORK FOR FREE?
RIGHT ON.
SO, WHO'S THIS?
YEAH, WHO'S THIS?
Okay, Scott, think fast think fast think fast.
UH... NOBODY!
→SIGH←
FORGET IT.
Well, that could've gone worse, I guess...

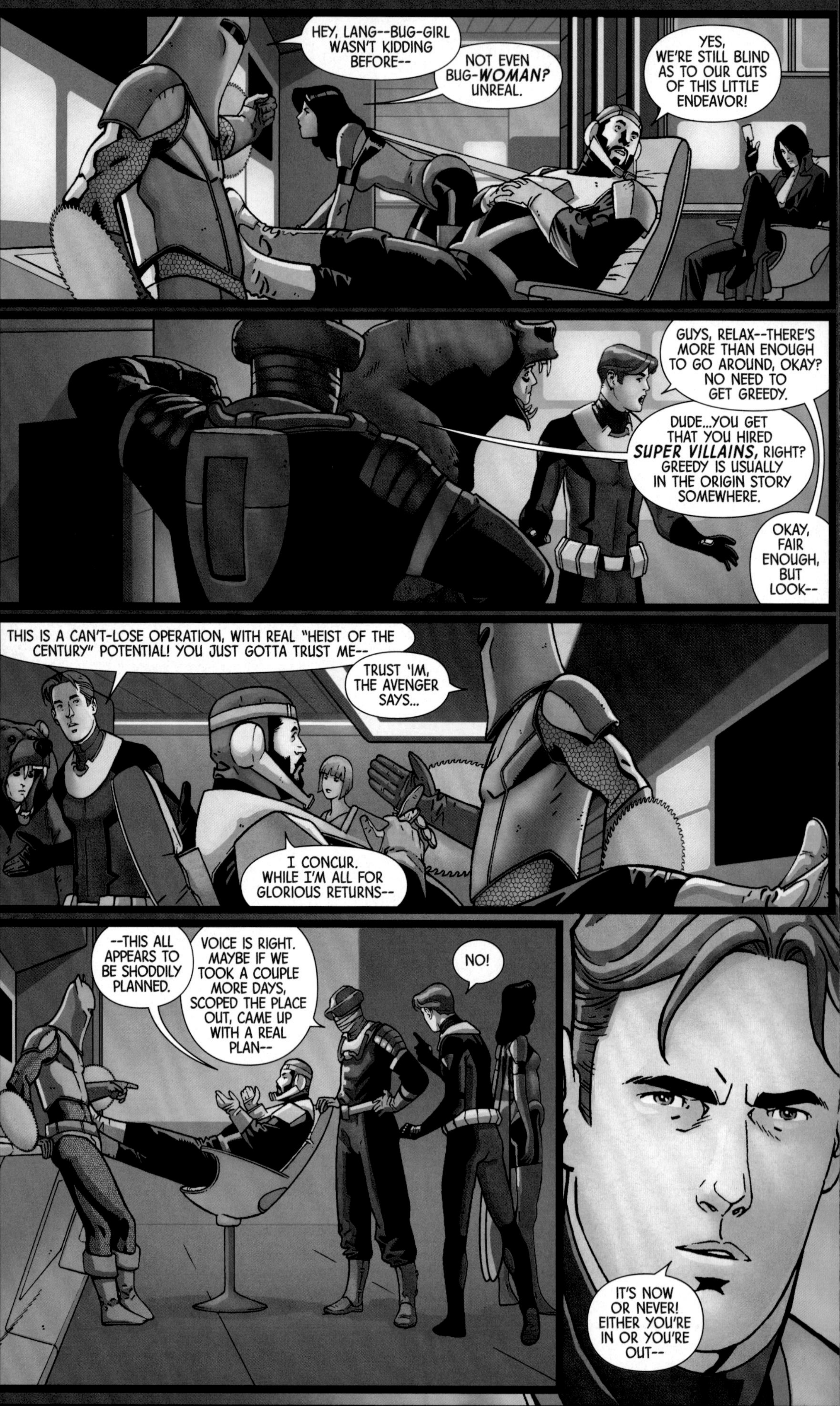
HEY, LANG--BUG-GIRL WASN'T KIDDING BEFORE--
NOT EVEN BUG-*WOMAN?* UNREAL.
YES, WE'RE STILL BLIND AS TO OUR CUTS OF THIS LITTLE ENDEAVOR!
GUYS, RELAX--THERE'S MORE THAN ENOUGH TO GO AROUND, OKAY? NO NEED TO GET GREEDY.
DUDE...YOU GET THAT YOU HIRED *SUPER VILLAINS,* RIGHT? GREEDY IS USUALLY IN THE ORIGIN STORY SOMEWHERE.
OKAY, FAIR ENOUGH, BUT LOOK--
THIS IS A CAN'T-LOSE OPERATION, WITH REAL "HEIST OF THE CENTURY" POTENTIAL! YOU JUST GOTTA TRUST ME--
TRUST 'IM, THE AVENGER SAYS...
I CONCUR. WHILE I'M ALL FOR GLORIOUS RETURNS--
--THIS ALL APPEARS TO BE SHODDILY PLANNED.
VOICE IS RIGHT. MAYBE IF WE TOOK A COUPLE MORE DAYS, SCOPED THE PLACE OUT, CAME UP WITH A REAL PLAN--
NO!
IT'S NOW OR NEVER! EITHER YOU'RE IN OR YOU'RE OUT--

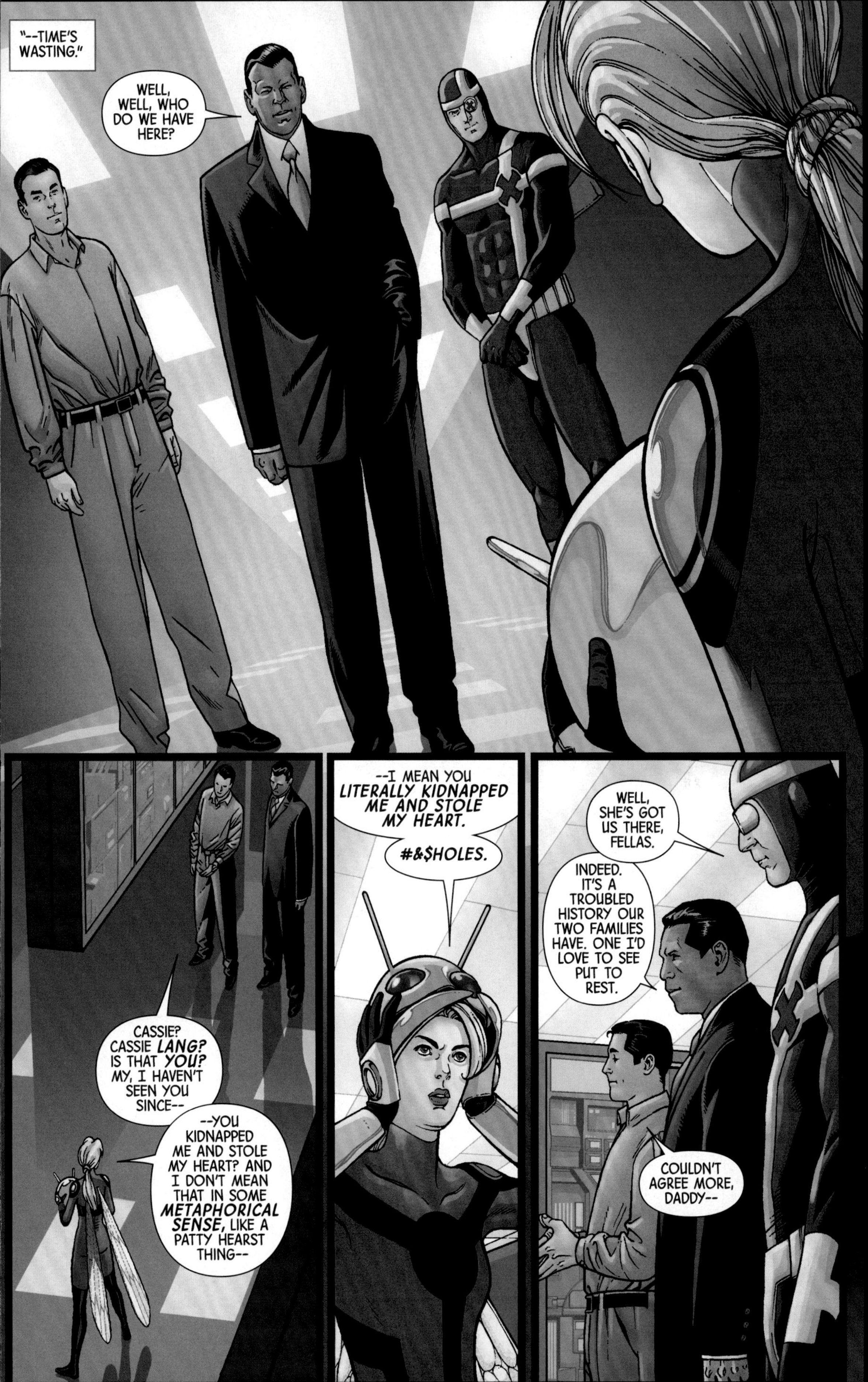
"--TIME'S WASTING."
WELL, WELL, WHO DO WE HAVE HERE?
CASSIE? CASSIE LANG? IS THAT YOU? MY, I HAVEN'T SEEN YOU SINCE--
--YOU KIDNAPPED ME AND STOLE MY HEART? AND I DON'T MEAN THAT IN SOME METAPHORICAL SENSE, LIKE A PATTY HEARST THING--
--I MEAN YOU LITERALLY KIDNAPPED ME AND STOLE MY HEART.
#&$HOLES.
WELL, SHE'S GOT US THERE, FELLAS.
INDEED. IT'S A TROUBLED HISTORY OUR TWO FAMILIES HAVE. ONE I'D LOVE TO SEE PUT TO REST.
COULDN'T AGREE MORE, DADDY--

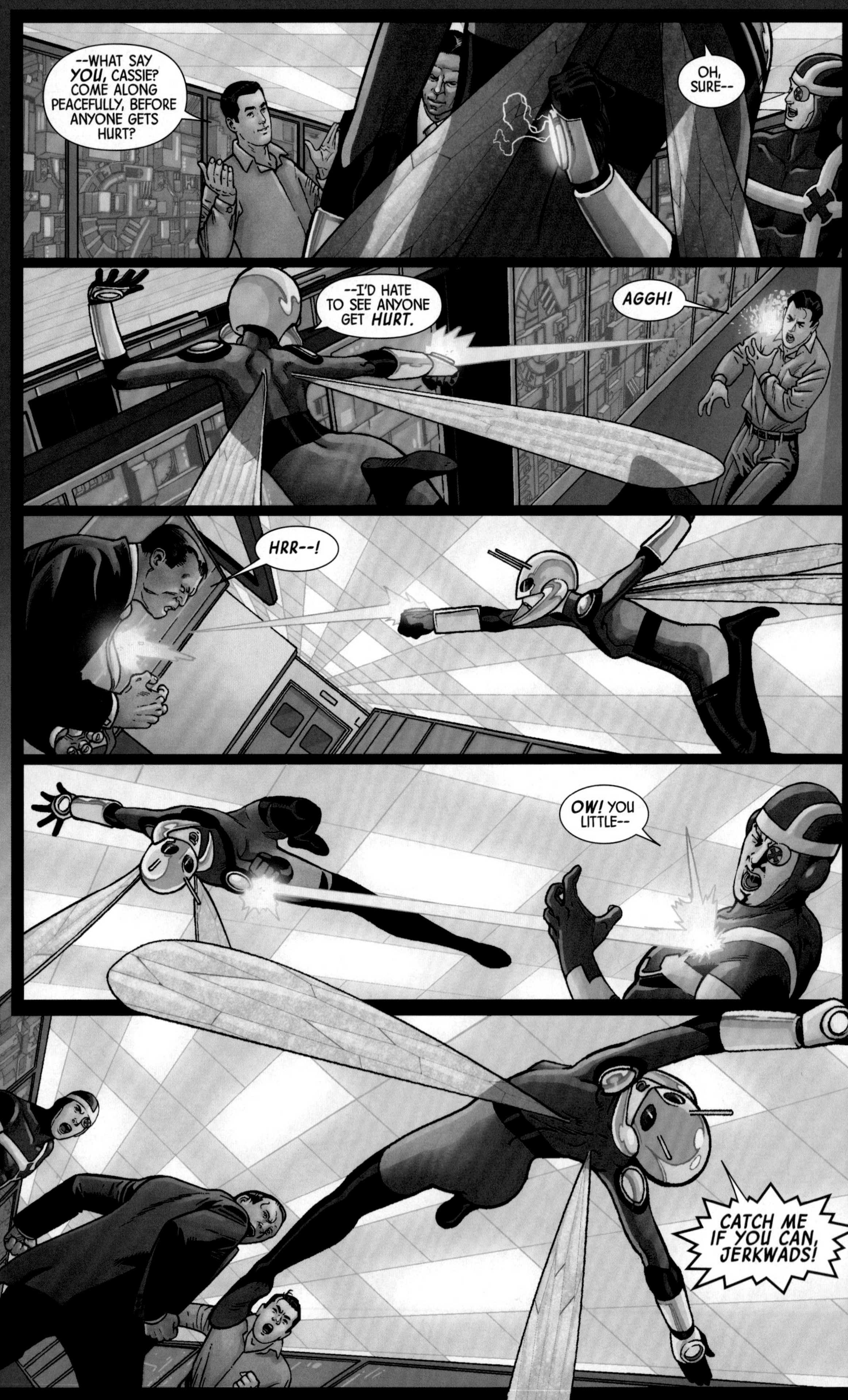
--WHAT SAY YOU, CASSIE? COME ALONG PEACEFULLY, BEFORE ANYONE GETS HURT?
OH, SURE--
--I'D HATE TO SEE ANYONE GET HURT.
AGGH!
HRR--!
OW! YOU LITTLE--
CATCH ME IF YOU CAN, JERKWADS!

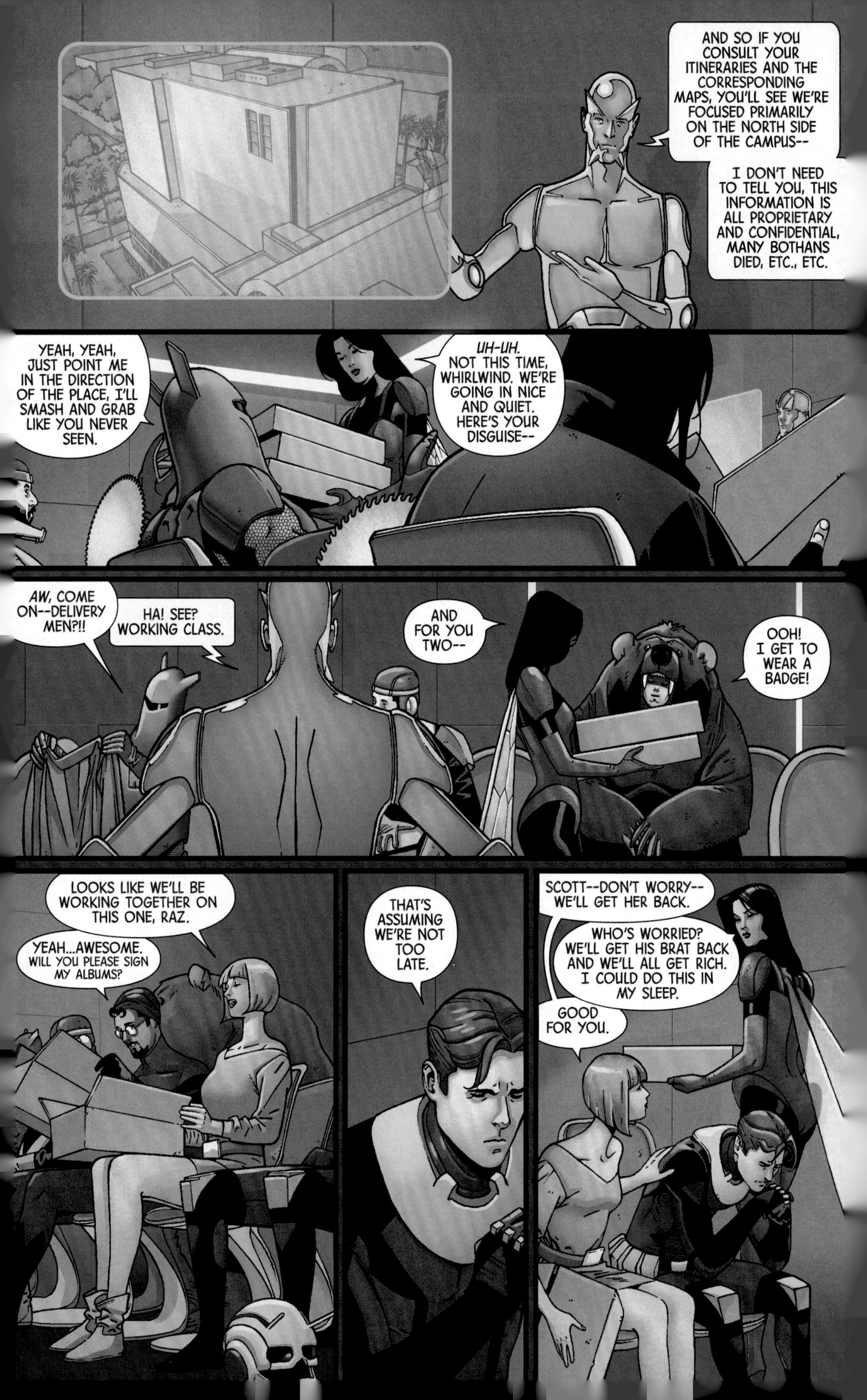
AND SO IF YOU CONSULT YOUR ITINERARIES AND THE CORRESPONDING MAPS, YOU'LL SEE WE'RE FOCUSED PRIMARILY ON THE NORTH SIDE OF THE CAMPUS--
I DON'T NEED TO TELL YOU, THIS INFORMATION IS ALL PROPRIETARY AND CONFIDENTIAL, MANY BOTHANS DIED, ETC., ETC.
YEAH, YEAH, JUST POINT ME IN THE DIRECTION OF THE PLACE, I'LL SMASH AND GRAB LIKE YOU NEVER SEEN.
UH-UH. NOT THIS TIME, WHIRLWIND. WE'RE GOING IN NICE AND QUIET. HERE'S YOUR DISGUISE--
AW, COME ON--DELIVERY MEN?!!
HA! SEE? WORKING CLASS.
AND FOR YOU TWO--
OOH! I GET TO WEAR A BADGE!
LOOKS LIKE WE'LL BE WORKING TOGETHER ON THIS ONE, RAZ.
YEAH...AWESOME. WILL YOU PLEASE SIGN MY ALBUMS?
THAT'S ASSUMING WE'RE NOT TOO LATE.
SCOTT--DON'T WORRY-- WE'LL GET HER BACK.
WHO'S WORRIED? WE'LL GET HIS BRAT BACK AND WE'LL ALL GET RICH. I COULD DO THIS IN MY SLEEP.
GOOD FOR YOU.

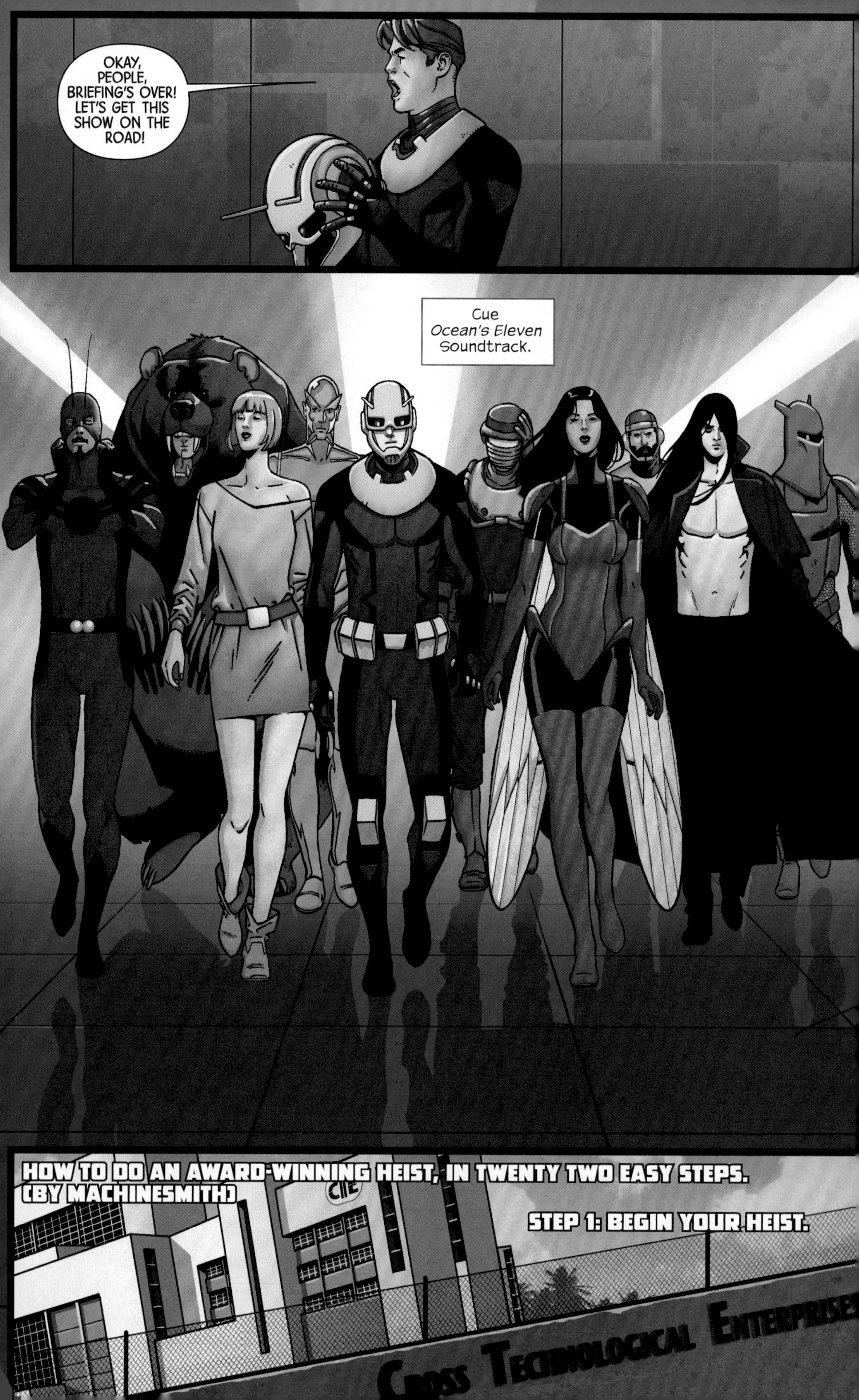
OKAY, PEOPLE, BRIEFING'S OVER! LET'S GET THIS SHOW ON THE ROAD!
Cue *Ocean's Eleven* Soundtrack.
HOW TO DO AN AWARD-WINNING HEIST, IN TWENTY TWO EASY STEPS. (BY MACHINESMITH)
CIE
STEP 1: BEGIN YOUR HEIST.
CROSS TECHNOLOGICAL ENTERPRISES

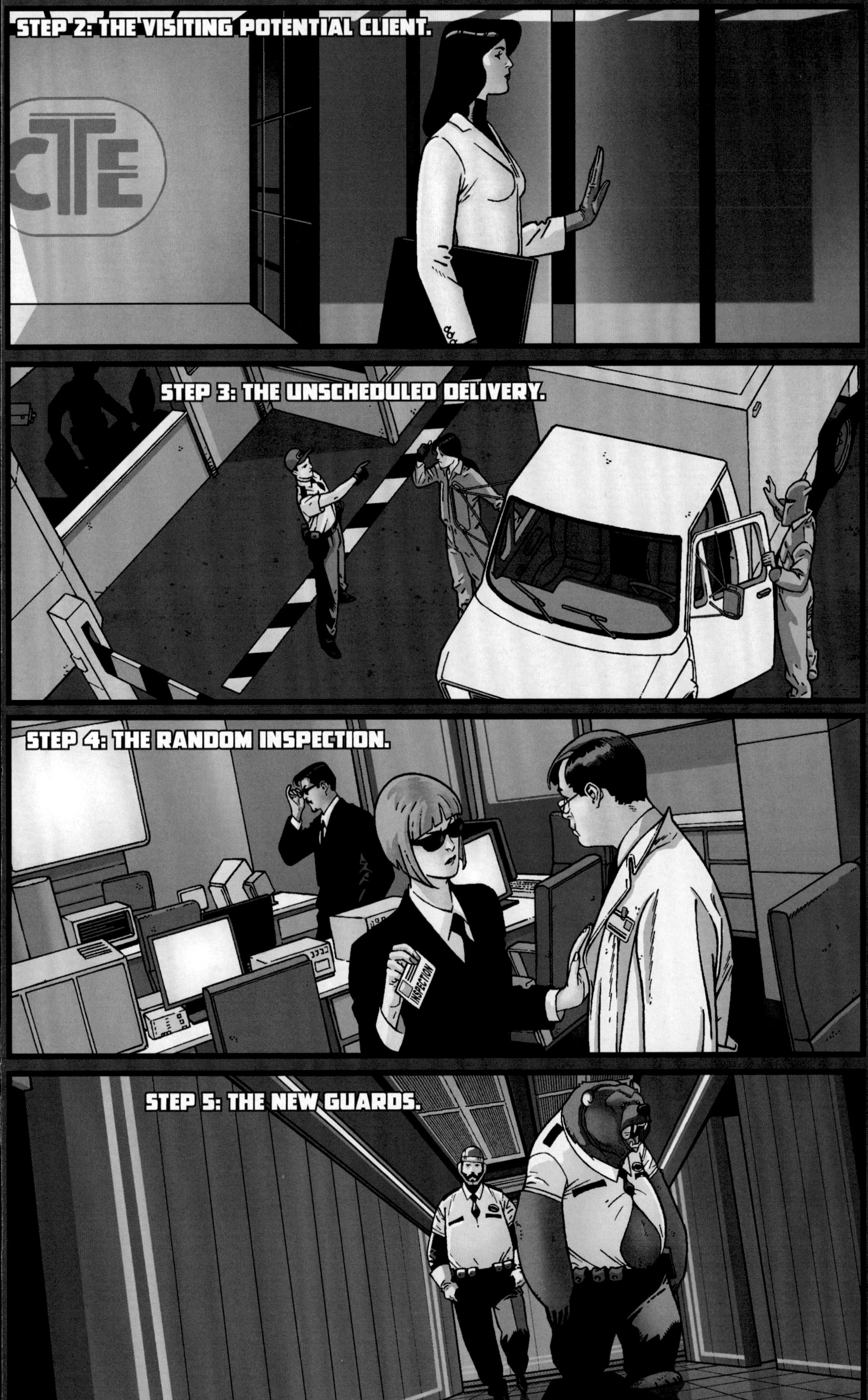
STEP 2: THE VISITING POTENTIAL CLIENT.
CTE
STEP 3: THE UNSCHEDULED DELIVERY.
STEP 4: THE RANDOM INSPECTION.
INSPECTION
STEP 5: THE NEW GUARDS.

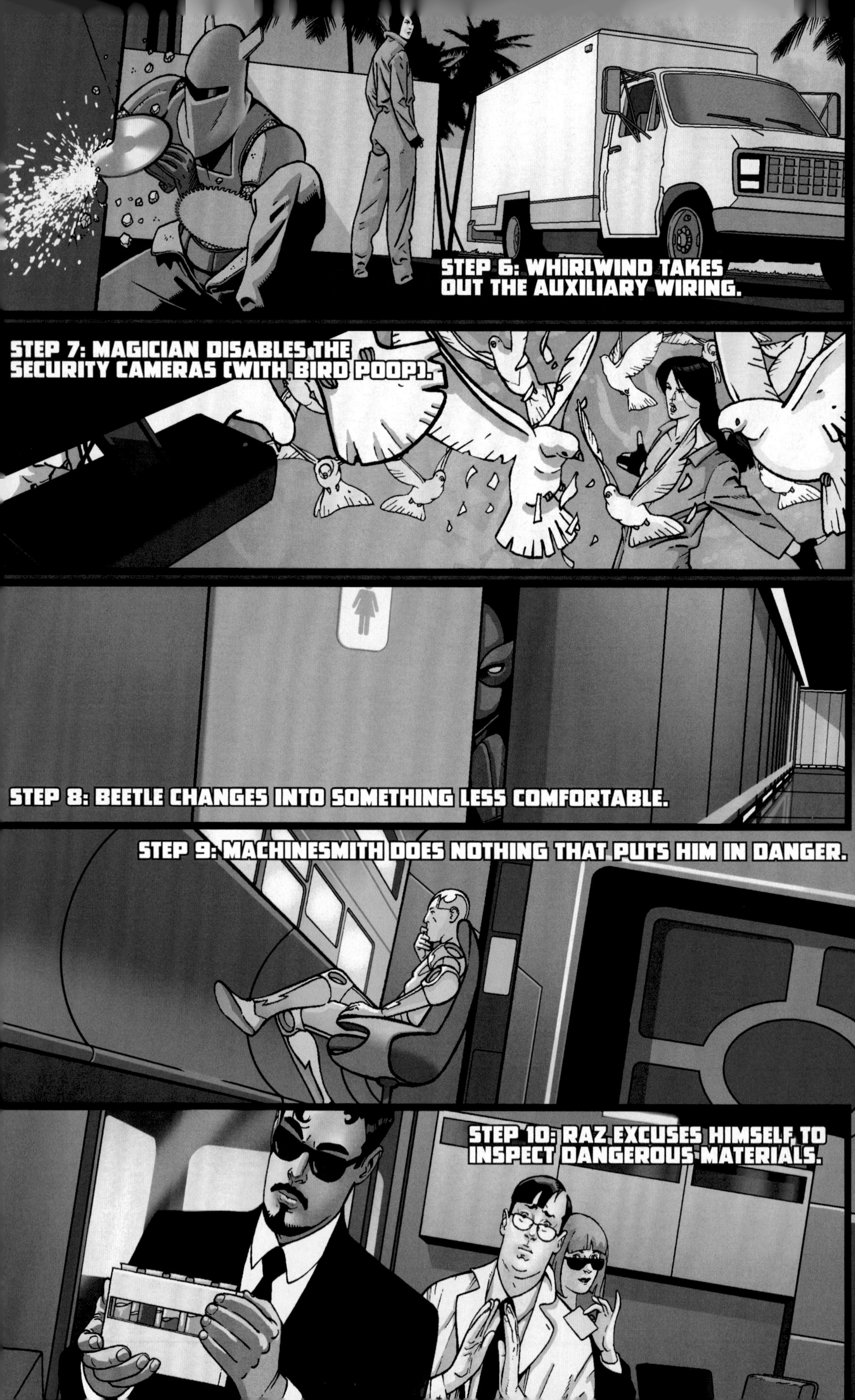
STEP 6: WHIRLWIND TAKES OUT THE AUXILIARY WIRING.
STEP 7: MAGICIAN DISABLES THE SECURITY CAMERAS (WITH BIRD POOP).
STEP 8: BEETLE CHANGES INTO SOMETHING LESS COMFORTABLE.
STEP 9: MACHINESMITH DOES NOTHING THAT PUTS HIM IN DANGER.
STEP 10: RAZ EXCUSES HIMSELF TO INSPECT DANGEROUS MATERIALS.

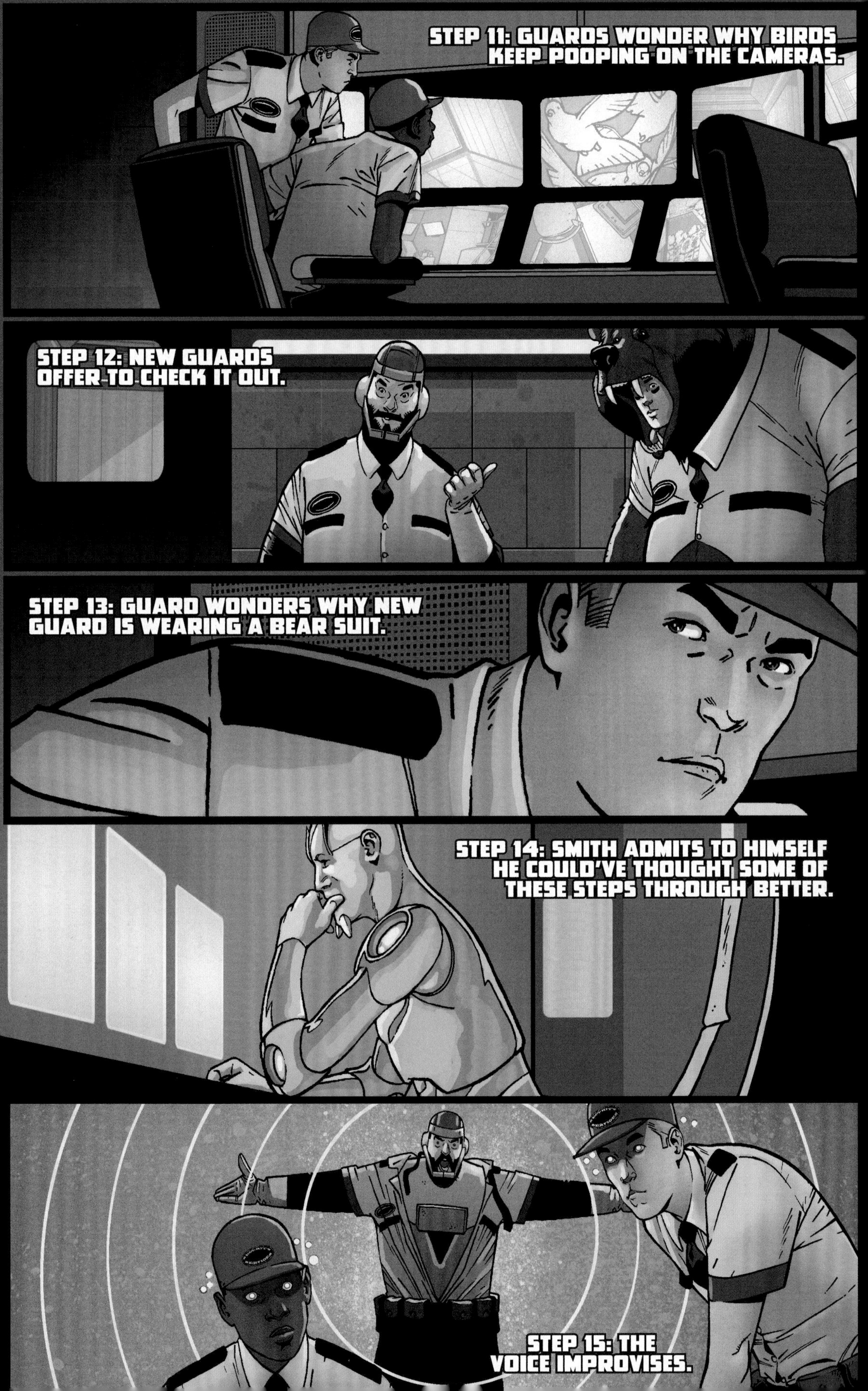
STEP 11: GUARDS WONDER WHY BIRDS KEEP POOPING ON THE CAMERAS.
STEP 12: NEW GUARDS OFFER TO CHECK IT OUT.
STEP 13: GUARD WONDERS WHY NEW GUARD IS WEARING A BEAR SUIT.
STEP 14: SMITH ADMITS TO HIMSELF HE COULD'VE THOUGHT SOME OF THESE STEPS THROUGH BETTER.
STEP 15: THE VOICE IMPROVISES.

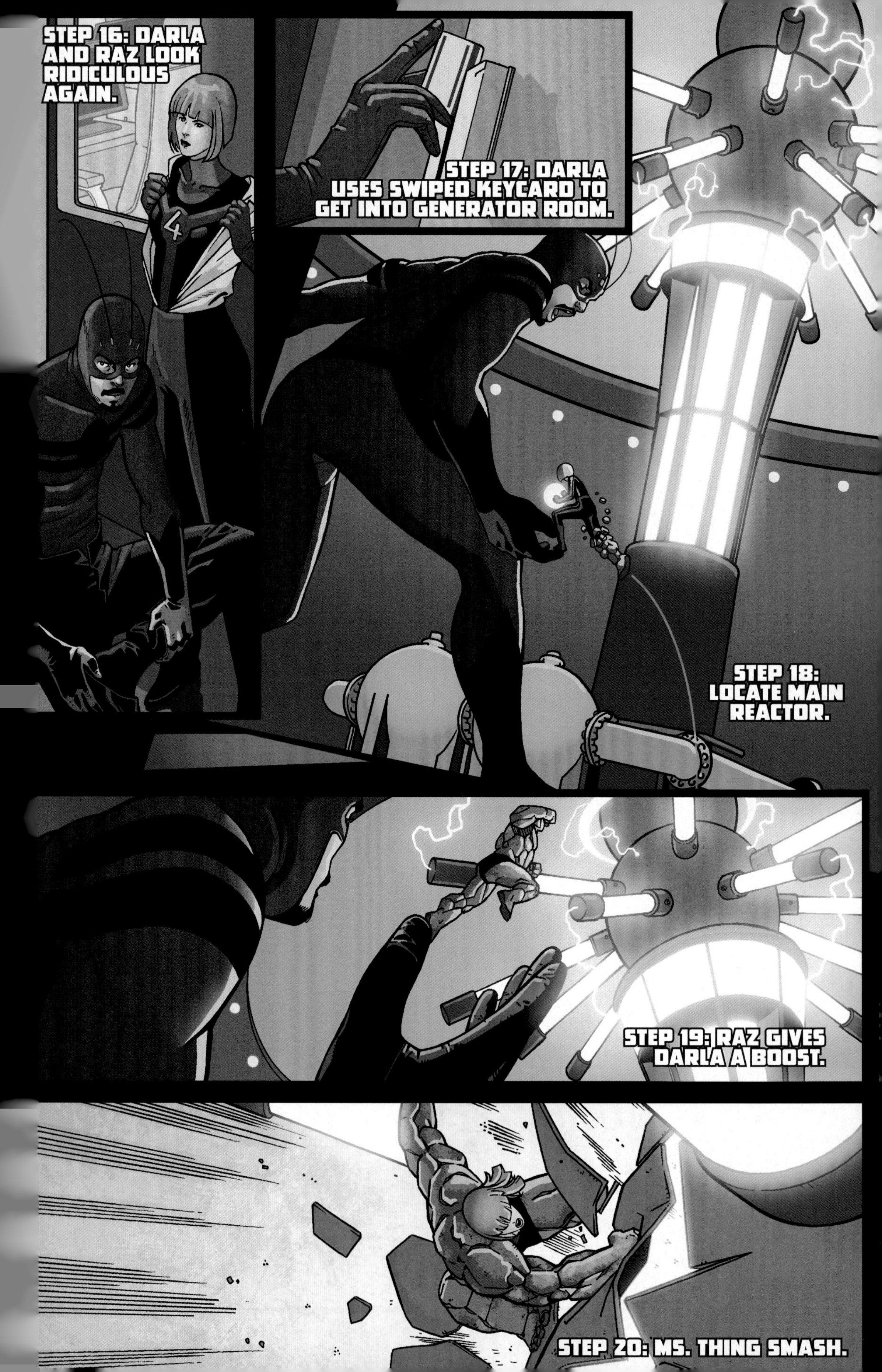
STEP 16: DARLA AND RAZ LOOK RIDICULOUS AGAIN.
STEP 17: DARLA USES SWIPED KEYCARD TO GET INTO GENERATOR ROOM.
STEP 18: LOCATE MAIN REACTOR.
STEP 19: RAZ GIVES DARLA A BOOST.
STEP 20: MS. THING SMASH.

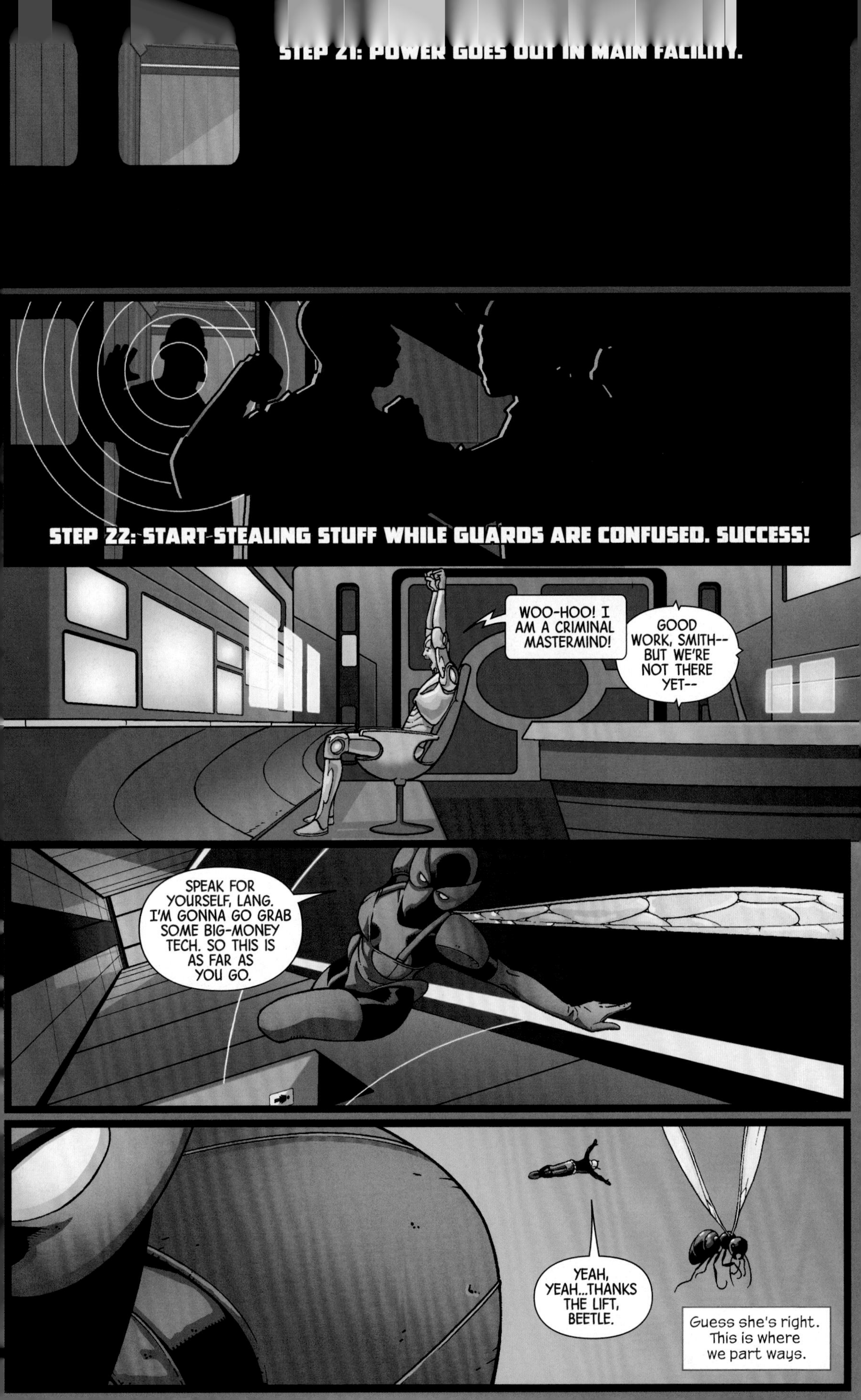
STEP 21: POWER GOES OUT IN MAIN FACILITY.
STEP 22: START STEALING STUFF WHILE GUARDS ARE CONFUSED. SUCCESS!
WOO-HOO! I AM A CRIMINAL MASTERMIND!
GOOD WORK, SMITH--BUT WE'RE NOT THERE YET--
SPEAK FOR YOURSELF, LANG. I'M GONNA GO GRAB SOME BIG-MONEY TECH. SO THIS IS AS FAR AS YOU GO.
YEAH, YEAH...THANKS THE LIFT, BEETLE.
Guess she's right. This is where we part ways.

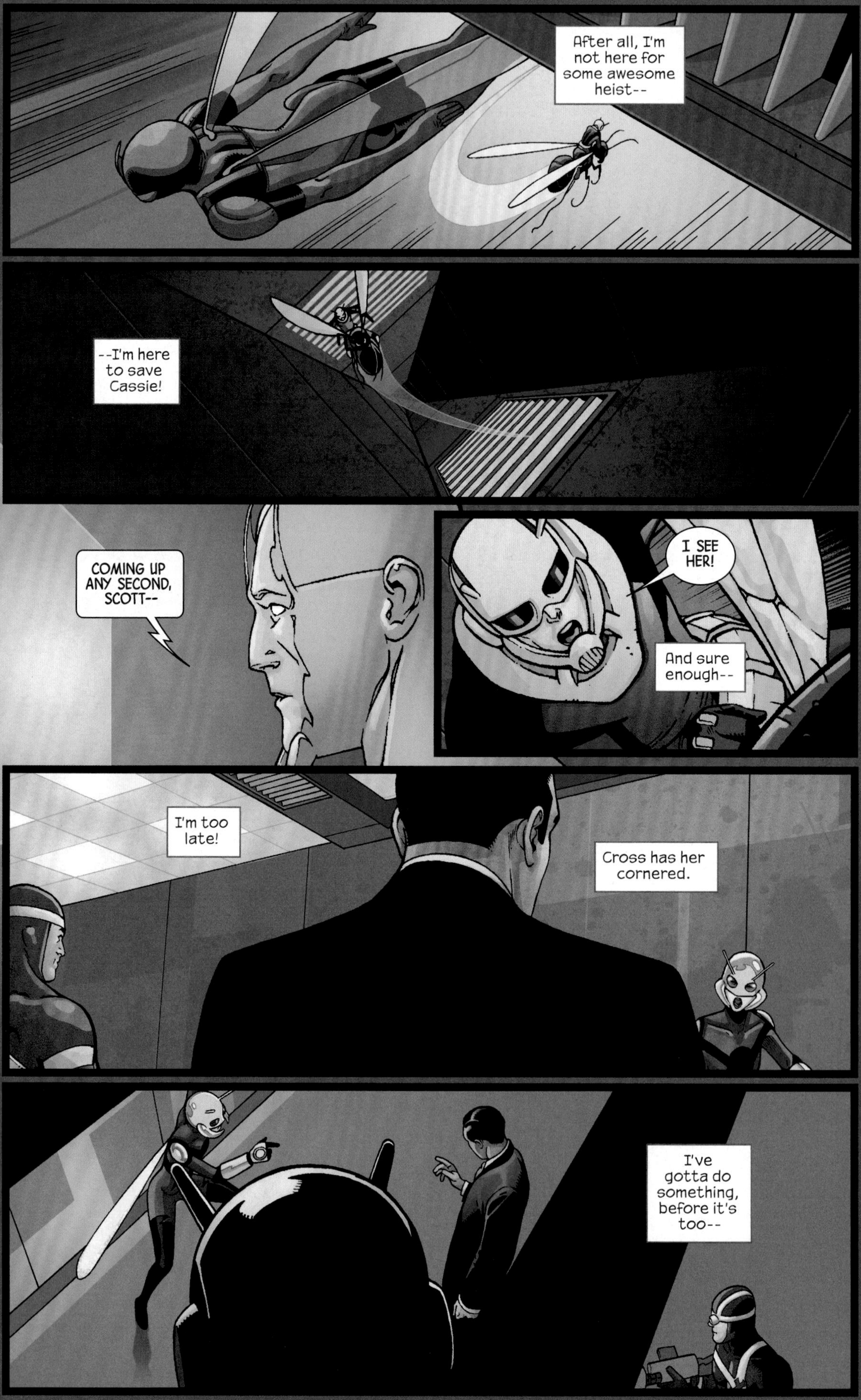
After all, I'm not here for some awesome heist--
--I'm here to save Cassie!
COMING UP ANY SECOND, SCOTT--
I SEE HER!
And sure enough--
I'm too late!
Cross has her cornered.
I've gotta do something, before it's too--

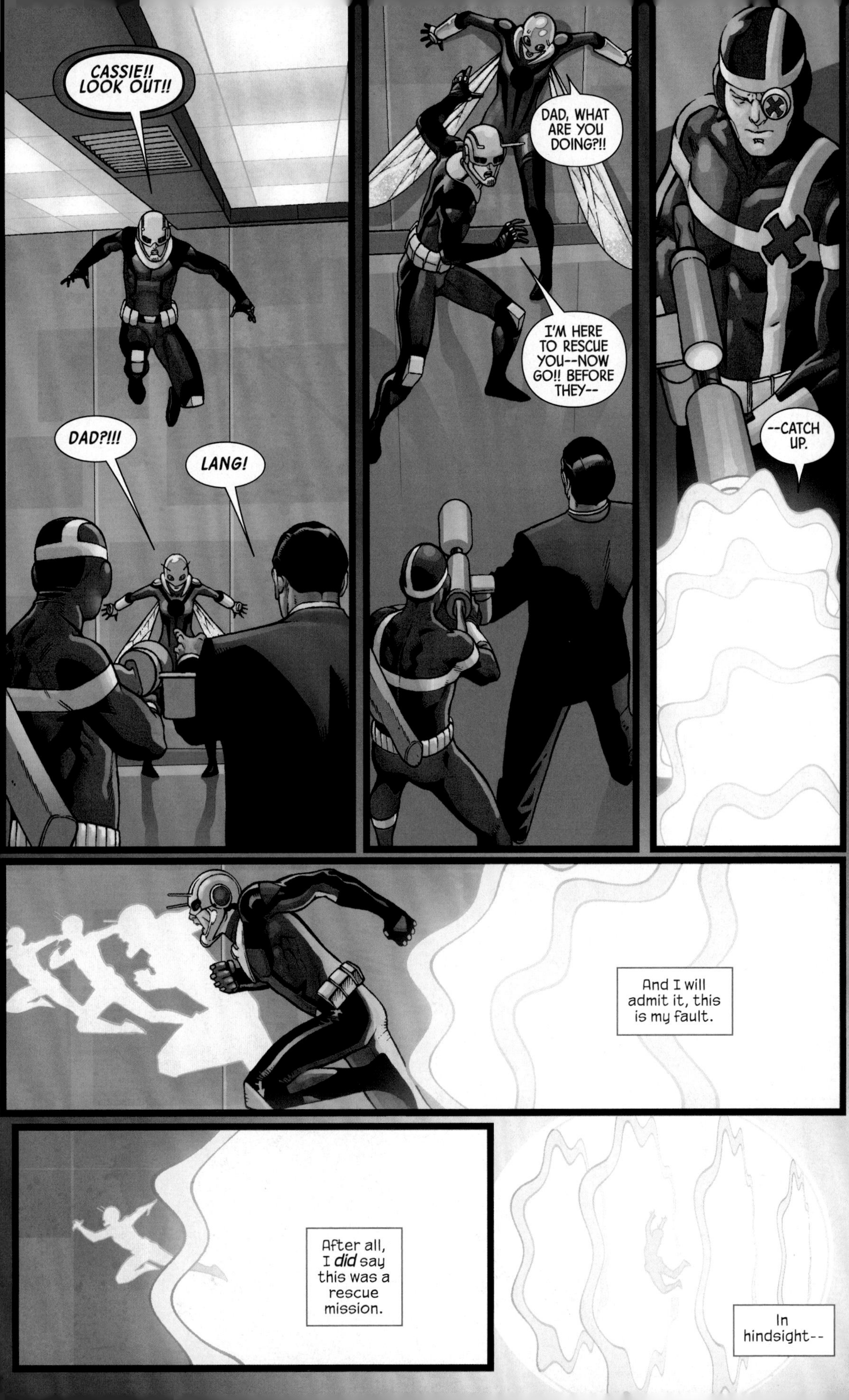
CASSIE!! LOOK OUT!!
DAD?!!!
LANG!
DAD, WHAT ARE YOU DOING?!!
I'M HERE TO RESCUE YOU--NOW GO!! BEFORE THEY--
--CATCH UP.
And I will admit it, this is my fault.
After all, I *did* say this was a rescue mission.
In hindsight--

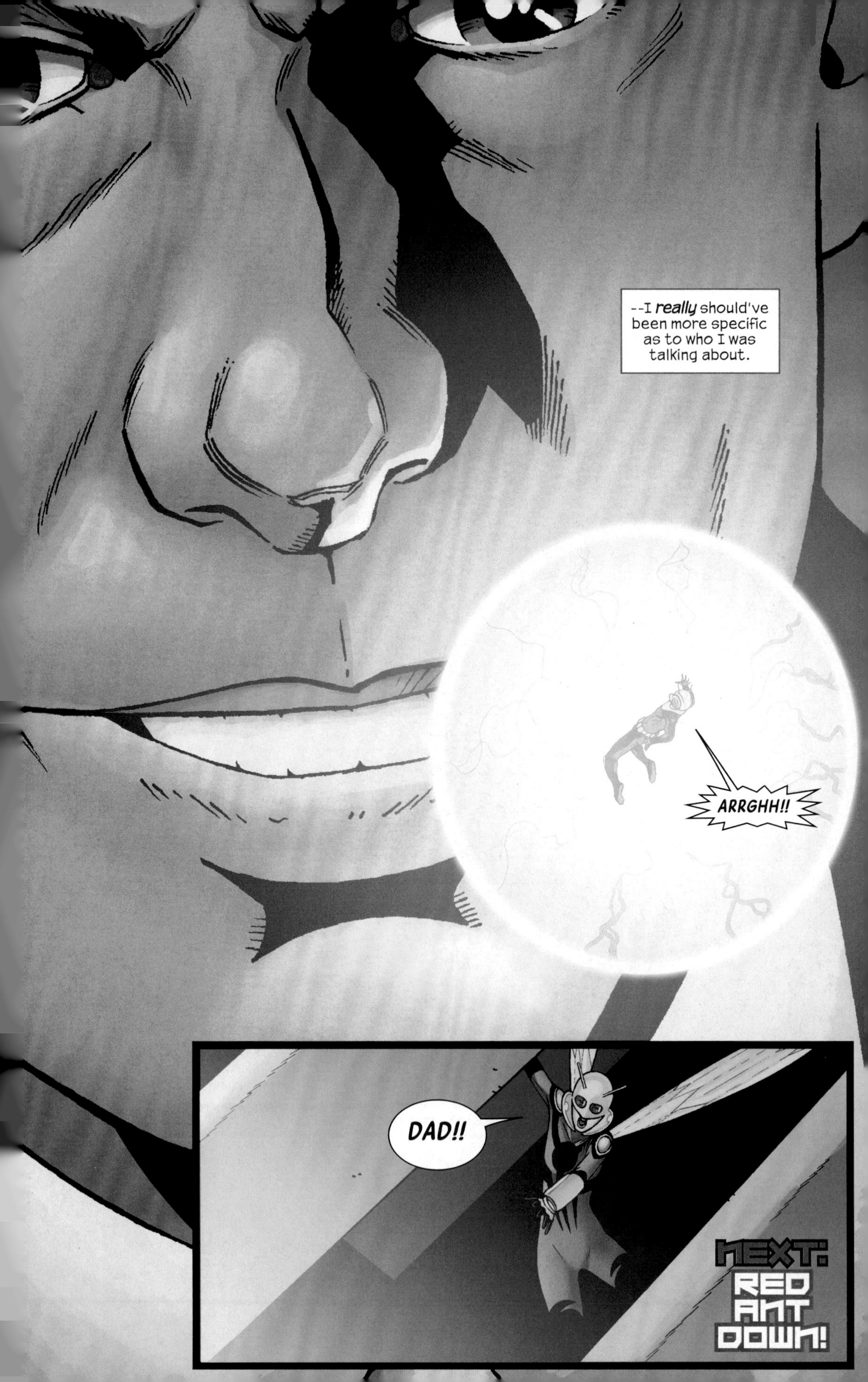
--I *really* should've been more specific as to who I was talking about.
ARRGHH!!
DAD!!
NEXT: RED ANT DOWN!

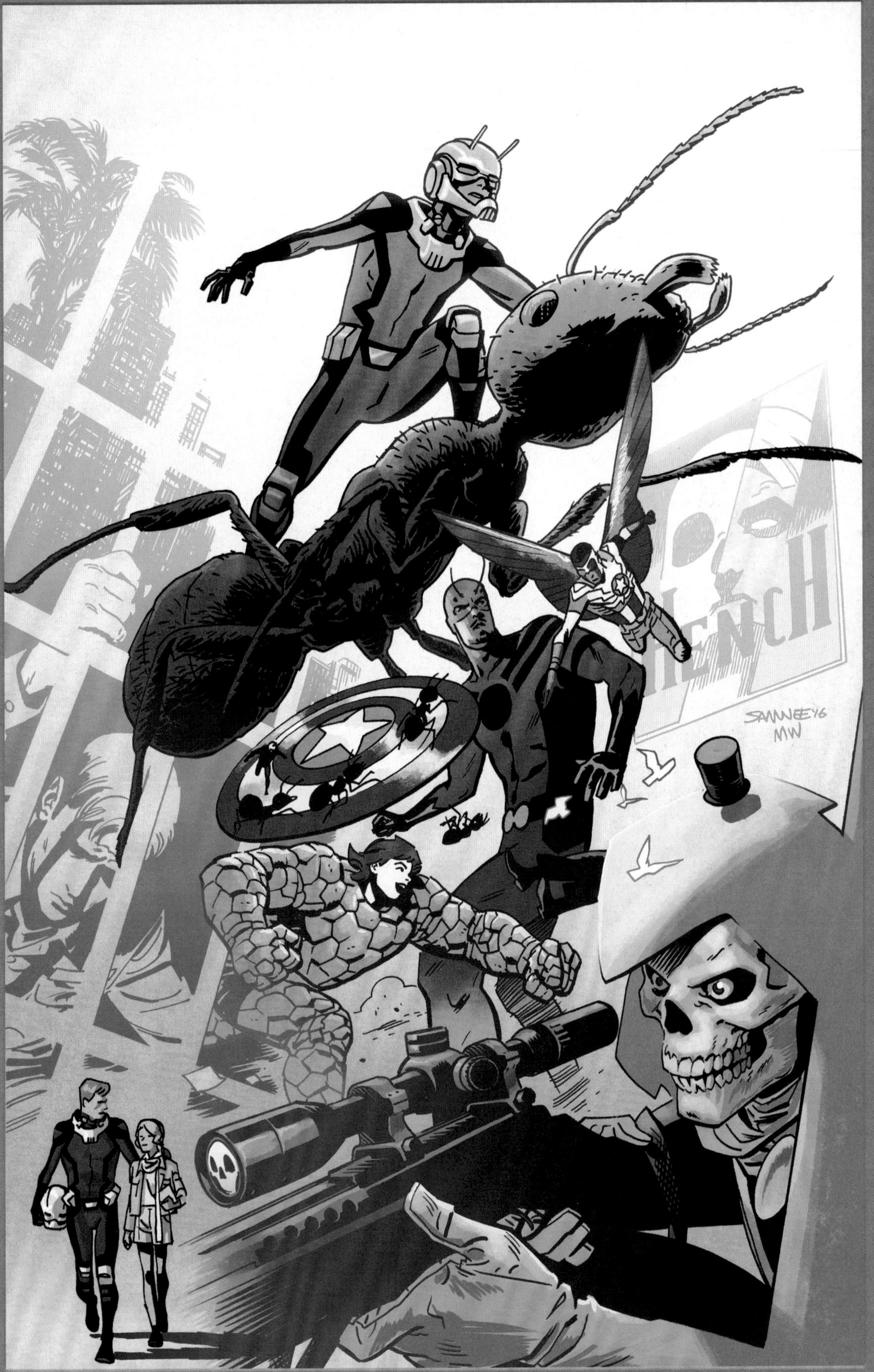
HENCH
SAMNEE '16
MW

#7 STORY THUS FAR VARIANT
BY **CHRIS SAMNEE** & **MATTHEW WILSON**

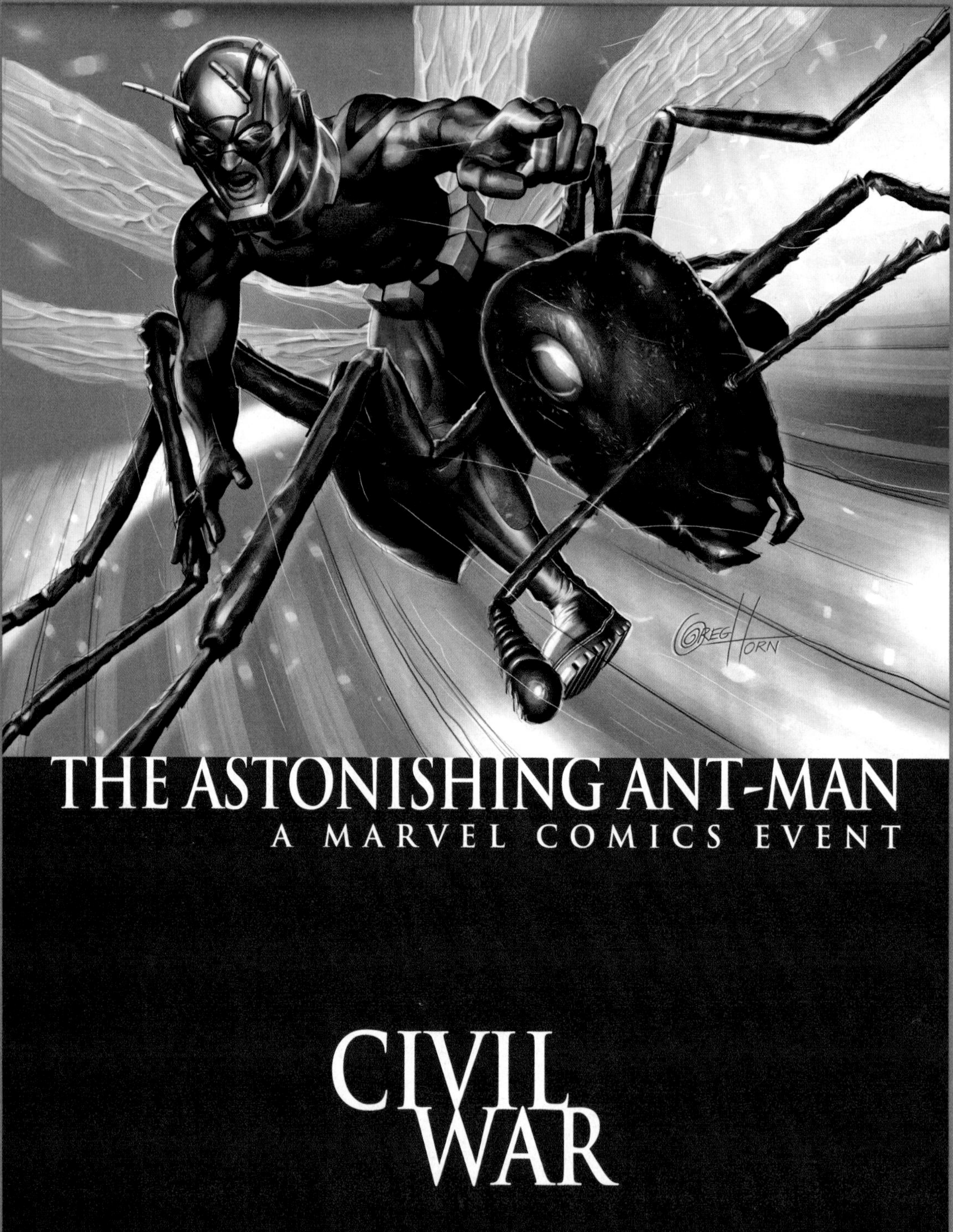
Greg Horn
THE ASTONISHING ANT-MAN
A MARVEL COMICS EVENT
CIVIL WAR

#7 CIVIL WAR VARIANT
BY **GREG HORN**

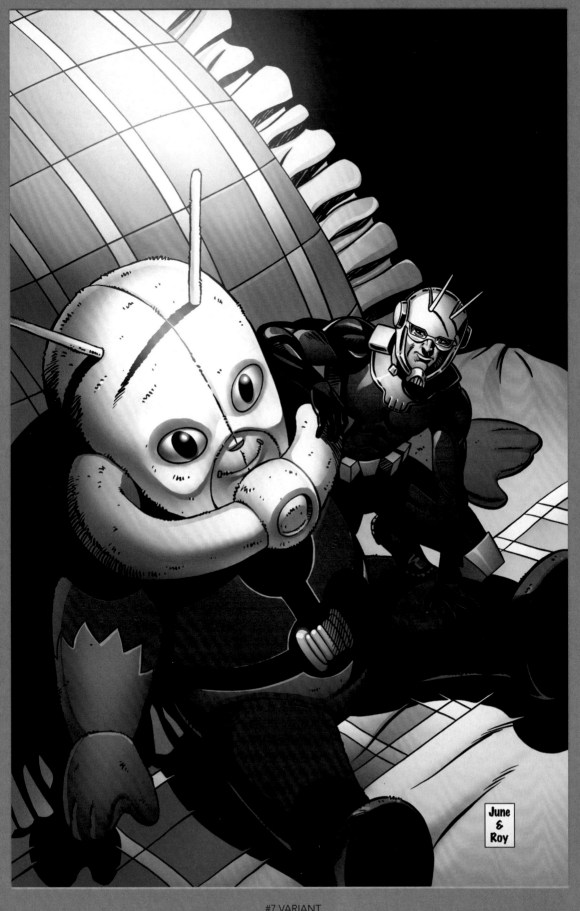

#7 VARIANT
BY **JUNE BRIGMAN, ROY RICHARDSON** & **FRANK D'ARMATA**

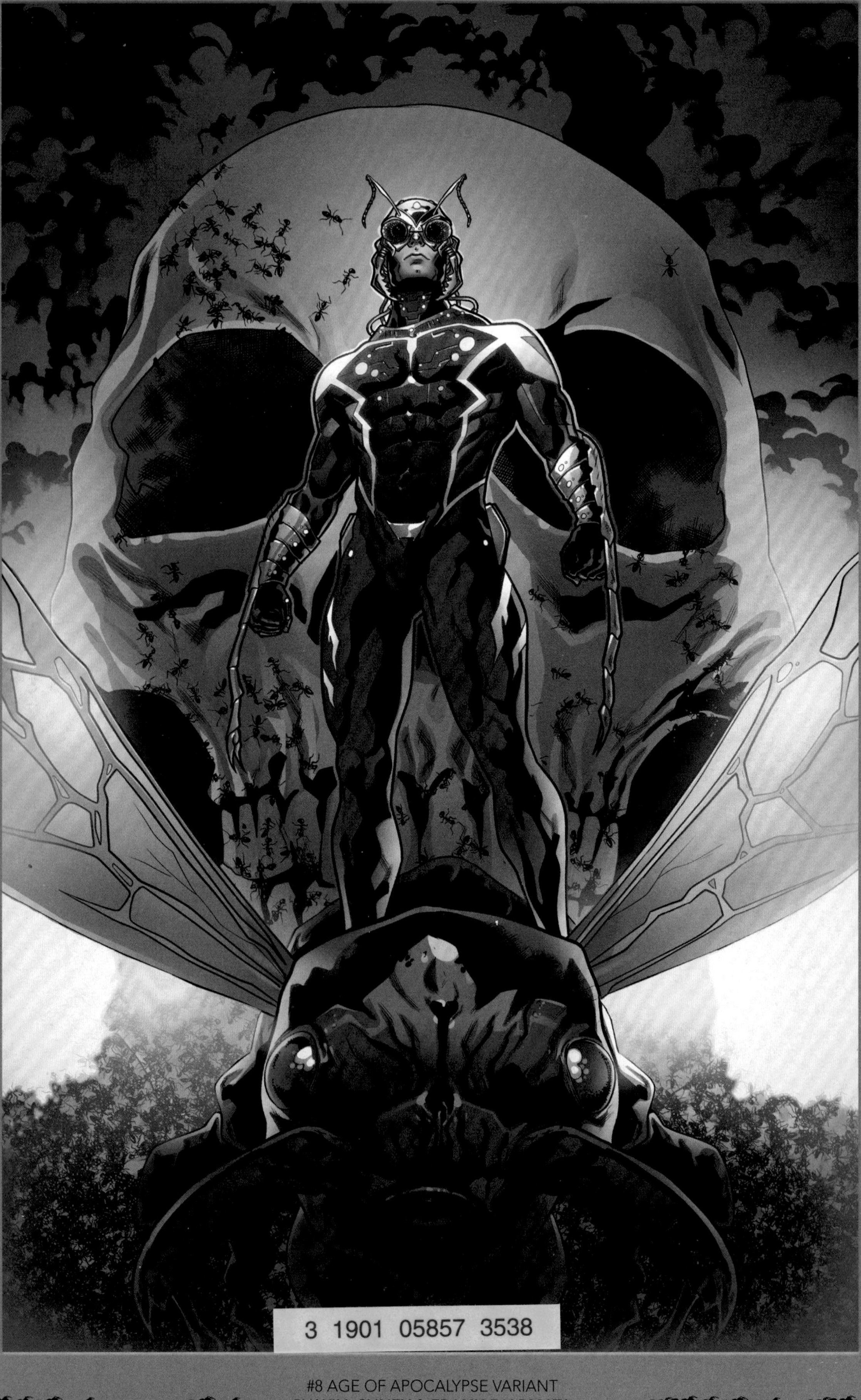

#8 AGE OF APOCALYPSE VARIANT
BY **WILL SLINEY** & **FRANK D'ARMATA**